TRAVELS ON THE
DANCE FLOOR

D0302199

This edition published in 2010

First published in Great Britain in 2008 by
André Deutsch
An imprint of the
Carlton Publishing Group
20 Mortimer Street
London W1T 3JW

Text copyright © Grevel Lindop 2008, 2010
Design copyright © Carlton Books Limited 2008, 2010

The right of Grevel Lindop to be identified as the author of this work has been
asserted in accordance with the Copyright, Designs and Patents Act 1988

All rights reserved. This book is sold subject to the condition that it shall not,
by way of trade or otherwise, be lent, resold, hired out or otherwise circulated
without the publisher's prior written consent in any form of cover or binding
other than that in which it is published and without a similar condition
including this condition, being imposed upon the subsequent purchaser.

A CIP catalogue for this book is available from the British Library.

ISBN 978-0-233-00298-9

Typeset by E-Type, Liverpool
Printed and bound in the UK

TRAVELS ON THE DANCE FLOOR

Grevel Lindop

André Deutsch

Also by Grevel Lindop:

Poetry
Fool's Paradise
Tourists
A Prismatic Toy
Touching the Earth (Books I-IV)
Selected Poems
Playing With Fire

Prose
The Opium-Eater: A Life of Thomas De Quincey
The Path and the Palace: Reflections on the Nature of Poetry
A Literary Guide to the Lake District

As Editor
British Poetry Since 1990 (with Michael Schmidt)
Thomas Chatterton: Selected Poems
Thomas De Quincey: Confessions and Other Writings
The Works of Thomas De Quincey
Robert Graves: The White Goddess
Graves and the Goddess (with Ian Firla)

For all my salsa teachers, who work hard
to make the world a happier place.

✳ PREFACE

Many people have helped with the making of this book and the journey it recounts. Above all I must thank my dance teachers: in the Caribbean region, Geldys Morales Feito (Havana), Gustavo Farias and Zuleika Piña (Caracas), Victoria Laverde (Bogotá), Carlos Estacio and Maira Castillo (Cali), Alina Alderete (Panama City), and Norma Rivera (San Juan); and in the UK, Debbie, Tony, André, Gary, Mo-ji, Charifi, Les and Lorraine, Tina and Alex, Paola and Lazaro, Juan and Susan.

Among the innumerable people who showed me kindness on my travels, I owe a particular debt to Mauricio Contreras Hernández, Rafael Quintero and Francisco Buckley "Bush", who showed me so much hospitality in their home cities; I also thank Owen Sheers and Maria Nuñez, who made contacts for me. Chris McCully gave me peace of mind by backing up the emails from which many details of the journey were reconstructed.

I'm profoundly grateful to Charlie Viney, my agent, who convinced me that the journey would make a worthwhile book, and whose friendship and enthusiasm offered unfailing support. Penny Phillips and Gareth Jones, my editors at André Deutsch, have provided invaluable expertise and – most importantly – shared my excitement about the project, as has Lydia Drukarz, publicity director.

I also give heartfelt thanks to my wonderful Spanish teachers at the Instituto Cervantes in Manchester, especially to Ana Castiñeiras and Maria José Anadón. That my Spanish remains less than perfect is, of course, entirely my own fault. I should have paid more attention in class.

My greatest debt is to my wife and dancing partner Amanda, who maintained an essential contact with reality while I was exploring other worlds. I only hope she can accept her presence in this book as generously as she accepted my absence from home. Without her, none of it would have been possible.

All air travel undertaken in the course of the journey has been rendered carbon-neutral by donation to Atmosfair, the gold-standard carbon-offsetting charity. Please visit atmosfair.com to see how you can reduce the environmental impact of your own travel.

Finally, my respect and gratitude to Ochún for her protection; and to Eleggua, who opened so many doors for me, and who fortunately has a sense of humour.

Grevel Lindop

❋Contents

✳ PROLOGUE

If I ask myself where it all began, the answer has to be: in Manchester, on a rainy Wednesday evening in January. The club was hidden away down a side-street in the Northern Quarter – that section north of the city centre where Asian and Jewish garment warehouses jostle with tattoo parlours, Kung Fu studios, "adult" video stores, vinyl record exchanges and the occasional anarchist café.

There my wife Amanda and I found our way to a worn wooden doorway under a bleakly-lit first-floor window full of tailors' dummies in formal waistcoats. The doorway was flanked by a pair of bright green neon palm trees, and over it a yellow neon beer-bottle gleamed invitingly through the rain. Amanda, always averse to spearheading our entrance into unknown spaces, pushed me through the door ahead of her. I found my way down a long flight of steps into a bland, sandy-coloured basement with lots of small tables, two dance floors, and a bar decorated with plastic signs advertising Latin American beers. TV sets hung from the ceiling relaying the Wednesday evening football. The place was almost empty. I bought two Coronas, each with a slice of lime wedged in its throat, and we sat down to see what would happen.

I wouldn't have been disappointed, to be honest, if nothing at all had happened. We were here – carried more by dogged determination than by enthusiasm – to fulfil a New Year's resolution. A friend had been recommending for months that we try salsa, and in a reckless moment, looking for something to provide a new sensation for the new year, we'd agreed to give it a try. We had found the class advertised on the internet, but as the weather worsened had almost changed our minds and stayed at home. Only my typically obsessive reluctance to abandon plans, and that odd impulse to throw a new factor in at the start of the year and see what would happen, made me insist on going, and helped me persuade Amanda to come too.

The idea of learning to dance was alluring and alarming. I'd loved dancing in the wild, individualistic (and now deeply embarrassing) hippie style of the late 1960s. Later on, Amanda and I had spent every Friday night dancing to reggae. But that was a lifetime ago; and in any case it hadn't been structured dancing, dancing with real *steps*. It was intuitive and fun, but it didn't pose any challenges or make any demands.

For couple dancing in an identifiable style, I had to go back to a set of memories I could now hardly bear to contemplate, memories of a few lessons in ballroom dancing, taken in early adolescence. What had I learnt? The waltz, certainly. Other archaic species like the foxtrot and the quickstep. Hours of acute mutual embarrassment shared with girls in long pastel dresses and their first make-up, partnered by pale clumsy youths in sports jackets. Everyone anxious and tongue-tied, surviving some of the last long, dull evenings before the Beatles and the tidal wave of rock swept away the final frosted vestiges of structure and formality.

But now, on that evening in Manchester, the club was starting to fill up. Beginners were summoned to "the small dance floor". Debbie, a blonde in black trousers, hooped gold earrings and a ponytail, lined us up and began to teach us our first steps, forward and back. "One, two, three (tap); five, six, seven (tap)..." Then the same thing, side to side. Then with an "open-out" movement – swinging to the left and the right, stepping back and pivoting at the hips. Heels clicking, Debbie strutted over to the DJ box and added some music. I recognized "*Oye Como Va*", but not the Santana version. It seemed a bit stodgy (no doubt she'd slowed it down), but it added some precision to our plodding and shuffling line-dance. Left, right, left (tap); right, left, right (tap).

That tap on the fourth and eighth beats was tricky. I kept forgetting and taking the extra step, colliding with the woman next to me or – worse – treading on her toes. Physical co-ordination has never been my strong point (I was useless at football), and having size 12 feet doesn't help. Nor, indeed, does an inability to remember the difference between right and left. Not that many of my fellow beginners were notably better off. Some seemed to have no sense of rhythm. Others were simply hampered by their footwear. Plenty of people wore ancient trainers – acceptable, but gripping the floor far too firmly to allow elegant footwork. One or two seemed to have dressed for an evening's dancing with an eye to the positively surreal. The girl, for example, in massively-buckled black motorcycle boots. Or the lady whose rubber flip-flops kept folding in half under her soles and tripping her up.

Still, we soldiered on – and soon it was time to partner up. We were organized into facing lines, male and female, shown the correct partner-hold and, keyed by instructions from Debbie, launched into practising our moves – forward and back, side to side, open out – in couples. At once, two things became evident. First, that there were far more women than men. Every two or three minutes, Debbie would shout "Rotate!" and each man would have to move leftwards to a new partner. The unpartnered women – half a dozen or so out of some eighteen – simply had to practise alone until the next man arrived. Glancing along the lines, I saw tall girls and short girls; black, white and oriental girls; elegant (and not-so-elegant) middle-aged ladies; and pretty student types. And I realized I was going to get to grips with every one of them. One hand lightly clasped, the other around the shoulder. This was starting to get interesting.

And that led to the second realization: that couple dancing is psychologically as well as physically challenging. A moment later Debbie confirmed this by giving us another instruction: to look into each other's eyes while we practised. Not at our feet, not over each other's shoulders. Into the eyes. At once the temperature went up several degrees. Physical contact is one thing; intimate psychological contact puts you into another dimension entirely. It quickly became evident that most people simply can't bear to look into the eyes of a stranger for more than an instant. It's just too intense. It goes against everything we've been taught. But in salsa it's vital.

Partly this is because, once beyond the most elementary practice steps, the sequence of moves in salsa is unpredictable. There's no fixed order, and ultimately no definable repertoire of turns, spins, slides, dips, breaks or whatever. The man decides what's going to happen, and he leads the lady. His obligation is to lead clearly, firmly and decisively; hers is to pay attention to his signals so that she's ready to go, in a split second, just the way he's sending her. All this requires constant alertness. You can't go off into a daze or a daydream. Salsa is a continual process of two-way communication. The partners' total attention to each other is vital.

And that, as all we New Year beginners learned that first night, is where the other function of eye contact comes in. For salsa is all about sexuality, all about the polarization of male and female. Whatever kind of gender-neutral "new man" a guy may aspire to be in other circumstances, when he's out there dancing salsa he has to be commanding, confident, and protective of his woman. And his lady has to be elegant, flirtatious and *sexy*. And this has little to do with physical good looks, and still less to do with age. It comes from inside, and it's summed up in the magic word *attitude*.

Salsa is about the body, and about the heart within the body. It's about passion made into movement; about the fast, elegant co-ordination of two bodies; and about the sexual polarity between them. There needs to be a bit of a smoulder between salsa-dancing partners when they're out on the floor. And there's nothing like eye contact for generating that heat. No wonder we beginners on that Wednesday night got a bit burned, and looked hastily away. We had a lot to learn.

But dancing in couples began to work its magic anyway. Once you're a pair, however apparently ill-matched, it's the two of you against the world. You share moments of comic dismay when something goes wrong. You smile conspiratorially. You apologize for a misstep and are assured that it's perfectly fine. You share mutual congratulations when for once something goes right. And every so often you remember to look into each other's eyes, and you smile again.

When we'd changed partners enough times for me to be dancing with Amanda once more, I asked her how she was getting on. "Okay," she said. "I keep getting the bottoms of my trousers caught in my heels."

"I need some different shoes," I said. I'd come out in brown leather shoes which felt clumsy here. I resolved to get some light slip-on trainers, ones with smooth soles.

At least Amanda and I weren't having any problems with the eye contact. It felt sexy, even just going "left-right-left" and back again. "This is fun," I said. And she said, "I think I'm getting the hang of it." Her long dark hair swayed and flicked around as she turned from side to side. Though she's as English as I am, Amanda has always insisted that she has "Spanish pirate blood" in her veins – a matter on which I keep an open mind. But as she danced, it began to look as if it might just be true.

At the end of the class we learned how to break back, moving slightly away from our partner, and how to turn the lady: the basic anticlockwise spin. It seemed a little tricky, and I had to be careful not to bump my partner's nose with my elbow. But we managed. Then it was all over, and Debbie was telling us to give ourselves some applause. We clapped our own efforts vigorously, disproportionately delighted to have survived: to have finished, to have learnt something new – and not to have to do it any longer.

Amanda and I decided to have one more drink before going home. The club had filled up, the main lights had been turned down, the DJ was getting into his stride, the spots and ultraviolet had been switched on and the main dance floor was heaving. We watched couples spinning and holding each other, breaking apart to do intricate footwork, rejoining and flipping effortlessly into elegant, complex knots and tangles like human metal puzzles, before unwinding and floating again on the rhythms of the music. Without knowing it, we were learning something else: that salsa is for watching, and that the watching is what draws you on.

Because from the day you begin – and always – you will see someone else doing something you don't know how to do. And you will want to find out how it's done, because it looks wonderful. How does that guy spin that girl round twice without (apparently) ever letting go of the hand he holds behind her back? How can that couple both have their arms crossed over their shoulders, and then turn inwards to come out with their arms crossed on their chests, without ceasing to hold hands? How can that girl spin seven or eight complete turns without stopping, becoming no more than a visual blur, and yet carry on with no trace of dizziness? And above all, how can they do everything so *fast*?

Watching those other dancers, I found I had an immense craving to do all these things myself. (Or at any rate, all the things the men were doing.) There were paunchy, middle-aged guys out there, built like Baloo the Bear, yet they seemed to dance weightlessly and with total relaxation. There were cool-looking Latin guys, and blokes who looked like the students I used to teach on my postgrad courses. There was a tall, bulky, Chinese-looking man with his hair in – yes – a pigtail. He looked like someone out of an old martial-arts movie, and he moved with matchless delicacy. I wanted to be like them and do what they were doing. And I wanted to spin those gravity-defying girls and bend them back over my knee as if they hadn't a bone in their bodies.

So we returned. In the following weeks we began to master some of the basic moves. We got used to dancing with other partners, both more and less experienced than us. In salsa, changing partners frequently is vital because each man – each leader – will have his own repertoire of moves, and his own way of dancing. If you stick to the same partner it becomes predictable: the lady doesn't have the challenge of responding instantly to unexpected leads, and the gentleman gets blasé because his partner always knows what he's likely to do. Staying sharp requires dancing with people who don't know your every move. And if changing partners adds a little erotic *frisson* (which it does), so much the better.

We also found things happening to our bodies. Amanda (who wasn't overweight to begin with) lost a stone and a half in a few weeks, and then stabilized at her new weight. It didn't take any effort; it was simply the effect of the dancing. I found that my posture gradually changed. Salsa gives you a new and different experience of your body. You learn (even I learned) to co-ordinate. You start to get some sense of poise. It wasn't always easy, of course. I'm tall (six foot four) and had always tended to stoop – the result, I used to tell myself, of subliminal signals sent out by all those short people who don't like anyone being that much taller than they are. After I'd been dancing for a few months, a male salsa teacher invited me out through a door I'd never noticed before, into a quiet back corridor of the club, and talked to me for ten minutes (or what seemed like ten minutes) about my bad posture. He told me to look at the ceiling for a while when I was dancing. I gave it an occasional try – it turned out to be harder work than gazing into women's eyes – and after a few weeks found I was no longer stooping. My whole way of standing and walking had changed.

Meanwhile we were hearing about other clubs and deciding to try them. We found a class in a tiny café, hidden away even deeper into the Northern Quarter, between a vacant site used as a car-park and a pub favoured by transvestites. The café was stuffed with Cuban memorabilia. Old gramophones, guitars, suitcases and bicycles hung from the ceiling. There were revolving fans and plastic palm trees and a sign advertising halal curries (which they didn't serve) and six TV monitors showing old, silent Tito Puente videos while the speakers played the best salsa music in town.

We found a class in the basement of a Spanish restaurant, where the teacher – who could have made a living as a stand-up comedian – taught the most intricate moves we'd yet encountered. And we didn't want to give up the weekly class we'd started with. So we found ourselves going to salsa two nights a week. Then three. And sometimes going out just to dance, no class involved. That meant four nights. By the end of three years, it was hard to get enough.

And I began to wonder what salsa was like in the countries of its origin, its heartland. In Manchester it seemed a well-rooted but still exotic import. What would it be like to dance in the places where salsa was as natural as breathing, where it evolved and interacted as part of a whole culture?

Every so often one of the dance teachers would disappear for a couple of weeks, returning with some new moves brought back from Cuba or Puerto Rico. Mythical places, I felt, patterned with sunlight, colour and music; and with just a dark edge of possible danger to sharpen the outlines. Places where you could find real salsa – and who knew what else? Not just Cuba, not just Puerto Rico. Where else did the tracks on our *Salsa Clasica* CD come from? Venezuela. Panama. The Dominican Republic. Colombia. Why not visit all of them and find out what they had to teach?

At last I put the idea to Amanda.

"You're crazy," she said.

"We could both go," I said. "Why not?"

"I hate hot places," she said. "Besides, there'd be bound to be some crisis with the family." (The youngest of our children, I should explain, is now over twenty-one.) "And as for you, you're too tall. You stand out. You'd definitely be kidnapped. Or come back with a tropical disease. Or someone will plant cocaine in your luggage and you'll spend the rest of your life rotting in jail."

"If I stand out that much," I countered, "why would they plant the drugs on me? Anyway, I don't wear expensive clothes, my watch is a kids' one from M&S, and I can speak some Spanish. No one's going to kidnap me."

"If they do, don't expect me to ransom you. Oh, and if you die out there I'm not paying for them to fly your body back to England. Got that?"

"Fine," I said.

"Anyway," she said, more thoughtfully, "if I went away, what would happen to all the guys I dance with in Manchester? They'd miss me."

That seemed to be the clinching argument. But for me, the idea had a life of its own; it wouldn't let go. From a fantasy it became a possibility, and then a plan. First, I'd go to Cuba – the Mecca of salsa; then I'd make my way along the mainland, through Venezuela and Colombia (taking in Cali, Colombia's salsa city), to Panama. After that I'd island-hop, visiting Puerto Rico and the Dominican Republic, before ending with a visit to Cuba-in-exile, the Latin quarter of Miami.

And suddenly, somehow, here I am at the hideous and unreal hour when all long journeys seem to begin – five o'clock – on a dark and freezing Manchester morning, having a last cup of tea and listening for the sound of the taxi that will take me to the airport.

I've packed my best white trainers – the ones I wear only for dancing. They're so light they make me feel as if I've got wings on my feet, and I associate them with good times. Susan, one of my dance teachers, has given me a bulky letter to deliver to Ernesto, a friend of hers in Havana. To read, I've got Borges's *Historia universal de la infamia*. (Blessings on the name of Borges: a literary genius who uses simple sentences and plain vocabulary, a miraculous gift for those whose Spanish is ambitious but rudimentary.) My toothpaste, nail-clippers and other requisites for hijacking an airliner (we're still under the shadow of 9/11) are safely stowed in my hold baggage, an immensely sturdy rucksack which the sales assistant assured me was the type used by foreign correspondents at the BBC. (Since I bought it from a shop opposite the BBC building, this could well be true. And if it's good enough for John Simpson, it's good enough for me.)

And I've got the condoms.

"What on earth are these?" I asked, when Amanda produced the box some days before.

"They're condoms, dickhead. What do they look like?"

"But I'm not going to have sex with anyone."

"How do I know that? Anyway you can never tell. What if you're overwhelmed with desire? You might be desperate. It could happen. At least if you get into a situation where you can't control yourself, you can practise safe sex."

"Are you saying I've got a licence to lose control and have safe sex with someone?"

"You'd better bloody not. No, but just in case."

So the condoms – a packet of twelve – are now packed, along with the T-shirts and jeans and the medical kit. I don't really like to think about whether or not they might get used. Do I want to use them? I don't know. I find it's a kind of mental no-go area. But I know they're in there: the cellophane wrapping unbroken, like the pin firmly in place on a hand grenade.

And then from outside comes the unmistakable rattling diesel throb, and a black cab illuminates the rainy darkness with the wan yellow glow from its sign. I kiss Amanda, heave my luggage onto my shoulder and open the door.

CHAPTER ONE
✳Cuba Libre

The flight to Havana was delayed, so instead of landing in mid-afternoon, we've touched down late at night. I come down the steps from the plane into the hot damp darkness feeling a blend of excitement, apprehension and immense fatigue. My eyelids are swollen, my ankles ache. Part of me feels bouncy and alert, ready for anything and excited to be in Havana at last. Yet somewhere deep inside, I'm aware of a seething current of exhaustion that threatens at any moment to well up, knock me over sideways and make me sleep for ever. I follow a straggling line of fellow-passengers across the tarmac to the glass terminal building.

Manhandling my bag from a disorganized heap that seems to have fallen off the carousel, I join a long queue behind a red line on the floor. Here I wait my turn to step up to a glass booth, where an immigration official who looks like a twelve-year-old boy in uniform stares unsmiling from me to my passport photograph and back. He scrutinizes my entrance permit intently. I wonder if it contains some awful mistake. I recall having problems with the tiny spaces given for squeezing in those long Havana addresses where you must give not only the house number and district, but also the names of the intersecting streets on either side of your particular block – all this to be written in capitals, under the warning that any irregularity in completing the permit will result in its rejection. At length he asks me the purpose of my visit. I tell him "*Turismo*" and he gives me a broad grin. "Enjoy your visit," he says.

I walk through customs to join the queue for money-changing, and exchange some *libras esterlinas* into Cuban *pesos convertibles*. Then I retreat to a quiet corner, where I stash most of them in my money belt and the rest in my rucksack, uncertain which is the more secure. I've been told both "Don't carry anything on you in the street", and "Never leave anything behind in your room, even if there is a safe". I'm keeping my passport and the bulk of my money next to my skin – but who knows how safe that is?

I edge my way into a seething crowd that seems to move in all directions at once: hauling wheeled cases, whistling to attract the attention of friends, shepherding children, wielding crutches, puffing ecstatically on a first post-flight cigarette. At first there are signs up in the roof saying TAXI, but soon they disappear. I plod on and am starting to despair when a tall, pleasant-looking young man appears at my elbow. "Taxi?" he asks. I breathe a sigh and resign myself. "*Sí*", I say. I know it's a basic rule that you never take an unauthorized taxi, but my entire nervous system is overloaded. I can't face any more searching.

The young man strides ahead of me through the crowd, out through some glass doors into the car-park. A couple of rows back is his yellow Fiat (or is it a Lada?). He heaves the trunk open. The lid has some rusty dents, but then I wouldn't expect to find immaculate cars here. He's very helpful with the luggage and insists on putting everything in. It's a vast relief to feel it lifted off my back. I get in and find there's another Cuban in the rear seat. He greets me ceremoniously and we shake hands. The two of them put their heads together over the address I give them. I tell them it's a *casa particular* – a private house that rents rooms – not a hotel. I ask how much the ride is going to cost, and the quoted fare sounds reasonable. So we launch into the traffic.

Scrunched up in the passenger seat, I peer out as best I can. I glimpse harsh street lighting, hurtling lorries, battered concrete buildings, pulsating (and ignored) traffic-lights, clusters of young people grouped around motorcycles. There are brightly coloured, striped murals on the ends of buildings. I register a vast image of Che Guevara on the side of a tower block. Half my brain takes this in, while the other half maintains a desultory conversation – my name, my work, where I come from, English football teams. *Chicas Cubanas*, I'm told, are *muy guapas*. Very hot indeed. Would I like them to arrange for me to meet a pretty Cuban girl? They can fix it, no problem. No, thanks, I tell them. Yes, certainly I like beautiful girls, I'm already married to one. Et cetera.

The driver tells me they have to stop to get some gas. Oh right, I think, this is where they're going to ask for extra money. But they don't. We pull in at a distinctly run-down service station which seems to be partly a bar, populated by a few young men in jeans and T-shirts drinking from beer-bottles, and a larger number of girls with long hair and very short skirts who lean against the petrol pumps chatting and flicking the ash off their cigarettes into puddles of oil on the tarmac. Maybe these are the hot chicks my driver recommended. My fellow-passenger leans forward over the back of my seat and goes on talking to me about Cuba – until the driver returns, slams his door, and we drive on.

Suburbs start to show up, yellow streetlights patterned by the leaves of dusty trees, wide unkempt pavements patched with dry grass, iron gates sheltering low houses that recede into shadow. We crawl through a grid of streets – Havana suburbs are built as a matrix, avenues cutting across one another at right angles – Linea, Calzada, 3rd, 5th and so on – identified by names or numbers cut into the faces of little stone pyramids set at each street corner, so the driver has to crane from his window to scrutinize the pyramids until he gets to the right junction.

We come to rest in front of a dark house guarded by tall gates of wrought iron backed with rusted sheet metal. I can see the number on the gatepost. The driver lifts out my bags and hands each one to me with elegant courtesy. I pay him, adding a tip, then watch the car recede into the dimly glowing distance before I turn to the gate. It looks as if it hasn't opened in fifty years and might be the entrance to a mausoleum.

There's a bell-button at one side; I press it without much hope and wait, listening to the unceasing musical scrape of the cicadas. I'm just wondering whether to press again when a dim light shows from somewhere inside and I hear shuffling footsteps, then the sound of much complicated unlocking. One of the gates swings back a little way and a man, cautious and stooping, in pyjamas and something that looks more like an old overcoat than a dressing-gown, stands in the space revealed. He has glasses and a long, troubled face. He welcomes me in, explaining that they've been expecting me, his wife knows about everything and we'll settle it all in the morning. I start to ask about breakfast, but he waves this and all other concerns aside. We agree that they'll call me at eight (though all hours have now become meaningless to me).

He takes me round the side of the house to a back door that leads to my *habitación*. It's just big enough for the bed to fit in. There's a straw mat, a mirror, a chest of drawers and a scratched and chipped ghetto-blaster on the windowsill. There's a tiny bathroom with a shower at the back. A vast ceiling fan hangs over the bed. Well, it's pretty basic – to be honest, rather more basic than I'd expected from the website I used to book it. But right now, the crushing necessity, the thing every cell in my body wants, is to sleep. The room is stiflingly hot. I tell my host I'll be fine and he shuffles off, leaving me to play around with the plastic knob that operates the fan. It takes a while to coax the fan into turning at a pace that takes some of the heat out of the air without roaring like an aircraft propeller, but I manage it. Then I unstrap my rucksack, drag out some night things, and collapse into the darkness.

When eight o'clock comes I pull some clothes on, just in time to catch my landlady – a smiling broad woman in an apron and slippers, very concerned about the lateness of my flight and whether I've slept – and negotiate about breakfast. It's coffee, fruit (papaya, guava, mango), bread, fried eggs if I want them, and hot milk. (I soon discover that milk is a much-prized drink in Cuba, a country where there are few dairy cattle and people are often short of protein. I'm lucky to get it.)

I eat at a small iron table in the yard, among flowering shrubs in pots, under an array of strings and wires which I guess will carry washing later in the day. High walls in every direction hide any trace of Havana's suburbs apart from the windows in the tall neighbouring buildings. But I'm feeling pretty pleased with myself – and it's only when I start to unpack that the true meaning of last night's taxi ride becomes clear. I notice that the envelope given me by Susan, which I've carried in the centre of my rucksack, doesn't look quite right. Surely it was smoother than that, and more neatly stuck down? I dig further in among my clothes. An envelope that held around a hundred pounds sterling is still there – but it's empty. My stomach lurches. I scrabble around, but the money is gone. I examine Susan's package again. It's been opened and everything it contained apart from the letter has been carefully removed, and the paper stuck down again – neatly but not quite neatly enough. How the hell did that happen?

Then I remember the stop at the gas station. Of course: beautifully simple. The driver stops for gas, his friend keeps me talking, the driver pretends to fill the tank and meanwhile checks expertly through my luggage. No wonder he was so politely eager to help with my bags. He was making sure they went into the trunk where he could get at them. And how neatly everything was strapped up afterwards so there was no sign of any tampering. A tidy, expert job. And thoughtful. Nothing taken but the money (and whatever else Susan had packed for her friend). Just as well most of my cash and documents were in my money belt. If you take an unlicensed taxi, I say to myself, that's what you get. Or worse. Welcome to Cuba.

Later I'll have to break the news to Ernesto that whatever he was expecting from Susan has, through my stupidity, been stolen. But just now I can't face it. And I'm due to meet my dance teacher at noon. So I dig out my street map of Havana, throw my white trainers into a backpack and set out for the Teatro Neptuno, where we've arranged to meet. The walk through the suburbs is dreamlike. Playful Art Deco houses sporting wavy lines of coloured tiles or circular windows: a modernist version of Toytown, alternate with ornate, crumbling baroque mansions. Every so often there's the spectral, vine-covered shell of a house that has simply collapsed from within. The concrete pavements are cracked and have patches of dry, yellowish grass growing through them. I pass smart-suited workers and schoolchildren carrying little briefcases, their immaculate clothing a weird contrast to the patched and splitting buildings.

I've chosen a route that leads to the Malecón, the grey waist-high sea wall that runs for miles along the frontage of Havana keeping the waves from battering the buildings – though in several places groups of men with concrete-mixers are repairing breaches made during the summer hurricanes, when the waves hurled themselves right across the road and smashed into the lower storeys of the buildings on the other side. Most still have their ground-floor windows criss-crossed with heavy-duty adhesive tape to minimize the damage from shattered glass if wind and water should decide to punch their way in again. It's high tide now, and as I walk along beside the Malecón irregular waves from the turbulent water keep smacking into it, sending towers of spume over the rampart onto the pavement, where the water drains away through huge gratings and back into the sea.

The sun is already hot. I'm tired with walking so when I reach the main urban area, Centro Havana, it hits me with full intensity. Between high, raddled buildings cut dead-straight streets, narrow as canyons, filled with a haze of traffic fumes. Fiats and Ladas are everywhere. So are the classic cars famous from the travel brochures: great hulks of Plymouths and Dodges, dented, filled, rusted, much repaired, many of them matt in texture as if they've simply grown too old to shine any longer, or painted with house paint complete with brush marks. Every one trails a cloud of blue smoke to mix with the black fumes from the diesel trucks.

The buildings are a fantastic vision of every possible architectural style, all of it cracked and crumbling. Curling iron balconies are adorned with birdcages, washing, bicycles, old TV aerials. The narrow pavements are plentifully daubed with the leavings of the packs of friendly stray dogs I've encountered every few blocks on my way into town. Elaborate classical façades, moulded with flaking stucco nymphs holding swags of fruit and foliage, adjoin concrete 1940s shop-fronts which have lost their plate-glass windows and had them replaced with sheets of plywood. Mysterious hammerings come from cavernous ground-floor spaces behind metal grilles.

Every so often there's a gap where a building has simply disappeared, the walls on either side of the gaping hole shored up with vast slanting timber props. A four-storey-high fig tree flourishes inside one such space; another is filled with stacked breeze blocks and scrap iron. I pass an open door, inside which is an immaculate white marble staircase. Peering in and taking a few steps up, I see that the flight takes a half-turn and opens into empty sky. There's nothing at the top; it's just a dream-staircase, a detail from a surrealist painting.

And all the time people pour past me, people of every colour and physique, mostly dressed in jeans or denim shorts and T-shirts. Here and there an old person sits, cigarette in hand, in a cheap kitchen chair set out on the pavement. I quickly realize that there's no typical Cuban physique. Truly every height, build and colour is here. Some people are as pale as I am; every shade of pink, brown and black is represented. No one takes the slightest notice of me.

I've arranged to meet Johannes García, Director of the Conjunto Folklórico Nacional de Cuba, in the entrance to his headquarters, the Teatro Neptuno, which is situated (naturally) on Neptuno, between Escobar and Lealtad. Spotting a tiny sign with the street name in rusted cast iron, I turn the corner and start to look for numbers. There are fifty or so to go. Ahead of me an elderly lady in a wheelchair pushes herself gamely along in the carriageway, against the current of cars and bicycles, which circumvent her perilously. I walk up alongside and ask if I can help. Where is she going? Only a few blocks, it seems. So I bend to it and get the knack of keeping a steady pace over the unevenly tarmacked road surface. And a few minutes later, I am sailing with the steady momentum of the wheelchair past the Teatro Neptuno where Johannes García and associates sit in plastic garden chairs under the flaking blue-and-white stucco arch of what must be an old cinema, recognizing me at once, waving and calling out, while I shout that I'll be back in a moment, just as soon as I've taken this lady and her wheels around the next corner.

When I walk back to the Neptuno, Señor Garcia gets out of his chair and we go through the introductions. He's tall and wiry, very dark and very ceremoniously formal. My *profesora*, he tells me, is to be Geldys; and with a bow and a sweeping gesture he ushers forward a lovely young black woman with her hair in braids. She wears a black-and white tracksuit and trainers, and smiles broadly as she shakes my hand. She will show me, Señor Garcia assures me, everything I need to know. I am in her hands.

Geldys raises her eyebrows and nods, then invites me to follow her. Instead of heading into the depths of the theatre, as I'd expected, we go down the steps and along the street. Where are we going? To her apartment, she tells me, for my first lesson.

I almost have to run to keep up with her through a maze of streets, turning a corner here, crossing to the shadowed side there. At one point she grabs my elbow gently to save me from stepping in front of a fuming diesel truck loaded with timber. Finally we get to a hot narrow street sloping down to the sea. On either side are tall doorways in high flaking façades of brown and ochre, studded with the usual metal balconies. Geldys slips a key from the pocket of her silky tracksuit bottoms and unlocks a beaten, blistered brown wooden door, its rim scarred with past forcings, pitted and scabbed with the remains of old locks and hasps. Inside, the air is cool, damp, dusty. A big black umbrella leans beside a rusty fuse box from which emerge tangled electric cables. She beckons me to follow her up a tight spiral staircase of white stone. It goes up and up. Every so often there's a small landing with a door. I stop by one to get my breath back. When we reach the fourth floor Geldys produces another key, unlocks another cracked and damaged brown wooden door, and stands back to let me enter. She follows, shuts the door and slams a big iron bolt across.

We're in a light, bright room with a floor that looks like stone. There's a formica table with some stacking chairs, and an old wooden cabinet full of plates and china ornaments, its shiny top covered with photos and cheap souvenirs – a miniature plastic Eiffel Tower, glittery pictures of the Alps, a "snowstorm" globe. There's a silvery plastic CD player. Opposite, a curtain on a string partially hides a sink and a twin-tub washing-machine.

Geldys is changing her shoes, so I take off my sandals and put on my white trainers. She admires them, calling them my "*preciosas tenis*" – a word dating, I guess, from the days when trainers were just tennis-shoes.

Then we get started. Geldys positions me in front of her – I have to learn to stand firm in the disconcertingly direct gaze of her dark eyes – and tells me to do exactly as she does. She presses a button on the CD player and salsa music starts up – something percussive and halfway towards rap. And from that moment Geldys begins systematically to exercise, and retrain, every muscle in my body. First it's just the neck: we turn our heads – left, centre, right, and back again, over and over again, first slow, then fast. Then it's shoulder movements. Chest. Arms. Hips.

It's clear I can throw away everything I thought I knew. Geldys starts from the assumption that I know nothing and deconstructs my every movement. We work for two hours, and at the end of it I haven't actually taken a dance step. Instead I've started to develop a new sense of my own body, a new kind of internal map.

The key, Geldys makes clear, is first of all the chest area, in fact the heart, *el corazón* – that organ mentioned in the lyrics to every salsa track. I have to find the internal point of balance at the centre of the chest, and swing from there, as if it's a kind of pivot. And Geldys isn't shy about showing me how. She grabs my neck, my waist, my shoulders, the sides of my chest, with hands firm and practical as a baker's kneading dough. She tilts my ribcage gently up and down, to and fro. When I don't seem to be getting the message, she grabs my wrists and plonks my hands solidly on either side of her stocky torso, where I grip on, feeling the firm protrusion of her breasts under her T-shirt while she undulates with a kind of floating motion around that elusive centre point. I start to get the feel of it and swing freely for a few beats – delighted shrieks of "¡*Eso es! ¡Okay! ¡Eso es!*" – before I lose the knack and revert to jerking my shoulders up and down.

But gradually it starts to come. My centre of gravity changes; I begin to find that it's possible to loosen up and let the different parts of the body flow, or float, to the music, almost independently. I realize I've had a habit of holding my body tightly together, as if afraid the bits of me would somehow come apart if I didn't keep them together in one tense mass. But this is like becoming pleasantly weightless, floating from a point at the middle of the chest that miraculously supports everything else. That is, until I lose it once again. But we keep at it, pausing only for *un refreco* (a plastic bottle of cheap cola) at half-time. Geldys is smiling, patient, encouraging. The time goes too fast. When we finish, she gives me exercises to practise for the next day – in front of a mirror if possible – and sees me to the head of the marble stairs. I kiss her on both cheeks – I can feel her warmth, she's sweating almost as much as I am – and head off down into the darkness. Out in the blinding light I cross the pitted carriageway and look back up at the balcony. Geldys is there, leaning over, waving. I wave back, turn the corner into Trocadero and lose sight of her.

There's a vague uneasiness at the back of my mind, though, and I trace it to the knowledge that I shall have to call Ernesto and confess that I've lost the consignment of goodies entrusted to me by Susan. I am not looking forward to making that call.

But I know I have to make it, and I do. When Ernesto answers, he's puzzled about who I am. I manage to explain that I'm a friend of Susan's, and he suggests I come over. I'm not sure whether he's quite grasped my story about the theft, but I go down to the Malecón and hail a cab. It's a vast coffee-and-cream Plymouth, completely matt as if every trace of its gloss has been polished away with fine-grade sandpaper. There are two ladies – slight, middle-aged and well dressed – already in the back, but I climb in alongside them on cream leather seats networked with an astonishing craquelure. We head across town. The car is air-conditioned, so we're cool despite the glaring afternoon light reflecting off the concrete road surface. Salsa music pounds from the car radio.

San Miguel, between Soledad and Aramburu, turns out to be a brown stucco block in a long narrow thoroughfare full of the usual street life: four guys leaning earnestly into the innards of an old blue Packard, its huge hood propped precariously on a length of timber; kids circling on bicycles; a small pack of yellow stray dogs trotting purposefully along the pavement. The entrance to number 19 is a dark passage guarded by a rusty metal grille. There's no bell or knocker. As I peer into the depths, a small brown boy wearing just a pair of shorts appears from nowhere to swing on the grille and ask if I want Ernesto. He pulls the gate open and I follow him in. He calls ahead of us down the passage in an accent I can't understand. The passage is like an alley: once inside I can see the sky above, and several storeys of tenements stretching high above us. The boy leaves me to wait outside a door while he goes in. Beside me, a stocky chap dressed in swimming trunks – good clothing for the afternoon heat and humidity – bends over a plastic washing-up bowl, rinsing his back with cold water from a green hosepipe. He straightens up and shakes my hand, introducing himself as a friend of Ernesto's.

A moment later the boy re-emerges, followed by Ernesto, who's tall, wiry and black, with a round, melancholy, wrinkled face and delicate features. We shake hands – his arms are as long and skinny as mine – and he welcomes me inside. As we go, he introduces me to his wife, a powerful-looking lady as broad, stocky and stolid as Ernesto is slender and animated. She wipes her hands on her apron to take mine, and kisses me on both cheeks. She's busy cooking on a gas stove right in front of the door – so close that I almost walk into the hot pans as I enter the apartment.

Further in, there's a small space with two wooden armchairs and a mat, on which is a mass of small boys, tumbling over one another, yelling. They have to yell because of the noise from the TV, which is showing one of the Spanish channels broadcast from Miami. It's technically illegal in Cuba to watch these channels, but everyone does. In one corner is a pair of huge, dark red conga drums. (Seeing me eyeing them, Ernesto tells me he's a drummer but hasn't worked for the past eighteen months.) Beside the TV table are the richly painted and gilded statues of two Catholic saints, male and female – blue eyes, glazed rosy cheeks, golden crowns, long crimson robes. They're three feet tall and very striking. Around their feet are candle stubs and bowls of fruit.

Ernesto clears the small boys from the floor and invites me to sit down. He disappears, returning a moment later with a bottle of rum and three glasses. He pours with concentration, and while he does so the man who was taking the hosepipe shower outside arrives, now clad in T-shirt and shorts. We shake hands again, and he's named as Agustin. We chat a bit and, bracing myself, I explain to Ernesto about the theft. He picks thoughtfully through the package I've brought. Alice's letter is intact, but the money and paracetamol she had enclosed have been removed. Paracetamol is in short supply in Cuba, so it's a grievous loss. I feel terrible for having let it happen, but Ernesto takes it philosophically. These thieves are very clever, he says – always coming up with some new dodge; it's impossible to avoid them entirely. If it hadn't been this, it would have been something else.

The TV rumbles and shrills in front of us. Agustin and Ernesto are talking together, glancing at me from time to time. Agustin gestures at me with his thumb and tells Ernesto, "You should ask the *santos* about him." Turning to me, he explains, "Ernesto is a *santero*, you know? He's a good one, he knows a lot. Very powerful."

"You want me to consult the *santos* for you?" Ernesto asks, eyebrows raised. "Yes, come on – why not?"

The *santos* are the Afro-Cuban gods, the Yoruba deities brought to Cuba by the slaves and then merged with the Catholic saints venerated by their captors. Well, a talk with the *santos* is fine by me. I shrug politely, and agree: why not?

Ernesto goes over to confer with his wife. Then he disappears up a small spiral staircase at the back of the room. After a minute or two he comes back carrying a stool, a cushion and a brightly coloured beach towel. He turns off the TV.

I watch as Ernesto unfolds the towel and spreads it on the stone floor. It is pristine, apparently brand-new, and it depicts, in red, black, white and bright blue, the familiar image of Postman Pat and his cat Jess. Ernesto places the stool at one end of the towel, and the cushion on the stool. He asks me to take my shoes off, and indicates the stool with a wonderfully graceful gesture. I perch on it while Ernesto sits cross-legged at the other end of the towel. He begins to chant in a deep-voiced, reverberating, rhythmical drone. After two minutes or so he stops abruptly and asks for the name of someone in my family who has died. I give my father's name – wondering ruefully what he would make of all this – and the chanting resumes. My father's name duly crops up amongst a rapid-fire torrent of deeply vibrating syllables. After a couple more minutes Ernesto stops again in mid-flow. "Another who has died?" I give him my mother's name and the chanting rushes on again.

Suddenly Ernesto produces, as if from nowhere, a string of what look like large flat beads, though I soon see that they are in fact small oval sections of coconut shell, each like the bowl of a teaspoon in shape and size, dark on the outside and painted white on the concave inner surface. There are eight of them, held together with small links of iron chain. Ernesto hands me a white oval pebble about an inch long, and a dark seed the same size. He tells me to hold them between my hands and shake them, mix them up. I begin the shaking and as I do so Ernesto takes the chain of coconut ovals by its middle and drapes it – almost throws it – onto the towel, creating two parallel lines of shell pieces, randomly black or white. He tells me to hold out my fists, shell in one and pebble in the other. When I do, he taps one fist, then the other. I open them and he glances at the pebble and shell. "No good. Again!"

I start rubbing and shaking again, scrambling the small lumps over each other to randomize them as effectively as possible. Ernesto drapes the chain again, taps my fists again. This time we do better. He reaches behind him, where I now see there is a small cloth bag on the floor, and gets out a school exercise book and a biro. He makes a note, and then on we go. We end up with four valid throws, which Ernesto notes in his book as four pairs of circles, black and white in different combinations.

He ponders the result. Then he gives me his diagnosis, throwing it out in abrupt phrases. I must take care of my legs, he tells me: I might have an accident affecting my legs or knees. I must wear light, brightly coloured clothes. Dark clothes won't bring me luck, especially not black. And I must change my clothes often: that way I will confuse evil spirits or enemies. I shouldn't eat heavy meals last thing at night – it's bad for *la presión*, my blood pressure. My wife will bring me luck. I shouldn't listen to people who might tell me bad things about her. I have a supposed friend who is envious of me. When I write a book, this person says to himself, "*¡Ojalá!* If only I could write such a book!" And his heart burns with envy. This person may try to harm me. I must not tell him my plans. Oh, and for me the god Eleggua – the oracle god, the god of travel, the guardian of the home – takes the form of the *caracol*, the sea shell. He's my protector; he'll take care of me.

The reading over, Ernesto smiles up at me, delighted. I thank him and he carefully folds up Postman Pat. Agustin, pouring more rum, looks at me expectantly. "How was it?" he asks. Did the *santos* give good advice? Ernesto's pretty sharp, yes?

"*Fenomenal*," I tell them. Amazing. Great advice. And I'm going to watch out for that false friend.

Next morning at ten I'm outside Geldys's apartment, ready for my lesson. The pitted brown door is locked, there's no bell, and when I knock with my knuckles I can tell the sound isn't travelling. I cross the narrow street and sit in a doorway, looking up at the fourth-floor shutters and cultivating patience.

After a couple of minutes I see a shutter opening. Geldys leans over the balcony, waving. She brandishes some small object as if she wants me to look at it. Then she tosses it down into the street. I check for traffic and run out to retrieve it. It's a small white sock, perhaps a child's, with something heavy inside it. Easing whatever it is out, I find it's the door key. I cross the street, let myself into the cool, damp darkness of the stairwell and trudge up the four marble flights. Geldys is waiting for me at the top. She beams and embraces me firmly. "*¿Como estás?*" I kiss her on both cheeks and follow her in.

As before, we start with loosening-up exercises – neck, shoulders, chest, waist, hips, knees – but this time we also do some dance steps. The correct partner-hold (palm vertical, pressing against the partner's palm but not clasping her hand), then the forward-and-back step. Soon we move on to the *dile que no* – the cross-body step – which seems effortless with Geldys's firm guidance, little nudges and pushes just where they're needed, until I get the hang of it. Before long I'm leading her with only the occasional word of warning. And then we're on to the *enchufla* (where the man spins his partner anticlockwise, then reconnects), the *enchufla doble* (where the lady gets half an anticlockwise turn, is caught and sent back before being spun completely round) and – great excitement! – the *enchufla doble a la moderna*, which involves giving the lady a half-spin, then walking around her in a circle while turning her again before sending both partners independently into a spin away from each other. All this is accompanied by hot salsa music from the bootleg CDs on Geldys's player, and by perpetual counting to make sure I get every step in the right place at the right moment. It's exhilarating and exhausting.

Just as we're collapsing into the armchairs with our bottles of cola, there's a piercing whistle from the street. Geldys heaves open one of the shutters and a shouted conversation follows, culminating in the tossing-down of the key, this time enclosed in a plastic spectacles-case. She unbars the door and a small boy runs in and hurls himself at her, followed by a lady who is an exact, though slightly more lined, replica of Geldys. I'm introduced to Geldys's mother (Geldys charmingly addresses her as "Mima") and her nine-year-old son Esven, who bows delightfully while we shake hands ("*¡Encantado!*"), stares at me with big eyes and then skips off to the back of the apartment. I chat with Mima a little.

Mima is as pretty as her daughter, and tells me she used to dance a lot of salsa. She still dances quite a bit – it keeps her young, she says. She also scolds Geldys about being late: apparently Geldys has to get to the Teatro Federico García Lorca, where she's rehearsing dance numbers for a Cuban opera that's opening in a few weeks' time. I begin to realize just how hard Geldys works. She has other private pupils today, besides rehearsals. She does all the odd jobs too: earlier she mentioned that when the water-pump goes wrong, she's the one who fixes it. (There's no water pressure in Havana; each building has its own electric pump to fill a metal tank upstairs.) As I leave, Mima is starting to cook; I can smell fried chicken from behind the dividing wall that partly separates the back half of the apartment – where I can just glimpse three beds, as well as a cooker, a dressing-table crowded with make-up and plastic bags, and a hundred other things, all crowded together. Our dancing has used nearly half the apartment. In the other half everything else, the rest of life, has to go on.

I've heard that there's dancing every night at the Hotel Florida, so I walk along the Malecón a few blocks to the main tourist district, ignoring voices from the shadows offering me genuine Havana cigars, or a Cuban girlfriend. A soft, golden full moon floats above the sea, surrounded with faint, misty rings. I find myself wondering whether Amanda's looking at it too; she always notices the moon. Then I realize it's unlikely – there's a five-hour time difference.

The Florida turns out to be an elegant colonial building, the *discoteca* a dimly-lit bar with a small band playing traditional music while the clientèle gathers. I take a *mojito* and survey the room, slightly apprehensively. There are certainly plenty of Cubans here, but they all seem to be men. And there are plenty of women, but they all look like European tourists. I'd hoped to dance with *Cubanas*. Still, it's early days and a bit of practice won't go amiss. I choose a sofa and sit down to sip my cocktail.

In due course the band packs up, the lights go down a little, and salsa starts playing. A few couples get up to dance. They're good – lots of rhythm, fluid movements, precise timing – but I think I can cope and I know I've got to take the plunge. When the DJ puts on one of those tracks that simply defy you to keep still, I take a deep breath, go to a neighbouring table and ask a pretty, blonde woman, maybe in her late thirties, if she'd like to dance. She accepts, and we head out onto the dance floor.

My first real dance in Cuba! In between the more energetic moves we snatch a conversation in Spanish and I find out she's from Norway. After that we use English – not that the energy of the dance leaves much scope for words. She moves nicely, she follows the leads well, and I can feel a new flexibility and spontaneity in my own movements. Geldys's hard work is paying off. It's exhilarating.

When the music fades I take my partner back to her table and ask another lady onto the floor. It turns out she's Norwegian too. In all, I dance with five Norwegians, and it doesn't take me long to see how things work, and to understand my own place in the ecology of this particular venue. These European women aren't here to dance with an Englishman, however Cuban his style may be. Like me, they want to dance with Cubans – but there aren't enough to go round. I'm a pilot-fish accompanying the sharks: with each new track, the Cuban guys take their partners out onto the floor, and I follow, asking the ones who are left. I notice that I'm the only non-Cuban male – in fact the only white male – who's dancing. Towards the end of the evening, I pass a tall young Cuban chatting to a group of lady tourists. He reaches out to put his hand on my wrist. I brace myself nervously but he raises an eyebrow, nods seriously, and tells me, "*Bailas bien*." ("You dance well.") I shake his hand and thank him. Cuban courtesy, of course, but perhaps his compliment means something.

I've established a pattern, and try to follow it. I have a lesson with Geldys every morning, and in the evenings I go to a club or a dance hall to hear the music and practise my moves. In between, I lie on my bed to read, or sleep, or listen to the radio. Fidel Castro has been ill and in hospital for months. Power has been handed over to his brother Raúl. I ask people how things will change. Everyone has a different opinion. My landlady thinks Raúl will be more flexible. Maybe he'll negotiate an end to the American embargo that makes trade so difficult for Cuba. Life will get a bit easier. Other people tell me the opposite: Fidel was always ready to discuss; Raúl is more authoritarian, a real dictator.

A taxi driver sorts it all out for me. "*Cuba es como una pelicula*," he tells me as we lurch through a huge junction, slaloming around pot-holes and just missing the back end of a *camello*, a colossal bus built like an articulated lorry. "Cuba is like a movie: for negotiations, for politics, you have the good guy and the bad guy. The open hand and the closed fist." He takes both hands off the wheel to demonstrate. "Underneath, they know what the score is. I believe in my heart that things will change. Already things become a little better. *Soy optimista*. And what use is there in being a pessimist? In my heart I'm content, and that's what counts." He places his open hand on his chest. Once again, the heart, *el corazón*: the key to everything.

Often I go out just to gape at the endless cornucopia of wonderful architecture, or wander around the array of second-hand bookstalls in the Plaza de Armas. I pick up a detective novel by Leonardo Padura. Harder to read than Borges, but maybe I'll graduate to it. And I feed my addiction to Borges with a tattered copy of his essays, *Siete noches*. There's a chapter on the *Arabian Nights*. Back in my room, remaking my bed after a siesta, it strikes me how much pulling the sheet over this bed is like closing the cover of an old book. I feel a poem springing to life. I search for paper but can't find any, so I pick up *Siete noches* and scribble on the blank leaves at the back:

> Our bed is a great book. Open those covers –
> soft and floppy as the hide of a giant folio,
> patched and stitched – and inside are the stories
> of our thousand and one nights, the incandescent
> conceptions of our children, dreams and memories
> time can't wash out, nor the wringing of hands...

I find I'm writing about the bed I share with Amanda at home. I also realize how much I'm missing her. I go out to one of the hotels to check my email, paying for ten expensive minutes at an old, slow computer. And yes, there's a message from Amanda. "There was a beautiful full moon last night," she writes, "with rings round it, golden at first…" So she did notice that moon after all.

In the evenings I try Club la Red, the Karachi Club, and the Café Cantante, a small basement club where some fine local bands perform. And in these places I get to dance with the Cubans at last.

The difference is noticeable. The Europeans I've danced with tend to be preoccupied with elaborate moves. They want to be spinning and turning all the time. The Cubans are different. They follow the leads all right, but they don't give the impression of being familiar with all the moves I know. They dance more simply, maybe more subtly, and they move in the rhythms of the music like fish in water. I dance with chunky middle-aged women out for the evening in groups; I dance with slender young girls, apparently still in their teens, who ask their parents' permission before going with me to the dance floor. It's good practice for me, because invariably they seem to want clear and very firm leads – I almost have to shunt them around when I want them to execute a cross-body step or a spin – but once given a good shove, they go beautifully. And the dancing seems to happen at a deeper level than I'm used to. We don't have to do a lot – just move to and fro to the music and change our holds from time to time – but I can sense their bodies talking to mine. There's a whole conversation going on at a subliminal level to which I'm only just becoming attuned.

This connects with things Geldys has said to me. One morning, showing me a certain way of rolling the shoulders gently in time to the music, she told me, "If you're just waiting somewhere, and there's music playing, you can do this while you sit. It's a way for your body to enjoy the music." "*Para disfrutar la música.*" She demonstrated, and as I watched I could see that for her the body enjoys (*disfrutar*) music the same way it enjoys food – physically. You don't just listen with your head; you consume the music with your body, and you have to move a little to help it flow through. I begin to understand that there's a whole realm of experience, a whole intelligence of the body, that I'm starting, belatedly, to learn.

I'm walking down San Miguel when I notice a red pick-up truck at the kerbside. Someone is standing up in the back, and when I get closer I recognize Ernesto. He's lifting two live goats, a nanny and a kid, one in each hand. They're both tied by the feet, and it's by the feet that he lifts them. He shouts to me and I wave. He climbs down from the pick-up and strides into the dark entry of an apartment building, swinging the two goats like sacks. I carry on down the street – but turn when I hear him yell again. Now goatless, he rubs his right hand carefully on his jeans before shaking mine. Would I like to come for dinner in the evening? He has a little surprise for me, he says. Something very special. And hey, if I've got a minute… He beckons me to follow him, and we go into the building, and up two or three flights of winding stairs.

At the top there's an open door, and through it a noisy room with half a dozen people sitting around watching the inevitable TV. Ernesto introduces me to a buxom brown woman dressed in white from head to toe: white shoes, long white skirt, white blouse and cardigan, white lacy cloth wrapped around her head as a turban. I've seen people dressed like this in the streets and been told that they are dedicating themselves to *santería* – training for the priesthood. She's a *santería* priestess. She looks at me placidly. I reach to shake hands but she steps back, fists closed, forearms crossed on her chest. I guess that she isn't supposed to touch men, or strangers, or something, so I smile and give her a nod. She and Ernesto talk for a minute or so, then Ernesto gives me a wink and I follow him back onto the street.

That evening, while his wife cooks dinner, Ernesto shows me his *santos*, or more properly his *Orishas* – the Yoruba gods. The two colourful Catholic saints by the TV set represent San Lazaro, alias Babalú Ayé the healer; and Santa Barbara, female form of the very male Changó, god of fire and thunder, who once disguised himself as a woman. Just inside the front door, in an inconspicuous dusty corner, Ernesto points out Ogun and Eleggua. They look like part of the household junk (of which there's plenty). But no, that brown jar full of bits and pieces is the house of Ogun, god of all things metal – knives, cars, railroad tracks, you name it. Ernesto picks up the house to show me. It's a clay pot full of iron objects, all brown with rust. He pulls them out and spreads them on the floor.

There are knife blades of all sizes, nails, pieces of chain, small iron ingots, an ancient padlock, a big octagonal nut ... too many items to count. There's a thing like a giant nail, square in cross-section and with a flat square head, which Ernesto tells me is a railroad spike – very old, he adds proudly. The prize exhibit is a hefty iron spring, some nine inches long and three in diameter. "*Desde un carro*," Ernesto explains. "From a car." It's a shock-absorber. He puts the spring back into the pot as a kind of central spine and arranges the other ironware around it until the pot is crowded as before. But Ogun also has his own tools: Ernesto shows me a small shallow dish, little more than a saucer, that sits beside the larger pot. It contains exquisite tiny tools a couple of inches long. Unlike the miscellaneous old iron in the pot, these are silvery and shining. There's a little jagged saw cut from thin white sheet metal, a tiny hammer, a hoe, an anvil and other tools cast in lead or solder. They're like toys, perfect for a Christmas stocking. But taken with the contents of the pot, they represent Ogun, and in front of them in small jars are offerings of some nameless sticky liquid.

Beside Ogun, in a shallow earthenware dish, sits Eleggua, in the form of a coconut with a face roughly carved on it: just two eyes and a mouth cut into the shell. "My Eleggua is the *coco*," Ernesto explains; "yours is the *caracol*" – the sea shell. Eleggua has to be kept just inside the front door because he guards the house. Contemplating Eleggua's cockeyed cheeky face, cut into the dusty pelt of a moulting coconut, I wouldn't be inclined to trust him an inch; but Ernesto tells me he's one of the most important of the gods. He likes offerings of sweets and cigars.

Dinner is fried beef with cassava. Ernesto's two sons wander in with Agustin. Chairs are pushed back, straw mats are spread and we sit around on the floor to eat. The cassava is delicious and tastes like buttery mashed potato. The Señora offers me the dish. "Eat like a Cuban," Ernesto encourages me when I don't take enough. "Grab all you can get!" We drink cola, and afterwards some coffee and rum. Then Ernesto reminds me that he promised a surprise. "We're going to ask the Orishas to purify you, get rid of any bad luck that might be hanging around, any sickness, any problems. The Orishas will help you, they'll become your protectors. I spoke to the *santera* yesterday and she says it's fine."

Well, this should be interesting, I reflect. Remembering those goats, I rather hope they're not going to kill any animals. But the ritual Ernesto and Agustin have in mind doesn't seem to involve sacrifice. What it involves is my taking my shirt and shoes off and standing in a white chalk circle about eighteen inches in diameter, drawn on the floor just inside the closed front door of the apartment. The chalk circle is filled with small white chalk crosses, and on these I plant my feet.

Ernesto begins chanting – the same deep, reverberating chant that I've heard before, but this time it's interrupted by other voices, high-pitched or questioning. I guess that several spirits are involved, and that Ernesto is letting them speak through him. Then I realize he's talking to me. "*¡Girate! ¡Girate!* Turn round! No, no! Against the watch! Against the watch." After a moment's puzzlement I understand he means anticlockwise, so I hastily change direction and revolve steadily, being careful to stay inside the chalk circle. Agustin swigs some rum from a bottle and then, making his mouth into a small circle, abruptly blows in a single explosive puff so that the rum is vaporized and blown over my body. He repeats this several times. It smells good and it's cooling; a pleasant experience on the whole. He takes a cigar stub from a dish on the floor near Ogun's house, lights it and blows tobacco smoke over my skin. Then he produces a bunch of leafy green herbs, with which he gently beats me, or rather flicks me, all over the body as I turn. Ernesto tells me to stop moving. The herbs are placed at my feet in the chalk circle. "Trample them," Ernesto instructs. "Do it hard – go on, really lay into them. The harder, the better luck!" So I trample the green bunch as hard as I can, try to tread it to a pulp against the stone floor. "Okay," they say. "Enough. Enough."

Ernesto tells me to go upstairs and wash. I follow him up the spiral staircase onto a kind of mezzanine, more a platform than an upper storey, forming a tiny bedroom. There's a double bed, another set of congas, and in the corner a primitive shower – just a tap, with pipe and shower-head above. He gives me a towel and I take a cold shower: pleasant enough in the warm, humid atmosphere.

When I come downstairs Ernesto questions me. "How do you feel? Different? Much better?" I tell him truthfully that I feel fine. I feel good. I can't say I notice any vast difference, but never mind. Ernesto is busy wrapping up the trampled herbs, and some other small things I can't see properly, in a piece of white cloth. He hands me the bundle and tells me that I have to take it and throw it into the sea, making sure that no one sees me do it. He tells me the bundle now contains all the bad influences, bad luck, bad spirits that were driven out during the ceremony.

"And now," he says, "I have something else for you. Wait." He goes upstairs and comes back with a white plastic bag, which he places carefully on the floor. He takes out a saucer-size earthenware dish, in the centre of which sits a large sea shell – the conical kind, with curved, horn-like protrusions flourishing away from the pink lips of its opening. But this shell has a face. Its open side has been filled with a greyish, cement-like substance and onto this, in turn, little cowrie shells have been stuck, forming eyes and a mouth. I know at once who it is.

"It's Eleggua," says Ernesto. "Your own Eleggua. He'll guard you, and answer your questions if you need to know things. You should take him home and keep him on the floor in your house. Just give him some rum from time to time to keep him happy."

Clearly a considerable honour is being done me. I thank Ernesto profusely, and (having by now some idea of how things work here) give him and Agustin some *dólares* in recognition of the time and effort involved in preparing all this. Agustin crosses himself with the notes – and as he does so everything goes black. There's a collective groan. It's a power cut.

"Happens all the time," says Ernesto. "Except in Havana Vieja, where the tourists stay. They never get the power cuts. We get them every few days…" He scrabbles around for a plastic lighter, then lights candles.

I tell everyone it's time I went and got some sleep. I shake a lot of hands and kiss the Señora. I say I think I'll walk back along the Malecón and watch the sea under the stars.

"How much money have you got left?" Ernesto asks.

Wondering what's up, I feel in my pockets. "Practically none."

"Got a camera with you?'"

"Right now? No, I haven't."

"Fine, you're safe. You can walk back along the Malecón."

The next evening I go to the Casa de la Música, the powerhouse of *salsa* music in Havana. It's a big night, as Cuba's most famous salsa band – Los Van Van – are playing. Los Van Van have been together for thirty years, they've toured the world, their performances are the salsa equivalent of a concert by the Rolling Stones or the Who, and you can see them here every few weeks for ten dollars – cheap for tourists, but a week's white-collar wages for Cubans.

Still, there are those who can afford it. The queue stretches right round the block, and everyone is smartly dressed: Cubans retain many charming formalities that have vanished elsewhere on the planet, and T-shirts are banned from clubs, theatres and even cinemas in the evening.

The doors are supposed to open at ten. Finally, at ten-forty, there's a stir up ahead. People start shuffling up the pavement and are summoned forward in twos and threes to buy their tickets. We go into the foyer, where I'm stopped by a bouncer who runs me over elegantly with a metal-detector which he flourishes like a magic wand. Of course it goes off, because I'm wearing a big brass belt-buckle. Once that's been checked and pronounced safe, I'm in.

The Casa de la Música is a cavernous dark space with a stage at the far side, and several stepped levels of floor. I'm on the upper level, and down below, in front of the stage, is the dance floor itself. There's a bar at each side. The air-conditioning, as usual in Cuba, is full on, so it's freezing. But a dance or two will cure that.

I head for the bar and ask for a Cristal, the standard Cuban beer. They sell only Bucanero, its watery rival which comes in squashy aluminium cans, so I take one of these and return to my table. People continue to drift in, and a languid but perceptible mood of expectation builds up. A screen at the back of the stage is showing silent clips from one of Los Van Van's tours, while the DJ plays reggaeton, the abrasive Central American blend of reggae and rap.

The dance floor is dotted with people. Many just stand around, but a few begin to dance. The music improves. There are Cuban tracks: first Manolito Simonet, then Charanga Latina. Soon a lot of people are dancing: young Cuban couples undulating with a fluid, relaxed laziness, as if they hadn't a solid bone in their bodies; older couples turning and turning with small, precise steps that use the minimum of energy to generate the maximum of elegant style; groups of package tourists, with their dance teachers, moving from side to side with military regularity, practising their basic steps and hip movements. The unmistakable eight-beat salsa rhythm starts to permeate everything. It's a rhythm that somehow gets inside your body. I can almost feel it (maybe I can actually feel it?) affecting my heartbeat and breathing. The urge to get up and dance becomes overwhelming, a bodily imperative that has no truck with rational thought or decision-making, a physical process that simply has to happen. I make my way down the ramp past the tables towards the dance floor, scanning left and right for a possible partner.

I notice a table where a huge man is sitting surrounded by three young women. One of them catches my eye as I pass, so I go over and ask if she'd like to dance. She confers with Mr Big, evidently asking his permission. He holds out his vast flat palms towards me in greeting, nodding his approval, so I take her miniature hand and lead her down to the floor. She's slender and dark, with long wavy hair, and dances lightly and energetically. When the track finishes, I return her to her table and go in search of another partner. After two more dances I'm dripping with sweat, despite the freezing blast of the air-conditioning. A troupe of dancers in feathers is coming on for the brief floorshow that precedes the band, so I retreat to my table, sip my beer and sit back to watch the action.

A tall, striking black woman in a tight red dress wanders up and asks if she can take one of the empty chairs at my table. I invite her to join me. She's rather beautiful: she has dark, intelligent eyes and a high forehead, with a black velvet headband that throws her hair back in waves. She's slim, but the tight crimson dress shows her curves to advantage. No doubt she senses that I'm checking her out, because she asks me my name. She says she's called Estrella, and tells me that she usually dances with the resident floor show, but she strained a muscle in her leg and has had to take a few days out. I ask if she'd like a drink; she opts for a Cuba Libre, so I fetch it – a tall glass brimming with a darkly glittering mix of rum, cola and ice.

After some more conversation I realize that I'm finding Estrella distinctly attractive, and I say it's a pity she's hurt her leg because otherwise I'd ask her to dance. No, she says, it's fine, it's fully recovered, she'll be back working tomorrow. "Just feel," she instructs me. "It's fine, no?" She takes my hand and puts it firmly on the calf of her leg. "Go on, feel!" she says. "It's all right?"

I have to say that her leg feels absolutely fine to me. I can't find anything wrong with it at all. "So would you like to dance?" I ask.

Estrella explains that as an employee, she can slip in and watch the show for nothing, but if she's going to join the dancing she'll need to pay for her ticket like everyone else.

Privately, I'm amused – and sceptical – about this. I guess that like so many in this hard-pressed city she's looking for a few extra dollars, and I have to admit it's an ingenious little dodge. "And how much is your ticket going to cost?" I ask.

"The same as yours," she tells me. "Ten dollars."

I hand it over and she disappears, supposedly heading for the box office. In five minutes she's back and I ask her if she'd like to dance now. She opens big eyes at me, smiles and says yes, she'd love to. I stand up, she takes my hand and I follow her black patent high heels down the ramp to the dance floor.

Once there, we're so immersed in the music that the dancing largely seems to do itself.

It's a rare pleasure to have a partner who's tall, like me. I try not to think but rather just to float with the sound. Estrella is a superb follower: she takes my hints with almost disconcerting ease; I have only to give her hand the lightest of touches and she spins or paces around me as if she's weightless. And when occasionally I lose the plot, she simply continues with the drop-back step or moves forward and back until I get things sorted out. She has amazingly fluid and vigorous hip movements and doesn't seem averse to getting very close up to me as we do the turns. In fact she's soon pressing herself against me so enthusiastically that my main concern is to synchronize pelvic thrusts, and I have to remind myself every so often to break us apart into a *dile que no*, followed by an *enchufla* or one of my other carefully practised moves.

By the time we get back to our table, the stage is bustling with people, instruments and equipment. Los Van Van are imminent. We settle down to watch the show.

Los Van Van are astonishing. For a start, there are so many of them. There are at least fourteen people on stage. Three of them are on percussion, one with a full drum kit and two more with sets of enormous congas; there are two keyboard players, two violinists and a flute player; a four-man brass section including two trombonists; guitars and bass; and four singers, one of them a young woman. And they don't just play and sing; they dance continuously throughout the set. Every time the brass players are about to blow a riff they sashay forward in formation, a dance troupe within the larger dance troupe, punching the air with their notes and then dancing back. The percussionists oscillate continuously with fluid, flame-like movements, so their hands move on the congas in an effortless extension of the dance that's activating the rest of their bodies. The vocalists, singing in harmony or trading phrases to and fro, shuffle from side to side with perfect co-ordination, as precisely as if they were balanced on a tightrope. It's mesmerizing. And there's no break between numbers; one simply segues into another, co-ordinated by shared grins, winks and nods or at times just by magic, since often they seem to communicate telepathically.

The unbroken, insistent flow of music, an all-embracing wall of sound that becomes more and more intense and dominating, has a strongly hypnotic quality. Los Van Van play continuously for two hours, finishing with one of their biggest hits, "La Cabeza Mala". The music gradually focuses itself to a single riff, repeated over and over and over again. "*Te pone la cabeza mala... Te pone la cabeza mala...*" It seems to be inviting everyone to enter a collective trance, a timeless physical rhythm that simply doesn't ever have to stop.

I notice some change in the movement of the crowd at the front of the stage. A plump woman in white – white turban, white blouse, white skirt – is climbing the steps onto the platform. A *santería* priestess. The music continues unbroken, but some of the musicians move sideways to give her space. She unfolds a white cloth and spreads it at centre stage. I can see her arms moving about; she's reciting or singing something. As the riff continues, unstoppable, over and over and over, people begin coming up out of the audience and onto the stage. They throw money onto the white cloth. Some bring handfuls of notes; they cross themselves with the notes and then add them to the pile. Still the riff continues. Over and over and over. Everyone is in a trance. The pile of money continues to grow. The priestess waves her arms. People bow, people kneel, people climb onto the stage, they cross themselves with handfuls of pesos or dollars and they add them to the heap.

But I'm also preoccupied by something else. Estrella is now sitting very close to me indeed. In fact she's pressing her thigh firmly against mine. She reaches under the table and takes my hand, interlacing our fingers together. Then she gives me a coy, half-amused look and leans her head on my shoulder. We move together in time to the music. She starts kissing my neck. As Los Van Van's set reaches its climax, as the priestess declaims and the possessed musicians articulate their endless rhythm and the pile of money is gathered up and bundled away in the white sheet, I have to admit that it all feels extremely pleasant.

Quite suddenly the band finishes. There are no encores; the musicians simply walk off amid huge applause and the DJ settles in again. Reluctantly I peel myself away from Estrella and go to the bar for another beer and another Cuba Libre. When I return, she snuggles up to me more closely than ever. She puts her mouth to my ear. "Do you like me?" she asks in a whisper. And of course I can only nod. "For eighty dollars," she tells me, "we can spend the night together."

Aha. Okay, right. I guess I've been a bit slow. I notice now that most of the surrounding tables are occupied by male tourists, and that each tourist has an attractive Cuban girl wrapped round him. Evidently this is all part of a recognized game plan. I wonder how difficult it will be to extricate myself.

In the event, though, it turns out to be surprisingly simple: another little bit of Cuban magic. I explain to Estrella that, much as I like her, I don't think her proposal is really a great idea. She doesn't seem at all put out. "Are you hungry?" she asks. I tell her I'm not, but ask if she is. Yes, indeed – she rubs her tummy expressively with her hand. Could I buy her a sandwich? I'm very willing, and she says she'll fetch it from the bar herself. I get out a handful of cash and she picks out a ten-dollar bill. She says, "I'll be back," kisses me and vanishes into the crowd. I wonder what she's expecting to find in that *bocadillo* of hers – caviare and gold dust? In Havana, even a tourist can buy two decent meals for ten dollars. But I have a feeling Estrella's sandwich doesn't exist.

And sure enough, her Cuba Libre stands untouched on the metal table for half an hour. I watch while the ice melts and the beading of condensation evaporates from the glass. Then I drink it myself.

Not all my new acquaintances are so easily shaken off. For some days, Eleggua has been sitting in the corner of my room, watching my every movement. I've decided that I'm uncomfortable with him. I had an odd feeling about that shell from the moment I saw it, and now I know why. I've seen one like it in a display of objects seized by customs. It's illegal to import them to the UK, and I doubt if the excuse that it's a religious object – indeed, a god – will get me far. Moreover, I'm pretty sure that the brownish substance crusted around Eleggua's slitty little conch-shell eyes is blood. From what creature I don't know, but I'm not happy with it. How can I get rid of him? I suppose I could drop him into the nearest skip, but I'm reluctant to offend him. So I pack him carefully into his white plastic bag, and take him along when I go to Geldys for my morning lesson.

Geldys summons her mother.

"Has he been fed?" Mima asks. I lift Eleggua gingerly out of his bag and she examines him critically, especially around his eyes. I hear her mutter the word *sangre* – blood. "Yes," she says. "He's been fed. There will be places you could leave him – maybe the corner of a street, maybe the seashore. But only a *santero* will know. It's dangerous to leave him just anywhere. It could bring terrible bad luck. You must go back to the *santero*. Explain that you can't take him home, and ask him to look after Eleggua for you. He won't be offended. It's the only way."

So, feeling a little sheepish, I take Eleggua, in his bag, back to Ernesto. I explain that UK customs won't let him in, and I ask Ernesto to take care of him. Ernesto seems perfectly happy with this, especially when I leave a donation sufficient to keep Eleggua in rum and cigars for the foreseeable future. I shake hands with Ernesto, give Eleggua a wink, and leave.

And suddenly it's my last day in Cuba. I'm taking the evening flight to Caracas. Venezuela is waiting. I feel so much at home in dirty, battered, beautiful Havana, I can hardly believe I'm already leaving. I take my camera over to Geldys's apartment, catch the key and let myself in to climb the four flights and take pictures of the family. I promise to email from my next destination. I kiss Mima, I lift Esven off his feet, and when I embrace Geldys I find it hard to let her go. She's taught me so much and she's become part of my life. I'm almost surprised to feel tears coming into my eyes.

I give her one more squeeze and then it's time to descend the long, winding staircase. Outside, I cross the street and look up at the three smiling, vigorously waving figures. I wave back and kiss my hands to them before I turn the corner.

As I finish packing, I find a small white cloth parcel under my clothes. I realize I just have time to take my sins, my bad luck and all those evil spirits and consign them to the ocean. I've been putting the task off because, irrationally, I can't help feeling furtive about throwing this stuff into the sea. Still, I slip the parcel into my pocket and set out.

It's near sunset and the lights are starting to come on. Old ladies in armchairs sit in ground-floor rooms watching the illegal TV from Miami under the bleak illumination of a single neon tube. Outside the dark entrance to an ornately crusted art-nouveau apartment building, a group of men on battered tubular chairs play dominoes, their gaming-table a four-foot-square board that rests on their knees. I make my way down to the Malecón. The grey concrete rampart is wet with spray, and a brisk jagged wind punches my face at intervals. I wonder whether my sins are going to be blown straight back in my teeth when I try to send them out to sea.

As I walk on westward in the direction of the harbour, there are fewer and fewer people. The Malecón is now the domain of solitary fishermen: every hundred yards or so, a man sits on the pavement or leans against the wall, dodging spray and judiciously managing a hand line that floats behind him in the warm breeze across the sidewalk.

Despite the wind, the sea is fairly calm, an angled indigo surface broken here and there into white marbling. The Malecón takes a bend to the right, and I reach a point where there are no rocks on the seaward side. The grey wall drops sheer down into the ocean. There are no fishermen, no stray figures headed my way to beg a dollar or offer me a special deal on cigars. The wind cool on my face, I lean over the wall and carefully toss the white bundle out above the bluish-grey water. It floats for a moment before tilting a little, dimpling with a glaze of seawater and starting to dip under. Very slowly it sinks, its colour changing from white to pale green, then to a bluish-grey blur. I watch it drift further and further down, smaller and fainter until there's nothing to see except the limitless shifting depth of the water. To my surprise, I feel as if a huge weight has been lifted off my shoulders.

I look again in both directions. No one has seen me. I have an hour before it's time for my taxi to the airport. It's a fine evening and the lights ahead look inviting. I walk on along the Malecón towards the harbour.

CHAPTER TWO
✳ THE PEANUT'S LIKE THAT

It's morning when we reach Caracas. In the glass terminal building I join one of thirty enormous queues, shuffle through passport control and collect my rucksack from the carousel. Needing Venezuelan currency, I go to a kiosk to change some US dollars and am dazed by the vast number of bolívars I receive in return. I can't begin to take in these hundreds of thousands, let alone estimate whether I've received the correct amount. I take it on trust. However, remembering my arrival in Cuba, I go to an information desk and ask a lady in a blue uniform how I can tell which taxis are safe. "They're all safe," she says brightly. This was the one response I hadn't expected, and I'm not sure how reassuring I find it. "Really?" I say, no doubt looking rather blank. "Okay, fine." I step out of the terminal and stand at the pick-up point for a few minutes, watching other people getting into shiny black four-by-four taxis. The taxis all look pretty much the same, so I take the next one.

Away from the airport, the road winds steeply uphill between clusters of concrete shacks. We're heading into a *barrio*, a shanty town, and as we continue to climb I can see the hillsides below covered with an irregular and precipitous pastel-coloured mosaic of concrete shacks with corrugated-iron roofs. Little box-like shelters coloured pink, blue, green or white spill down every incline and into every gulley, tilting and tumbling down the red-earth slopes like a many-levelled house of cards caught in the moment of collapse. Here and there, tangles of rusted wire and greyish debris on the inclines suggest that some really have collapsed.

At the roadside, partly dismantled or burnt-out cars stand on jacks or breeze blocks. Refuse spills from piles of torn black plastic sacks, and stolid women stand, arms folded, in front of makeshift houses little taller than themselves, watching us pass.

I've heard that there's a tunnel between the airport and the city, so I ask the driver if we're taking it. "This time of day, the tunnel's blocked with traffic," he says. "We're going over the mountain."

The concrete shacks thin out and disappear. The road continues to climb, with a succession of hairpin bends. We are now above a vast tract of forest. Below us stretches an immense wooded gorge, and beyond it more abysses and rocky chasms. The hillsides beneath us, and the depths of the great rocky clefts that split them, are piled with lush, green foliage – a carpet of treetops. Out of this, at intervals, protrude immensely tall, spindly trees, the bushy green of their tops crowned with masses of bright pink flowers. A little further on others appear, dotted at random across the forest canopy, topped with vast clusters of daffodil-yellow flowers. As the car twists and turns, I glimpse entire green mountainsides splashed with these wonderful yellow patches.

Still the road winds on and we rise into a realm of cool white mist, which blows in drifts and rags across the road. The driver turns off the air-conditioning and opens the windows. Cold air floods in. The bends in the road have no marking or edging, only sometimes a row of concrete blocks between the tarmac and the lip of the gorge, which drops straight into the forested depths below. Up here the trees are swathed, draped and buried under immense masses of vines and creepers, everything fighting to reach light and air – a chaotic green battlefield punctuated with explosions of flowers. Occasionally we pass warning signs: *¡CURVAS FUERTES!* or *¡CURVAS PELIGROSAS!*

We are over the summit, below the mist and descending rapidly when suddenly a vast bowl opens among the mountains to our right, a saucer-like hollow filled with red-tiled roofs and, beyond them, a grey blur of skyscrapers. The driver gives a sideways jerk of the head. "*Trafico*," he says with satisfaction. I peer down. Along the valley stretches a line of ant-size stationary vehicles: the traffic from the tunnel, gridlocked.

Soon we're entering another *barrio*. Here some of the houses are still in the course of construction and I can see how they're built. Vertical concrete beams have the spaces between filled in with hollow red clay bricks that look as fragile as a waffles or wafer biscuits. Cables draped irregularly over the roofs suggest there's electricity. I wonder about water and sanitation. I also wonder if they have earthquakes here. If they do, these houses wouldn't survive a minute.

And again, outside the houses, there are cars standing everywhere – cars with one, two or more wheels missing; cars without engines; cars in every stage of dismantlement and disrepair from the merely battered down to burnt-out sepia metal shells like the husks of dead insects. A vast mass of old tyres stands on a street corner, stacked in ribbed black columns.

We emerge from the *barrio* and almost at once the taxi slows to a crawl. We're in a huge traffic jam, and for the next three-quarters of an hour we labour fitfully through the city, embedded in the hot and fuming mass. I have plenty of time to read the hoardings as we pass. Red, yellow and blue signs from the Revenue Department are everywhere, telling people about the good things (parks, roads, the environment) their IVA – the equivalent of our VAT – is paying for. I deduce that IVA is a sore point in Venezuela. Less ingratiatingly, there are posters announcing a zero-tolerance policy on tax evasion. The concrete retaining walls of the canyon-like underpasses carry enormous, amateurish murals depicting President Hugo Chávez and extolling his programme of "Bolivarian Socialism". My hotel is on the Prolongación Sur (South Extension) of the Avenida de las Acacias, but this Acacia Avenue is no suburban backwater. It's a six-lane highway fed by approach roads that pour ever more cars into our congested path. It's a relief when we turn off at a vast intersection and drive down the Prolongación itself – a road almost empty of cars – to pull up in front of the Hotel La Mirage.

I've chosen the hotel for its cheapness and its nearness to Caracas's dance-club district, so at first sight I'm pleasantly surprised by its elegant exterior. It has a shiny blue-and-white sign with three stars, and a glass door marked RESTAURANT. The impression, however, lasts no longer than the time it takes me to lug my bags over the threshold. The slow-moving, thickset man behind the reception desk surveys me bleakly. He has no knowledge of me or my reservation. It doesn't seem to matter: the hotel is almost empty. No, they can't take payment by credit card. I must pay cash – and at once. Where am I from? England? He gestures at a plastic sign on the wall which gives the hotel rules in translation. "The payments have been daily," it says wistfully. "No admittance visits in the Room." I can see the inner entrance to the restaurant: the doors, fastened with a rusty chain and padlock, look as if they haven't been opened for years. I stand in one of the lifts for five minutes, pressing buttons, until a passing guest indicates to me that it's out of order. I try the other lift and have better luck: several buttons are missing but the one for my floor, the eighth, is there. I press it and the lift takes me to the seventh floor. I haul my rucksack out and climb the stairs to room 802.

When I get the door open I find a large, dark room with a tiled floor. It's pretty basic. There are no chairs: indeed, apart from the bed, no furniture at all except for an unsafe-looking table near the window. There's a built-in wardrobe and a small ensuite bathroom. The only other amenities are a TV set on a bracket, an air-conditioning unit which has lost its front panel so that it looks like the inside of a car radiator, and, fixed to the wall facing the foot of the bed, a huge mirror. The bed, however, is large, clean and comfortable, and the pillows are good. I lie there to enjoy them for a little while, and then for a little longer still.

When I wake up, it's early evening. The room is uncomfortably hot so I open the windows to let some cool air in. I've been aware of a muffled background rumble ever since I arrived. With the windows open this becomes the steady roar of continuous heavy traffic. The panorama outside my window is impressive. Not far away are the green slopes of steep mountains covered with forest. In front of them, spreading in all directions, is a chaotic array of concrete blocks of every shape and size, some formidably brash – one towering edifice has a giant, wavy-patterned red, white and blue ball on top, advertising Pepsi. Next to it is a skyscraper crowned with a scarlet-and-white Nescafé mug ten storeys high. There are buildings of Cubist tendency, from which segments jut out diagonally at odd angles, faced with green or bronze glass. My prize candidate for the ugliest is a monstrous khaki concrete wedge labelled La Previsora, whose summit displays the time in light bulbs, a hideous digital clock. Around the bases are great swathes of two- and three-storey buildings with roofs of tile or metal, so the concrete towers look as if they're wading ankle-deep in a sea of small houses and shops. Many of the towers are crowned in the early twilight with neon advertising, and at all levels the landscape is studded with vast banners the size of entire buildings, carrying giant photographic images advertising beauty products, health foods or the Latin American mobile-phone company

Movistar. And veering in all directions through this surreal assemblage are the *autopistas*, a maze of expressways on concrete stilts, along which pour ceaseless torrents of traffic.

My hotel's street, exceptionally, has a good many trees. A block away I can see a cluster of bushy green tops flaming with masses of scarlet flowers, among which small blue birds flit about. Over the tower blocks I can see three or four big, square-winged birds – eagles? vultures? – circling on thermals. But the traffic dominates everything. The nearest expressway is less than a hundred yards from my window and I watch it, fascinated. There's something hypnotic about its perpetual movement, like water flowing under a bridge. The noise is overwhelming, a sullen unbroken roar highlighted randomly by the buzz of a motorcycle, the chime of a car horn, the blast of a truck driver's klaxon. It pours on, resonant and unstoppable, the slanting concrete slip road turning to a gold stream of headlights as darkness descends.

Later I sleep once more, to wake at 3 a.m. with the traffic still thundering on, unchanged and relentless. And when I wake again just before seven it's the same, a little augmented by the approaching rush hour. During my time in Caracas it will never slacken.

I decide to get up and confront the city. It's sunny but still cool in the streets and I'm struck by the solemnity of the people I pass. It's very different from friendly, chaotic Cuba. Here everyone seems in a hurry, and if I catch someone's eye and smile, they stare blankly and walk straight past. Not finding anywhere inviting to have breakfast, I settle for a cup of coffee at an internet café which also rents phones. The proprietor is minimally polite but doesn't waste a word – just takes the money, tells me which computer and phone to use, and vanishes. I feel very much alone. I'm trying to contact Gustavo Farías, a local salsa teacher whose website I found before leaving England and whom I emailed without response. Now my call is redirected to his voicemail, so I leave a message (hoping he can understand my Spanish), sending an email for good measure to tell him I'll call later. Then I walk back to my hotel.

As I approach it I notice that there's a tiny café right next door. Leaving the hotel earlier I must have walked past without seeing it – easy enough, because it's just a tiled passageway open to the street, with room for three tables, and at the back a metal counter with a narrow kitchen beyond. There's a smell of good food so I go in. A pretty, smiling woman in a yellow T-shirt with an apron over her blue jeans comes to the counter. She has bronze highlights in her hair and a radiant smile – the first I've seen in Caracas. I ask if she can do breakfast and she laughs as she tells me about all the things they haven't got this morning: no eggs, no fruit but oranges, no meat, no proper breakfast things. In the end, from the little they do have, I order coffee, freshly squeezed orange juice and some slices of buttered toast.

I sit down and she brings it all to me. It may be minimal but it's delicious. The coffee comes in a thimble-size plastic cup but it's so sweet and strong that this is plenty. As I savour it I listen to her chatting with someone in the miniature kitchen. I notice she drops the "s"s from the ends of her words, so I ask if she comes from Cuba. "No," she says, "I'm from Colombia!" That must explain the smile. I tell her hers is the first smile I've seen since I reached Caracas and she laughs uproariously. "My name's Aïda," she says. "Like the opera?" I ask. "Yes, like the opera!" I'm starting to feel better about Caracas already.

I feel better still when I call Gustavo Farias again and he answers. He says he'll be delighted to give me salsa classes, and that since I don't know my way across the city he'll come to my hotel to meet me. I'm reluctant to drag him through this battlefield of cars and concrete but he's adamant. We agree to meet at 2 p.m.

When the time comes I wait nervously in the hotel lobby. Two o'clock comes, and then half-past. Just as I'm giving up hope, the doors swing open and a huge teddy bear of a man in a red T-shirt rolls in, beaming and holding out both hands in greeting. Gustavo is as tall as I am and many times my girth. His smile radiates warmth and friendliness. He introduces me to his companion Zuleika, a lovely lady in a gold-and-black patterned top. We hug and kiss each other, friends already.

Though hardly in the same league as Gustavo, Zuleika too is built on a generous scale. Both are black – unusual in Caracas, where most people's features suggest Hispanic-Indian ancestry. It's a relief to encounter such uncompromising friendliness and enthusiasm, and we immediately agree to find somewhere we can have a drink and talk. My hotel has no bar, and the one next door is closed. We head for the next block, the generous acreage of Gustavo's denim jeans swaying purposefully up the street, followed by Zuleika who floats along like a galleon in full sail, silky top billowing, until we reach the Hotel Gavial, where the bar is open and we find a table. I order a beer, Gustavo and Zuleika a lemonade – *un limón* – each. And we talk.

Gustavo wants to know how I come to be in Caracas, and is amazed and delighted to hear that dance is my main reason for being here. He asks where else I've been, and we indulge in a five-minute orgy of nostalgia about ravishing, disintegrating Havana, which he visited several years ago. He says he'd give me a lesson right now, but he doesn't have access to the studio this afternoon. He and Zuleika cast lingering glances around the empty space near the bar, but decide it wouldn't be realistic to try and start teaching me here and now. We agree to meet the following morning, by the barriers at the Colegio de Ingenieros Metro station – the subway being the easiest way to get around this city.

Gustavo also tells me that the best salsa club in Caracas is El Maní Es Así, which means "The Peanut's Like That"; it's a Venezuelan saying, equivalent to "*C'est la vie*" or "That's the way the cookie crumbles". Tomorrow, he tells me, they have a great live band playing. We decide to meet there, too. Having made these plans, we finish our drinks and leave. As we come out onto the pavement Zuleika points to a placard beside the door. The hotel is having a *fiesta* with live band and DJ on Saturday. Gustavo looks at the names, then stabs his finger decisively at the poster. "That'll be good," he says. "You should go."

There's little to do in my hotel room and I'm not tired. I decide that it would do no harm to take a look at El Maní Es Así, even though it's Tuesday and little is likely to be happening. It's still early, however.

Killing time, I wander up the street and into an "American Bar" that's attached to yet another hotel. It's a long, dimly-lit space walled with angled strips of mirror. I perch on a black bar stool and ask for a beer. The bar is empty apart from me, the barman and some girls in very short skirts who wander in and out by a door at the back. I slip into a daydream – about what, I don't know – until I feel a sudden puff of air on the back of my neck. I swivel round, and jump when someone says "Boo!"

A dark girl slides, laughing, onto the bar stool next to mine. She has a round, pretty face and soft features. Her skirt is split to the waist, exposing a beautiful thigh. Do I mind, she asks, if she sits next to me? I assure her I don't. (I can guess what she's here for; but at least it'll be more interesting than sitting alone.) She introduces herself as Malena and asks my name. I ask if she'd like a drink. She accepts gracefully and orders a cocktail. Soon we're having one of those stereotyped conversations about where I'm from, how long I've been in Caracas, et cetera. But I'm intrigued by her. She speaks beautiful Spanish, without the local accent. That, she says, is because she comes from San Cristóbal, in the Andes. "In the mountains," she says with a little toss of the head, "we speak the best Spanish. *Castilian* Spanish." She compliments me on my own Spanish, tells me I have beautiful eyes, and puts her hand on my knee. It feels good, and I have no inclination to remove it. I ask how long ago she left San Cristóbal.

"I've been in Caracas since I was sixteen," she tells me. "How old do you think I am now?"

I can see that she's not quite as young as I'd thought at first. Deliberately underestimating a little, I hazard, "Twenty-five?"

She laughs. "More." Eventually she admits to thirty-two, and guesses my age as forty-two, which I know is flattery. She asks whether I'm married. I get out the photos of my wife and family. She seems especially struck with the picture of Amanda. When I confirm that Amanda is *muy linda*, Malena looks at me reproachfully. "*No linda*," she rebukes me. "*¡Hermosa!*" ("Not pretty, *beautiful!*")

When we start talking politics, Malena becomes even more passionate. President Chávez, she says, is insane – *loco*. Also he's a crook. He talks about helping the poor but he's a rich man! He wears gold! Look at all his rings! It's a terrible thing to say, but she'd be delighted if one day he was assassinated! As for Blair of England, he's a psychopath. *Her* hero, a true liberator, is Simón Bolívar. Now there was a man! She gives me an eloquent account of Bolívar's plans for a free republic of all the Americas. Holding up one hand, she counts on her fingers the countries he liberated from Spanish tyranny: Peru! Venezuela! Colombia! Ecuador! Bolivia!

Suddenly she leans over and kisses me. Then she excuses herself to go to the *baño*. She's gone a long time. I think what a marvellous history teacher she would make, and I ponder the despondent last words Bolívar wrote in his diary. In English they fall neatly into two lines of verse. It strikes me that they'd make a good ending for a sonnet:

> America is ungovernable. Those
> Who serve the revolution plough the sea.

Eventually Malena emerges from the ladies' room, wearing a black coat. A solemn-looking black man sits near the bar entrance, and Malena walks straight past me to sit down beside him. Soon they are deep in conversation. I finish my beer and decide to leave. As I go, Malena turns and smiles at me. "Ciao," she says.

It's now twilight. I walk up the busy street and am just about to cross at one side of the intersection when I hear a shout: "*¡Eh, jefe!*"

Some instinct tells me, unpleasantly, that the shout was meant for me, so I look over my shoulder. On a traffic island to my left is a curious structure, made of canvas: a red awning like a large umbrella, and under it a waist-high red canvas barrier with *Sabana Grande Seguro* on it in white lettering. I've passed it before and assumed it was something to do with an insurance company (*seguro* can mean "insurance" in Spanish). Now I see my mistake. It's a police checkpoint, and in it are two men in navy-blue, military-style tunics. One of them gestures at me. He shouts again. "*¡Jefe!*" ("Boss!")

Police. Sighing, I turn back, check the traffic and cross to the island.

The man accosting me is about thirty. He's wearing baggy blue trousers tucked into military-style gaiters above heavy black boots. He has a long, melancholy face. There are gold badges on his tunic. He looks me up and down bleakly. "*¿Pasaporte?*"

I curse inwardly. Uneasy about security in my hotel, I've come out, for once, with both my passport and my money on me, and I have them in a money belt under my clothes. The belt is normally invisible, but to get at my passport I have to unbutton my shirt and expose it.

The officer scrutinizes my passport, then puts it down on a plastic table inside the canvas enclosure and gestures at my money belt. He wants to see what else I'm carrying. "On the table. Please." I take the belt off and unzip the various compartments. Receipts, airline tickets, money. "How many dollars do you have there?"

I give him an answer, deliberately underestimating. He taps the table and I reluctantly put the belt down, determined not to let it out of my sight.

The officer's companion, a chubby youth, comes forward. "Where are you from?" I tell him. "Purpose of visit?" Tourism. "Where are you going this evening?" I say I'm on my way to El Maní. The two of them confer.

"Your pockets, please," says the senior officer. I decide it's best to comply. Once my pockets are empty, the officer gives an order to Chubby and he frisks me very thoroughly. If I had anything hidden under my clothes, it would definitely be found. I notice that there are now four policemen in the enclosure. They're all wearing leather belts with holsters from which protrude the black butts of revolvers. The officer points to a white plastic chair. He wants me to sit down. "Shoes and socks," he says. Chubby kneels down. "*Disculpe*," he murmurs. At least he has the decency to apologize. I sigh, shrug, take off my shoes and socks. It occurs to me that they're looking for drugs.

While I put my socks and shoes back on, Chubby sits down at the plastic picnic table and starts laboriously copying details from my passport, asking me for clarification at every step. Surname? Christian name? Place of birth is Liverpool, right? Occupation? How long have I been in Venezuela? What country am I going to next? Where am I going this evening? "El Maní," I repeat wearily. Chubby brightens up. "You dance salsa? Me too!" Sensing a possible ally, I start to develop the conversation – but the officer cuts us off sourly.

"*Mira, amigo,*" he says, tapping the table. (I find it curiously chilling to be addressed as *amigo* by a policeman.) "Look, friend. There are regulations about how many American dollars you may bring into Venezuela. I have reason to think that you have contravened those regulations. It will be necessary for you to come to the station to have your dollars officially counted to discover if you are in breach of the law. If you are, you will have to pay a fine. Or a tax."

My heart sinks. This is going to be a long evening, and maybe an expensive one too. Quite possibly this tale about a limitation on dollars is nonsense, but it strikes me that in Venezuela – a country famous for currency crises and bank failures – it could be true. Since I've been told that in several places I'm visiting you can't rely on travellers' cheques or credit cards, I'm carrying far more cash than I would normally bring. And it's all in US dollars. I decide that the only policy is to stay calm and radiate serenity, which I do while we all sit on our little plastic chairs at the little plastic table and the evening traffic thunders around us.

I wonder, though, whether I can bribe my way out of this. "Maybe I can save us all some trouble by paying a fine right now?" I suggest.

The officer seems shocked. No, no, not possible.

"So what are we waiting for?" I ask.

"We're waiting for the *moto.*"

The *moto*? Ah, yes, the motorbike. They're going to take me to the police station on a *motorbike*? Good grief.

We relapse into silence and the waiting goes on. I wonder how many hours I'm going to spend here. Chubby is still slowly making notes on his pad. "Which hotel are you staying in?" Scratch, scratch. "Room number in the hotel?"

The other two policemen are lounging at the edge of the island beside the traffic-lights. When a black VW van pulls up at the lights they gesture to the driver. The van pulls over and the driver gets out. Soon they have the six passengers on the pavement and the van is being searched inside and out. The driver, a middle-aged woman, produces an enormous dossier of papers, big square pages covered with print and writing, blotched with elaborate circular rubber stamps. Some of the policemen leaf slowly through these at the table, while others go through the luggage compartments, examine the spare tyre and peer under the chassis with torches.

"What's going on?" I ask the officer.

"*Churros*," he says contemptuously. It means "fritters". A slang term for crooks? Idiots? Smugglers? Heaven knows. After a long search and much interrogation of the driver, the police are unable to pin anything on the *churros* and they're allowed to drive away. We settle down again on our plastic chairs. It seems we could be here all night.

Eventually the sheer boredom starts to get to me. "All right," I say to the officer. "So what are we going to do?"

He launches into a curious little speech. His accent is so thick I can't understand most of it but eventually I make out the word *regalo*. A present. Aha!

"Well," I say, "of course it would be a pleasure to give a small gift to the police. And how shall we arrange this?"

It turns out that he has farcically precise ideas about how it should be done. No one must see the money change hands, of course. But if he sits beside me and the money is passed under the table, that will be fine. And of course his colleagues must also be taken into consideration.

Meanwhile, having retrieved my money belt, I'm conducting a mental accounting process. On the one hand, these guys know I'm carrying a lot of cash. On the other, I want this to cost me as little as possible. I decide twenty dollars should be about right.

What follows is a scene straight from a Keystone Cops movie. Angry as I am, I can't help seeing the funny side. Officer seats himself beside me on plastic chair. I pass folded bills under table. Officer takes them, stands up and steps back, gazing innocently around at the horizon while Chubby takes his place. More dollars. Chubby pops out of his seat and the next cop drops into it. And so on. Once this sordid little assembly line has run its course, we are all, naturally, the best of friends. I pack up my belongings and prepare to leave.

"Wait," says Officer, holding up one hand. Christ, I think, what now? "These streets are very dangerous at night. It is not safe for you to walk around alone. You are going to El Maní? Okay, I come with you."

I groan silently. Am I never going to shake this guy off? It dawns on me that he's bored out of his mind. Going to a club certainly beats sitting on a traffic island all night, and now he's found an excuse to do it. Several alternatives occur to me. I can simply insist on leaving without him. Or I can go with him, then try to lose him in the crowd.

I could change hotels. But suppose I *have* infringed a currency law? It's conceivable. The police now have all my details. When it's time to leave Venezuela, if my name comes up on the airport computer as wanted for questioning in connection with a possible currency irregularity I'm going to be in deep trouble, and missing an unrefundable flight to Bogotá will be the least of it. I decide the best policy is to humour him. "Sure," I say. "Why not?"

The two other policemen have now gone, leaving me with Officer and Chubby. Officer shows no sign of moving.

"Are we going?" I ask.

"We're waiting for the *moto*."

Fuck the bloody *moto*, I think. I'm getting really irritable by now. "Why don't we walk?"

"You don't mind walking?"

I feel like telling him that if it were up to me, I wouldn't be showing up at El Maní with a police escort; but if I must, then at least walking will be a pleasure after those plastic chairs.

So we walk. As we go, Officer tells me again how dangerous this district is after dark. You can get mugged, you can get shot, you can get knifed. I can see this is important to him; it's the source of his self-esteem. He points out other police sitting at their checkpoints, little enclosures of red canvas like the one we've just left. "They all know me," he announces proudly. "I am their *jefe*!" *Jefe* – chief, boss – is a key word for him. "Now people have seen you walk through the district with me," he says sententiously, "they will respect you. They will know you are on good terms with a police officer." I think he actually believes it.

We turn up a side-street and come to a small building covered in green vines. There's a carved wooden sign: EL MANÍ ES ASÍ. It looks like a farmhouse or a country restaurant. We push through the double doors into a warm, dimly-lit interior. The walls and ceiling are of old, brown wood. Hams, sausages, corn cobs and bunches of onions hang from the roof beams. We climb onto bar stools. Officer gestures at the rustic décor. "*Gaucho*," he says approvingly. Salsa music is playing in the background, but the place is deserted except for the barman. I order beer and am surprised when Officer asks for a Pepsi. "Don't you want a beer?" I ask. "No," he says, "I'm on duty."

While we wait for the drinks we talk about salsa and he lists some of his favourite artists, most of whom are new to me. The drinks arrive. He asks me my name ("Rafael?" – "Like Rafael," I say, "but with a 'G'"); also what I do, what books I've written, whether it pays well. He tells me his name. It sounds like "Giordanan": not a name I've encountered, but he says it's the same as "John" in English. I ask him whether he likes being a *policía*. Yes, he says, but it doesn't pay much. And the hours are bad. He's on patrol all night tonight, then again tomorrow. He has a day off, then he's on duty for two days. Then it's back to nights again.

"But you'll get promotion?"

"No," he says morosely, staring at his Pepsi.

"But you have good friends in the force?"

He purses his lips and shakes his head slowly. Not really, he says. You can't trust people…

I show him the pictures of my family. He holds out his mobile phone, showing a picture of his two-year-old niece. I ask if he's married. Yes, he says. His wife is at university, studying pharmacy.

A car horn sounds outside. "My *jefe*," Officer explains. He gets off his perch and goes out, returning glummer than ever. Another drink? He has beer this time. "Twenty-two," he mutters. "Twenty-two, and he tells me what to do." His *jefe*, he explains, is only twenty-two years old but *he* has had promotion because he's been to university. We talk on, desultorily. No one comes into the club to dance: it's too early in the week. After half an hour we hear the car horn: the *jefe* again. Officer goes outside. I feel I'm getting the picture. Here he is in a boring, poorly-paid job with rotten hours, bossed around by a twenty-two-year-old who happens to have a degree. Even his wife is going to university. No wonder he has a chip on his shoulder.

He comes back. We have another drink. He gets emotional. "*Tu y yo*," he tells me, "we are brothers, Rafael. Brothers!" He flings an arm around my shoulders. Again I sense a kind of inertia about him. If I don't take action we'll be here all night. I tell him I'm getting tired, that the jet-lag is catching up with me. I need to sleep. "I'll escort you," he announces. "These streets are dangerous."

I accept the inevitable and we set out. A tall white church looms up in the lamplight. "*Iglesia*," my companion explains unnecessarily, pointing up at it. "I believe," he confides, crossing himself. When we reach the corner by his checkpoint, a hundred yards from my hotel, he stops. "From here, you will be safe," he assures me. Solemnly he shakes my hand. Then he crosses to the traffic island where he will spend the rest of the night on his little plastic chair under the red canvas awning, watching the traffic plough past, stopping a vehicle every now and then to search for something – anything – to alleviate the mind-numbing boredom.

Next morning I have breakfast in Aïda's café a little earlier. True to Caracas's domination by the car, the street is full of small workshops beating panels and charging batteries; in the café I'm surrounded by men in blue overalls spattered with paint and oil. When she brings my eggs and coffee, Aïda asks what I'm doing in Caracas. She tells me she loves salsa too. On a sudden daring inspiration I ask if she'd like to come with me to the *fiesta* at the Hotel Gavial on Saturday. Her face lights up. "*¡Sí!*" she says. I leave the café exhilarated.

I've arranged to meet Gustavo by the Ingenieros Metro station at 11 a.m. to have my first salsa lesson in Venezuela. But he isn't there at eleven, nor at eleven-thirty. I don't worry unduly because I've already learnt that in Venezuela it goes on being eleven o'clock until it's twelve, and so on. If you've arranged to meet someone at eleven and they show up at eleven-fifty, that's fine, because really it's still eleven o'clock. It's not a bad system, especially in a city with such heavy traffic. It's just twelve when a rotund figure in red finally comes through the barrier. Gustavo's smile is gone. He looks worried. In fact, he's distraught. It's the key, he tells me. He's lost the key to the room where he teaches his classes. Today he has not only my class but another one, this afternoon, and he can't teach them unless he can get into the room. There's a spare key but he can't contact the person who's got it. He makes another call on his mobile. No, no good. And there's really nowhere else we can do the lesson? No.

My disappointment is quite sharp. I've been hoping to dance and the frustration is hard to take. Rather than say just goodbye and drift off, I suggest we have lunch together. Gustavo agrees, so we return to the platform and take the train to Sabana Grande, where we make for a good restaurant I've discovered, fancifully called *El Rincon del Bucanero*, "The Buccaneer's Corner". We order drinks. Gustavo doesn't want a full meal, but I order steak and chips and he seems happy to share my chips.

He tells me he has three jobs. It's hard to make a living in Caracas. Besides teaching dance, he has a job in the Ministry of Culture, promoting Venezuelan music and dance. And he also likes horse-racing, so he takes groups of people to the races. What this involves I don't quite understand, but I don't get any elucidation. I ask what he thinks about President Chávez. Gustavo sways gently from side to side, balancing the issues. "The best thing you can say," he tells me, "is that some people now have access to a doctor, who wouldn't have done before. Other than that, well – " He quotes from a song by Los Van Van: "*Tiene cosas buenas, tiene cosas malas…*." There are good things, there are bad things. All those posters about "Bolivarian Socialism", he says, don't mean a thing to the average person.

I also want to ask Gustavo about María Lionza. She's a local goddess who, I've heard, has a big cult in Venezuela. Officially she's a Catholic saint, "Santa María de la Onza" – Saint Mary of the Jaguar – but really she's more like a *santería* deity, embodying a blend of Catholic, African and indigenous beliefs. She has a sacred mountain in Yaracuy, to the west, and she's said to ride on a tapir, followed by an army of lesser saints and heroes, a motley crew which includes Simón Bolívar, Dr Miguel Hernandez (a kindly local doctor who died in 1919 and is regarded in Venezuela as a saint, though uncanonized by the Vatican) and a number of Indian chiefs and black slaves, including, delightfully, Bolívar's nanny. Does María Lionza, I ask Gustavo, have a temple or shrine in Caracas?

No, says Gustavo. There's a festival for her every year in Yaracuy – there's miraculous healing, people go into trances, they walk over hot coals – but all there is in Caracas is a famous bronze statue. "And you can't get near it," he adds, "because of the *autopista*!"

"Can you see it?" I ask.

"You can see it, but you can't get to it because of the traffic. It's not far from here. Do you want to go and take a look?"

Of course I do – so we pay our bill and plunge out into the blinding sunlight and the crowds. We make our way down the Avenida Casanova, along the blazing concrete pavements, past a street corner where men in overalls sit on the kerb ripping the entrails out of old computers and TV sets, dropping the metal components into plastic bins for re-use and tossing the glass and plastic shells into a skip, where they land with a satisfying crunch. From the traffic-lights we walk down over worn grass alongside a slip road leading off the Autopista Francisco Fajado. Our pathway gets increasingly precarious. Cars and trucks hurtle past. We walk beside a buckled metal barrier, on a narrow triangular strip of dusty earth, which dwindles, thinner and thinner, as we near the carriageway. The sun makes my head throb, in rhythm with the repeated *thwack* of vehicle after vehicle rushing by.

The metal barrier ends. We stand just beyond it on the last spit of earth in the fork of the slip road. Gustavo points ahead. Hundreds of yards away, over six lanes of traffic, marooned on the central reservation of the motorway, I can just make out a square plinth, and on it the greyish figure of a naked woman, her arms raised vertically to the sky. She rides on something that from here looks like a cross between a pig and an elephant. There are wreathes and bunches of flowers around the animal's feet.

"How do the flowers get there?" I ask Gustavo.

"People risk their lives, running across the *autopista* at night to place them."

"Good grief." I think of the night-time traffic I've heard from my room. "They must be very devoted."

I take a photograph of the tiny, distant figurine. Perhaps I'll be able to get more detail by enlarging it on my computer at home. Then we turn back. I stop off at the internet café to check my email. Amanda tells me the central heating has gone wrong but has been fixed the same day. In the permanent sauna of Caracas it's hard to remember that such a thing as central heating exists. On a happier note, she lists the guys she's danced with at our usual club in Manchester. "I danced with one man who'd done a lot of street dance and hip hop," she writes. "He pointed out that a lot of men around us were doing the moves but not really getting into it heart and soul. Just wait until you're with me again, doing the moves you've learnt!"

I'm relieved that she's still having a good time. I tell her about María Lionza, and add, "There's a dance in the hotel up the road on Saturday. I've asked the lady who cooks my breakfast in the café to go with me." I think that's both true and tactful.

❋

I've developed a habit of evading police checkpoints. If I spot one ahead, I cross the street or take a discreet detour around the block; I wonder how many honest citizens of Caracas have the same habit. So this evening I reach El Maní Es Así without a police presence. Today the place is busier. A few people are at the bar, and further inside, where a group of tables has been pushed together, a dozen or so friends are having a meal. I get a drink and find a table. There's no dance floor as such, simply the tiled floor of the bar. The place glows in the warm, dim light: brick pillars, raw wooden beams, brownish walls studded with innumerable framed photographs of past singers, musicians and dancers. The small stage is bare except for two metal chairs and a stand with a disconnected microphone.

An hour passes and nothing happens. Salsa plays over the sound system. The people at the tables chat and laugh and order more drinks. Most of them are casually dressed, but there's one slim, elegant young man in a dark suit who looks as if he's come here straight from the office. He seems to be acting as master of ceremonies to a group, and he asks one of the girls to dance. To my surprise they don't seem to dance salsa. They make small, neat movements, with lots of stepping back and very few turns. Rather than putting an arm round her, the man holds his partner's hands and keeps passing her to and fro, from right to left and back again. I can't identify the dance. They sit down. After a few minutes another couple gets up and dances in the same style. Whatever they're doing, it's not salsa. I watch the steps closely but can't work out the logic.

At ten, the club is still largely empty and there's no sign of a band. I decide I'll give it until eleven and then leave if nothing's happening. But meanwhile I'm reluctant to leave without dancing at all, so when a highly danceable track comes on over the PA and several couples get up from the tables, I go over and ask a friendly-looking young woman if she dances salsa. "*Sí*," she says, smiling. She stands up at once. We find a space on the tiles and I put my arm around her.

It's my first dance in Venezuela, and I massacre it. I can't work out what's going on. I seem to be permanently out of step, and no matter how I try to adjust, I can't seem to correct it. I more or less manage to turn my partner, but when I try to put her into a *setenta* or reverse-arm, I can't do it. We're all over the place. Mercifully, the music soon finishes. She's polite enough to thank me warmly, but I go back to my table baffled and embarrassed. Perhaps she doesn't get out much; maybe she doesn't really know how to dance salsa. But I'm left feeling uneasy.

As eleven o'clock approaches I'm preparing to finish my last drink and leave when a man steps onto the stage and starts plugging in cables and arranging chairs. People are filtering past the bar into the space at the back. The club is starting to fill. The lights dim a little. I go for another drink, returning to see band members on stage unpacking instruments. The room gets ever fuller. At last I make out a bulky figure in a red T-shirt clearing a path through the crowd. A huge hand waves over the sea of heads. It's Gustavo. We embrace, and I fight my way back to the bar to fetch him a beer.

I return as the band, Guajeo, starts to play. The line-up is interesting and, I think, typically Venezuelan: three percussionists, with bass, guitar, flute and, instead of keyboards, an enormous set of marimbas, underpinning the music with a pounding, glassy resonance. There's a hugely dynamic girl with a broad face and long black hair, playing an electric violin. There's a tall, wizened, grey-haired male vocalist. The music cuts through the crowded space, the violin slicing the air with an urgent, jagged edge. The vocalist drives the music on and the other members of the band act as *coro*, singing the refrains behind him as he launches into the improvisation of the *montuno*.

The pulsing and rippling of the percussion make it impossible not to start moving. Almost everyone gets up and people start dancing, even though there's little more than a couple of square feet to each couple. Gustavo, standing next to me, begins to dance gently; he points down, signalling to me to join in. I start to dance alongside him. He's doing the drop-back step: back on the left, tap the right, replace the left; then back on the right and so on. Over and over again he does it and I do it along with him. Then he changes to the "open-out" step: a wider version of the same step where you turn the whole torso left or right as the foot goes back. He does this for a little while, then reverts to drop-back. We dance together, swimming in the music, feeling it pound and flow through our bodies.

Looking around as I dance alongside Gustavo, I suddenly understand. Everyone is using these two steps as the basis for their dancing. They simply don't use the "forward-and-back" step fundamental to Cuban salsa. They move into the turns (which they don't do very often) straight from drop-back. No wonder I couldn't dance with that girl. I was trying to take her forward and back while she was trying to swing from side to side. It's a revelation. Venezuelan salsa is different from anything I'm used to.

Gustavo watches me, nodding his approval. Dancing, he starts to clap the *clave*, the underlying two-bar salsa rhythm. Other people join in. The music drives us on, emphasized by the *dank ... dank ... dank* of the percussionist's iron cowbell, which comes in on the *one* of every bar. Everyone wants to participate; dancing or clapping, people become part of the music. The clapping is a fourth percussion instrument, a collective heartbeat urging the music on. We dance side by side, our footsteps setting up a complex pattern with the syncopated handclaps. Gustavo asks a young girl to dance. I watch him. Despite his impressive bulk he's precise, delicate, and light on his feet. He's a popular dancer and I watch him through several numbers.

By the time the exhausted band, dripping with sweat, put down their instruments and file off for a much-needed interval drink, Gustavo has given me a complete lesson in the basics of Venezuelan-style salsa. "Using these steps," he tells me, "you can dance with a woman." We go for fresh drinks. Gustavo seems to know everyone. All the way to the bar, women come up and kiss him; men shake his hand, embrace him, exchange banter. We fetch our beers and go back to our place near the wall at the edge of the floor. The band comes on stage again. "Now," says Gustavo, "you go and dance with a woman. Go!" His huge dark face looms at me, unprepared to tolerate refusal.

Another song is starting up. With a sensation – despite the heat – of jumping into a cold swimming pool, I plunge into the mass of people and make my way across the floor, looking for an unaccompanied woman at one of the tables. I see a pretty woman with a gipsy look and long dark hair, and recklessly ask her, "*¿Quieres bailar?*" She stands up, beaming, and we start to dance. She moves beautifully, swaying flexibly, and I find it's easy enough to take the drop-back as basic, then extend it to the "open-out" step, moving out of partner-hold and just taking first her right hand, then her left, neatly swinging her from side to side as we dance. As a variation, I return to partner-hold sometimes, gently taking us around in a small circle before returning to dancing on the spot, face to face. Occasionally I get a little lost, but she guides me. I can't do any real moves because I still don't know how to start them in this new style, without the *dile que no* I would have used in Cuba, but it's a delightful experience and once or twice she moves close enough for me to feel the magical, female warmth of her body. When the song finishes she smiles at me happily and laughs. I thank her, give her a small kiss on the cheek and make my way unsteadily back to Gustavo. He puts out a huge hand. "Congratulations," he says in English.

"*Mi amor*," says Aïda, laying her hand gently on my arm, "today we have no eggs. My friend has gone to look for some. You can have coffee now, but if you want eggs you will have to wait."

I sit at the outer end of the café, where it opens onto the street. The morning air is still cool, and on this side we're in shadow. A battered yellow lorry, its open back a construction of wooden slats, crawls up the street. A loudspeaker is attached to the cab roof with wires, and through it, in a melodious, metallic voice, the driver sings a song about tomatoes, onions, grapefruit. Each is the ultimate, the quintessence of its kind! Tomato of tomatoes, onion of onions, *¡pomelo de pomelos!* People come from houses and workshops to buy, among them the lady from my café. She soon returns, carrying a paper bag full of eggs in one hand and a plastic bag of vegetables in the other. In the café, a young girl is chalking the menu on a board in a careful schoolgirl hand. When she gets a word crooked, she rubs it out and writes it again. The lady with the bags pauses to say hello.

"Is that your daughter?" I ask.

"No, Aïda's. She's sixteen."

Perhaps I look surprised, because she confides, "Aïda is forty!"

She takes her purchases behind the counter, and soon my eggs are ready.

I explore the old centre of Caracas and discover the book market. It's underneath a concrete flyover. The traffic roars along on this vast overhead causeway, and in the long, shady concrete colonnade underneath, between the immense grey pillars, are nearly a mile of stalls covered with second-hand books, almost all in Spanish. It's a treasure-trove. Everything is here, from rare, beautifully-bound editions illustrated with historic engravings to sets of encyclopaedias and old schoolbooks. Most Spanish and Latin American writers are here. I hunt through stall after stall for Borges – who seems strangely hard to find. I'm intrigued by what I can deduce about Venezuelan reading habits. Translations of the *Kama Sutra* are frequent, as are North American self-help books: *Los Hombres Son de Marte, las Mujeres Son de Venus* turns up a lot. Harry Potter and Paulo Coelho are everywhere. Most stalls have the novelization of *Sin Tetas No Hay Paraíso*, a Colombian soap about cosmetic surgery. The title translates as *There's No Paradise Without Tits*, and the blurb reads "Never had she imagined that the happiness and future prospects of her generation would depend on their bra size." I turn over several editions of *Don Quixote* (I really must take the plunge one day).

Halfway along the book market the stalls stop. In the shadowed space beside a gargantuan concrete pillar are sixteen little tables, four rows of four, each with a chessboard. At each table sit two players, and at most are one or two spectators. Blind to the million books before and behind them, deaf to the resonant thunder of six lanes of traffic overhead, the chess players sit, radiating tranquillity and silence. Painted on the stony face of the concrete pier behind them are the words *Asociación de Ajedrez de Caracas*: Caracas Chess Association. It's a beautiful scene.

I wander out from the shadow of the overpass and into the searing sunshine, along a street crowded with stalls selling CDs and DVDs. Some have little TV sets powered by car batteries, showing movies. I emerge into the Plaza Bolívar, centre of the old city. Here trees cast a merciful shade, though between the patches of shadow a scorching heat reflects off the brownish-grey marble pavements. I sit on a stone bench to watch children on little scooters zip through a sea of pigeons, sending them up in clapping flocks. In the middle of the square the titanic statue of Simón Bolívar rallies us from his rearing bronze horse. The Art Deco City Hall offers an exhibition ("Caracas, Cradle of Liberty") with vast hoardings featuring the faces of Bolívar, Miranda (another nineteenth-century hero of the independence struggle) and Hugo Chávez.

I'm arrested by the sight of an earnest, toothless, brown-faced man in sunglasses and a woman's frayed blue denim hat, busy hanging cardboard placards from the railings around the square. I stroll over to take a look. The cardboard sheets are hand-lettered in red and black capitals. "BUSH HAS THE MARK OF ANTICHRIST!" announces the first one, in Spanish. The next goes into more detail: "BUSH IS A ZIONIST MASON! THE USA IS THE STUPID TOOL OF JEWISH ZIONIST MASONS!" Chávez, on the other hand, gets a good press: "JESUS SAID: GIVE AND IT SHALL BE GIVEN UNTO YOU. CHÁVEZ GIVES TO THE POOR COUNTRIES AND FOR THIS GOD WILL BLESS HIM AND GIVE MORE ABUNDANCE TO VENEZUELA!"

A small crowd gathers to read the posters. A board with a collection of yellowed press cuttings shows the paranoid prophet as a much-travelled man. Faded photographs catch him being moved on by the police in Ecuador, Colombia, Peru, Brazil. His name is Enrique Saume Ayala. Peruvian by birth, he's spent years wandering Latin America preaching his message, a bizarre blend of mystical Christian Socialism and fascist madness. "CARACAS IS FULL OF ELECTROMAGNETIC WEAPONS!" shouts another placard. The small print explains that lethal devices have been planted underground by the Americans. Chemical and radiological attacks are going on all around us. These include assassination by means of noxious car-exhaust fumes (something I can almost believe). Señor Ayala is now beyond the railings, debating with a group of passers-by, blue denim hat aquiver.

A card round his neck on a length of string reads 333 THE LAMB OF GOD IS A PERFECT COMMUNIST.

I'm reading about how the American Zionist Masons ambush people in the street and kill them by means of a secret technology, when Señor Ayala swivels round. Smiling encouragement, he reaches through the railings to shake my hand. "*¿De que país?*" he asks.

"*De Inglaterra*," I reply.

"Excellent," he says in a perfect, upper-class English accent. "Then we can exchange ideas. But pardon me one moment." He turns back to his debate.

I'm not certain that exchanging ideas is Señor Ayala's forte. Irrefutable circular logic in support of his views surely is. I wander off.

It's Saturday morning, and Gustavo has invited me to join his class in *rueda* – salsa circle dancing. We meet by the exit from the Metro and walk to a new concrete arts complex, a modern multi-level building containing galleries, theatres and practice studios. Gustavo's studio, a long room with wide windows, is already bustling. Teenagers sit against the walls, checking their cellphones and dragging dance shoes out of their rucksacks. Older people exercise, stretching stiff backs or flexing limbs. People are wearing everything from Lycra leotards to old jeans with baggy T-shirts.

Gustavo lines everyone up, men facing women. Zuleika starts the CD player and we practise basic steps, red-shirted Gustavo checking the line, swinging an arm in the air and shouting to keep us on the beat. His larger-than-life figure moves lightly and delicately. *Rueda* mostly uses Cuban moves, so we practise the "mambo" or forward-and-back, then the *guapea* (where the partners step back, then come forward to meet, pressing palms together). We also practise *arriba* (man moving straight ahead, lady backing away) and *abajo* (man moving backwards, taking lady forwards). We change partners often, so I dance with everyone – from plump matrons, who grin broadly as we march up and down the room, to waif-like, golden-skinned twelve-year-olds so shy they daren't look at me.

Gustavo organizes us into a huge circle, the *rueda* or "wheel" itself. We are twenty-two couples, so the *rueda* becomes an oval, filling the room. Zuleika starts the music. It's vital that everyone keep in step, so Gustavo calls out the beats while we practise *guapea* on the spot and then, after a couple of false starts, move off with *arriba*, men going forward so that we circle clockwise. *Rueda de casino*, to give it its full name, is controlled by a caller, in this case Gustavo, who shouts the moves so everyone in the circle can do the same thing. When Gustavo yells *¡Básico!* we pause for more *guapea* (except for the couple who didn't notice the call and collide with the pair ahead of them) until Gustavo shouts *¡Abajo!* and we start moving anticlockwise.

It's vastly exhilarating to dance in sync with forty-odd other people, the steps just sufficiently complicated to bind everyone into a sort of unstoppable dance machine. We work on *da me* ("give me" – I send my partner to the left, grab the next lady on my right and swing her across, continuing with the *guapea*) and then *da me dos* ("give me two" – the same, only I step to take the next lady *but one* on my right: easy to collide with other men unless everyone is very sharp). Sometimes we make mistakes or miss calls, but so long as nobody panics it's possible to pick up and carry straight on.

Gustavo shows us one more move: men circle anticlockwise on the inside of the *rueda* while women circle clockwise on the outside. It can be done either so you move along a certain number of places, or full circle until you reach your last partner again. There's something hilarious about the playful complexity of the process, about the edginess of juggling the dimensions: waiting for the next call, trying to keep in step, keeping the circle wide, enjoying a partner you may be throwing away any second when the word comes to grab another from the right. By the time we finish, everyone is sweating profusely despite the air-conditioning. Bottles of water come out of the rucksacks. People mop themselves and swig. The teens check their cellphones.

Gustavo, forearms glistening with sweat, mops his huge brow with a towel, and from a corner of the room he summons a tall girl of about twenty. He asks me to show him my Venezuelan steps. I do my best and he nods approvingly. "But," I tell him, "I still don't really know how to go from here into the moves."

"It's no different," Gustavo says. "You always start on the *one*. Look." Counting aloud, he does a couple of drop-backs and then spins the girl. "See? You try."

Nervously I take the girl into partner-hold, drop back a couple of times and then turn her. It works perfectly. I just have to remember to go straight into the drop-back again as we complete the turn. Exhilarated, I take her into a *setenta* – turning her clockwise, holding her left hand so that her arm goes behind her back, then turning her around me and into a partner-hold. It works! As we fall into the drop-back step, she tells me, pleased and surprised, that she's never done that move before. Gustavo beams. Leading a girl through a move she doesn't already know is the test. If I can do that, I've got the essentials.

I'm not going to tempt fate by trying more. I thank the girl and let her go. Gustavo pats me on the shoulder. When Zuleika has finished taking names and collecting payments we leave the building, but we don't head for the Metro. Gustavo says they've got something to show me. We cross several streets in the increasing glare of the sun and reach a broad façade painted primrose-yellow and geranium-red. A shining concrete fantasy of Moorish arches and minarets, it looks like a cross between a football stadium and an old-fashioned picture palace. The words *Nuevo Circo* are emblazoned in ornate lettering on a panel high over the central archway. Gustavo tells me it used to be the Plaza de Toros. Now it's being turned into an arts centre: the bullring will be a vast open-air auditorium for concerts; the interior will host exhibitions and films. Today is opening day.

In front of the main entrance an awning has been set up. People are dragging chairs and trailing electric cables across the dusty ground. The space is filling with people. We join them, sitting on concrete steps with chain-link fencing behind us. Under the awning a band assembles: teenage boys with percussion instruments – African drums, bongos, cowbells. Someone distributes bottles of water and sandwiches in plastic bags. The PA crackles into life with a dance track. There's a party atmosphere. A young man in black picks up a microphone and makes a long speech, with much repetition, about plans for the Circo. He urges passers-by on the street beyond the chain-link fence to come in and join us. Some do.

Then the teenage band starts up, an urgent, deeply-pulsing rhythm with voices of smaller, lighter percussion weaving above the booming wooden drums. The boys – they look between twelve and sixteen – clap and chant with young high voices, a strange haunting melody whose pattern keeps eluding me. They work their way through several numbers, each one intricate and powerful. The voices echo across the square from the loudspeakers. "It's from the coast," Gustavo tells me. "Where there are more *negros* and the music is more African." The power and complexity of the music, from such a young group, is astonishing and when they finish there's eager applause.

The next band has seven or eight members, all men: guitars, electric bass, several percussionists and a slight, tanned, wizened singer in a Hawaiian shirt. They play several dance tunes and move into up-beat salsa. Now things really come to life. The rhythms are steady, insistent, infectious. The crowd, excited, starts clapping the *clave* – the basic three-two syncopated rhythm of salsa. Then, after we've all clapped the *clave* for a while, Gustavo and Zuleika get up and start dancing side by side, doing the drop-back. I join them on the blazing, dusty concrete. We dance in a line, three abreast. Gustavo changes step; Zuleika and I change too, to stay with him. After I while I try something different; Zuleika and Gustavo immediately change as well. It becomes a game, as each in turn comes up with a variation: left foot over right; "Suzi Q" (two steps sideways with one foot crossed in front of the other, then reverse the pattern); right foot behind left… It's joyful and exhilarating, despite the heat.

We sit down again. The singer makes theatrical gestures, hushing the band to a pianissimo. He lights a cigarette, then with an air of great ceremony walks forward and balances it on the ground on its filter tip, vertical in the middle of the concrete space. There's a gentle breeze and I'm surprised the cigarette doesn't blow over. A thin thread of smoke rises up. There's a booming roll on the deep-toned African drums. The singer rejoins the band, gives a fiendish chuckle into the microphone and begins a song addressed to a *santería* priest, a *babalawo*:

"O Babalawo, Babalawo,
I need your help, I need your power!
I'll give you whisky, I'll give you a little money,
I just need a bit of your power!"

The musicians behind him sing the chorus – *¡Babalawo, babalawo aye!* – while he improvises over it. After several more verses he leaves the awning that shades the band, and dances with huge, slow steps – a stealthy prowl, miming mystery and caution – around the vertical cigarette. He rolls up his pupils until his eyes are completely white. He peers suspiciously to left and right, then abruptly arches back and flips forwards into a handstand, palms either side of the cigarette, which he grabs, lips around the filter tip, burning end inside his mouth. He springs neatly onto his feet and, with strange grimaces, mimes the chewing and swallowing of the cigarette. The band plays on as he dances back to the microphone to give one final fiendish cackle: "*¡Babalawo ahahahahahahaaaaa!*"

I half expect the cigarette to reappear, still smouldering; but it doesn't. Has he really eaten it? It seems so.

When I walk round to the café at ten that evening for my date, Maria tells me Aïda is still doing her hair and invites me to sit down. I find a chair and watch cars cruising past in the glittering dark, groups of excited people heading to one or other of the *fiestas* in the local hotels. Half an hour later, Aïda is still getting ready. "She's doing her make-up," says Maria, hurrying off to give help and advice. I feel quite nervous: I can hardly believe this beautiful Colombian woman has agreed to go out with me, and I'm determined to give her a good time, even though I haven't been in the country a week and there's so much that could go wrong. Will I know the etiquette? Will my dancing be good enough? Excited female voices are raised in the back room of the café. I take a deep breath and try to relax.

Eventually Aïda emerges round the counter and makes her way to me between the tables, wide-eyed and smiling. She looks wonderful. She wears jeans and a gold T-shirt, duskily gleaming gold eyeshadow and dark red lip-gloss. She is small and exquisite. "Are you ready?" I ask her. "*¿Vamonos?*"

She takes my hand. "*Sí*," she says.

We stroll up towards the Hotel Gavial. The street is full of people, walking in groups or couples, or standing around cars, CD players thudding. Disco music blares from bars and hotels. Boys on motorbikes, girls perched behind them, do thunderous U-turns to stand by the kerb chatting and revving their engines. At the Gavial we go into the dimly-lit club area. There's a large circular bar and a dance floor beyond it, glinting with chrome and mirrors. At the back, a band is setting up. We sit at the bar, and the barman offers us a range of drinks. With my limited Spanish and the deafening music from the disco I can't understand a word. I ask Aïda to take charge – which she's delighted to do. Cocktails appear: a strawberry-coloured extravaganza with cherries and a plastic umbrella for her, something lemony and full of crushed ice for me. We clink glasses – "¡*Salud!*" – and drink. It tastes good.

The place is filling up and couples are going onto the floor. After a few minutes of conversation (if you can apply the word to bursts of half-understood Spanish shouted to and fro over the musical bombardment) we decide to do the same. The DJ is playing *salsa romántica* so we dance easily, not too fast, swaying to and fro in what I hope is Venezuelan style, going gently through a few turns, circling neatly from time to time. It's relaxed but exciting: since leaving Havana I've scarcely danced except in classes, and now I have a real partner for the whole evening! Aïda is petite, energetic and light on her feet. She's also very pretty, and not averse to dancing close up against me. When the music changes to reggaeton she astonishes me with her energy. She stamps, gyrates, shakes her hips, waves her arms. She seems full of pent-up energy and to be enjoying herself enormously.

We sit down for another drink. To my surprise, Aïda confesses that she's not crazy about salsa. She likes it – "more or less" ("*ma' o meno*" as she puts it, dropping her "s"s Caribbean style) – but what she really loves is electronic music, reggaeton, house, hip hop, r 'n' b… Far from being a problem, this makes her the ideal partner. When we go back to dance salsa again I'm under no pressure to pile on one complicated move after another. I find she's not comfortable with those. Instead I get lots of practice at basic moves and simple turns, all of it on a foundation of Venezuelan-style drop-back and "open-out" steps. In between I enjoy going wild with Aïda, who does frenetic disco moves, pounding the dance floor and shaking her body. By the time the band comes on we're both, like everyone else on the floor, glistening with sweat. Caracas humidity finds its way in despite the air-conditioning. My back is soaked and Aïda's hands are slippery. I can see sweat trickling down her neck.

The band, dressed in black and orange, has the obligatory three percussionists as well as keyboards, guitars, electric bass, trumpets, trombone and vocalist. The music isn't original – it's mainly covers of familiar numbers by Oscar D'León, Hector Lavoe and the like – but it's full of punchy energy. When they slow down a little to play *salsa romántica*, Aïda glues her body against mine like clingfilm, with a layer of sweat providing an airtight seal. We sway and rotate in synchonization, pelvises locked together, my right thigh firmly gripped between both hers. I'm sorry when the music stops and the band takes a break.

We sit at the bar again and talk, though with the language barrier and the deafening music it's often nearly impossible to understand each other. There's one particularly strange moment, when she says what *sounds* to me like "*¿Por qué no traduciste a tu esposa?*" This is perplexing: I've come across *traducir* as meaning "translate", but she can't be asking me why I didn't translate my wife. I rack my brains. It occurs to me that possibly *traducir* may mean "betray": it's one sense of the English "traduce" – and isn't there a similar French word? In which case, she could be asking me, "Why haven't you cheated on your wife?" If she's making a proposition, it seems an odd way to do it, both complicated and tactless. But maybe I've totally misunderstood. I try to get clarification, but after shouting at each other through the music for a while we end up laughing and go off for another dance. There's no further mention of my *esposa*.

As we dance, Aïda crushes herself against me. If I were shorter, her cheek would be against mine. Instead, it's pressed against my neck and I can smell the fragrance of her hair. My left hand clasps hers, in standard partner-hold position, level with her right shoulder. During the slow numbers she moves it across and presses it firmly against her right breast. I feel no inclination to remove it.

At about 4 a.m. the lights go up and waiters start collecting chairs. We file out into the crowded street. I ask Aïda where she lives, whether I should get a taxi. "No," she says, gesturing up the street, "it's not far." We stroll on together amongst the groups of chatting revellers. Reaching the intersection, we wait while traffic passes.

"Do you live on this street?" I ask her.

"Oh no," she says, "it's a long way."

I'm puzzled. At last the lights change and I step out into the road.

"No, no!" she says. "Wait."

"But the *semáforos* have changed," I point out.

She gestures across the intersection, saying something I can't catch above the noise of engines. The lights change again. Another wave of traffic heads for us, led by a scarred and battered single-decker bus, its windscreen half covered with ragged strips of paper printed with the names of suburbs. It stops in front of us, doors open. Aïda squeezes my hand. "*Ciao*", she says, and steps inside. "*¡Ciao!*" she calls back. The metal folding doors slam shut and the traffic moves off again. She's gone.

I stare into the yellow light across the dusty concrete at the currents of cars and people. Then, having no alternative, I turn and walk back down the gentle slope towards my hotel. I'm perplexed and a bit disconsolate. I'm tired of being an ant in a concrete jungle, and Aïda made me feel special. I hadn't expected her to leave like that. Did she offer herself to me, and did I miss my cue? Or was my fevered imagination playing tricks? I'll never know. Well, I suppose sometimes the peanut's like that.

I sleep until nearly eleven the next morning, and wake feeling not too bad, all things considered. I go out looking for something to eat. The little café next door is closed with a shutter for Sunday. I won't see Aïda again. By the time she's in there, frying eggs and lighting up the morning with her smile, I'll be in a plane over the tropical forest, heading into Colombia. I wander past a couple of uninviting *luncherías*, then take the easy option and go to McDonald's for breakfast.

CHAPTER THREE
❋THE NEW COLOMBIAN DANCE SENSATION

The river is dark and fast-flowing. I sit in a clearing on the riverbank and watch the disc of the full moon straight ahead. It has a reddish tinge, its light glittering on the restless surface of the water and casting shadows under the bushes. Something darts from the undergrowth on my right. A black cat! It runs towards me and begins to circle me clockwise. But there's another. And another, and another. In fact there are dozens – hundreds – of cats, streaming from the bushes and dashing around me. They run fast and they close in, dancing, brushing my skin with their fur, a whirlpool of black cats. Then, as suddenly as they appeared, they veer away and stream back into the forest.

And I have to leave for my appointment. I have to see the woman. I can't go directly to her house, so I wait in the house next door. Sure enough, a slender woman with blonde hair comes in. She dances around me in a circle, close up, like the cats. I can feel the fabric of her dress and the warmth of her body. Somehow this isn't quite what I expected. "I thought you'd be naked," I tell her. She laughs. "I can't dance naked for you *yet*," she says, teasingly. And she leaves.

Now it's now time for me to go to the house next door, *her* house. I see her at once. She's not alone. There's a man with her, and a huge black dog. She smiles at me. She has something important to tell me. "This moon is the moon of copper," she explains. "Copper, because it comes between silver and gold." She gestures towards the man. "And now," she says, "you must kiss my companion."

I'm a bit troubled by this. But I needn't worry. The man bends forward and gives me the slightest brush on the lips, a mere formality.

We're not finished yet, however. "Next," says the lady, "you have to kiss my dog."

The dog is like a very large black Labrador. I have a dog at home, and I like dogs. I guess I can tolerate kissing it. I bend down and look into its beautiful, loving, dark brown eyes. The dog flickers its tongue out and gives me just the tiniest lick on my lips. No problem.

"And now," says the lady, "you can kiss me." She pulls me towards her in her arms. This time it's a real kiss. I can feel the pressure of her lips, the determined softness of her tongue. We kiss for a long time and it's very good. She smiles at me. "Look into my mouth," she says, opening it.

I look inside and something very strange happens. Her lower jaw seems to change shape, to elongate a little. There's something not quite human about it. A piranha? A cayman? I peer into her mouth. There are things inside: a rounded stone pebble; a small cylinder of polished bone or ivory, about the size of a chessman. And, astonishingly, I can somehow see through the back of her throat – instead of flesh there is empty space, the sky, and in the midst of it the copper disc of the full moon.

She closes her mouth and her jaw returns to normal. Once again she's a beautiful, blonde woman. She holds me at arm's length, a twinkle of amusement in her eyes, smiling as if to cheer up a favourite child. "Don't worry," she says. "If you're lonely, I'll send someone."

I wake with a soundless crash, my heart pounding, my scalp prickling, my skin covered with gooseflesh. I'm trembling, although I'm not cold. The pitch-dark room crackles with a weird energy, as if the whole place were charged with static. What on earth was that? Shakily I get out of bed and make my way over to the shutters. I can see tiny threads of light through cracks in the woodwork. I open a shutter, half-expecting moonlight to flood into the room, as in some Gothic novel. But no: there's just the pale electric light from a bulb in the courtyard, my fellow-backpackers' socks and T-shirts dangling from a washing line, and the orange-flowered creeper trailing in great swathes over the whitewashed wall opposite. I'm in the Platypus Hotel in Bogotá.

I switch on the light and close the shutter. The room has settled down: there's just cool air and a faint smell of damp from the old walls and timber rafters. For the present there's no chance of sleep. I find my diary, then climb into the hard, square, Spanish carved-wood bed, and write down my dream.

✳

The hotel stands in a sloping street of small buildings with tiled roofs and walls plastered in gentle, earthy colours. I sit on the edge of the pavement waiting for my contact, the poet Mauricio Contreras. Downhill I can see skyscrapers and urban haze, but up here we're on the edge of Bogotá, where the city began before it spilled down into the valley and beyond. From the top of the slanting street, forested mountains tower up into a cloudy sky. These are the foothills of the Andes, and the weather is fresh, mild, cloudy, damp.

I arrived late yesterday, and it was all very easy. I changed a few dollars for a dizzying number of Colombian pesos and was shepherded to an official taxi. The drive through cool, wet streets made me feel I was back in England. At the hotel I was taken across a courtyard and shown a chilly room with old wooden double doors and green-painted shutters, a bed with rough cotton sheets and a blanket. I slept, and I dreamed. And at last I slept again, waking to find that it was a public holiday. No one was answering the phone, and – so the hotel management told me – I shouldn't go out before noon because there were *manifestaciones* in the streets and riot police were on the rampage. So I sat in the courtyard with my fellow guests – backpackers from France, Australia, Norway and the USA – drinking free coffee and exchanging travellers' tales, until someone wandered in to tell us that the demonstrations were over and it was safe to go out.

In the late afternoon I tried to call a salsa school – the Academia de Bailes Actual – from the hotel office, but got no answer. So I dialled Mauricio's number again. This time he answered. The voice was a surprise. Since Mauricio was a friend of my friend, the young Welsh poet, Owen Sheers, I'd assumed he'd be young too. But his voice on the phone, deep and richly textured, conjured up an entirely different image: the poet as jowelled, grey-haired professional, perhaps in his sixties. I could see him clearly in my mind's eye – heavily built, wreathed in cigarette smoke, a tough, worldly sage whose stubby fingers were happier punching an old Olivetti than fiddling with a computer keyboard. We agreed to meet at eleven this morning, outside my hotel. So here I am now, waiting for Mauricio in the pale sunshine, admiring the neat brick-and-concrete pattern of the street – more like a garden path than a city thoroughfare – and watching the passers-by: chattering children, a couple of women walking their dogs, a pigeon pecking its way along the pavement.

And there, far off down the street, is Mauricio. He's unmistakable. Even from two hundred yards away he has *poet* written all over him. I forget my absurd telephone image. He looks to be in his late thirties. His slim, angular figure, hunched in a dark overcoat, trudges rapidly up the slope towards me, black-rimmed glasses glinting, dark, unruly hair flying. A sharp, intelligent smile lights up his face as he spots me. We shake hands and Mauricio launches into a rapid-fire monologue, gesturing at the buildings around us. When he pauses for breath I have to ask him to slow down. My Spanish simply can't keep up. Mauricio sways about, coughing with laughter, his eyes sparkling, and pats me on the back, apologizing. Then he sweeps me off for a tour of the neighbourhood, which is called La Candelaria. There are small cobbled squares, their corners shaded by spreading trees with gnarled, ancient trunks. High, pillared gateways lead into labyrinths of steep streets, almost free of traffic and irregularly lined with old houses plastered in blue, pink and ochre. There are street-corner cafés, and tiny bars in the recesses of shadowy courtyards.

And all the time we talk. About our mutual friend Owen, about our favourite writers, about our own work, about music. Mauricio knows the bars in Bogotá where they play the best salsa music. He's also an authority on the development of the music, and is full of surprising information. When I mention that I'm planning to visit Cali in a few days' time, he tells me that the frenetic style of salsa they do there evolved in the 1970s, when DJs in the city's clubs began to experiment by playing their Cuban 33 r.p.m. vinyl albums at 78 r.p.m. With the music going at more than twice its proper tempo, the dancers could really let rip. He asks me what I thought of Caracas, and I tell him about the traffic, my tangle with the police, and poor María Lionza, marooned on the central reservation of the motorway.

Talking of María Lionza reminds me of something. "Do you know a *mago*, a *brujo*, a *santero*?" I ask Mauricio. "A magician? A sorcerer? A *santería* priest? I've had an extraordinary dream. I need someone to interpret it for me."

Mauricio isn't the slightest bit fazed. "I do know a *brujo*," he tells me. "Let's see. I might be able to call him now. But what did you dream about?"

But I don't want to talk about the dream until I've checked it out with someone – preferably a *santería* priest – who might suggest how it could be interpreted. I explain as much to Mauricio, who gets out his *célular* to make the call. We stand on the pavement for a while, until Mauricio purses his lips and folds up his phone. "No answer," he says. "I'll try him again later."

He suggests having something to eat. We wander back towards the busy Avenida Jiménez and stroll through the crowds until we reach what looks like a fast-food restaurant, with a shiny metal counter and tubular chairs. But behind the counter a long line of chickens – twelve or fifteen of them – are roasting on a horizontal spit, rotating over a bank of glowing charcoal. We sit down. I leave Mauricio to do the ordering. The waitress brings a couple of local beers. Then the food arrives. There's a large metal bowl for each of us, two-thirds full of soup, and in the soup are half a roast chicken and half a cob of maize. She comes back a moment later with two more dishes. Each contains a mountain of rice, topped with thin slices of fresh avocado. There's also a green sauce, perhaps made with coriander. It's a seriously big meal.

I follow Mauricio's example, using a spoon for the soup and then tackling the corn and chicken with a combination of knife and fingers. It's delicious and there's far too much of it, but I eat as much as I can because meals are always unpredictable when I'm travelling; the sheer inconvenience of having to go out and find a restaurant every single time I'm hungry deters me from regular eating. One big meal a day is simpler, and I can always buy snacks in the street.

We talk about our families. Mauricio, it turns out, is divorced, and has a grown-up daughter who lives in Mexico, where he sometimes visits her. We agree to meet again later in the evening to go to a poetry-reading and then tour some bars.

When we've eaten a good proportion of the food, Mauricio has a word with the waitress. She goes away and returns a moment later, deftly folding together a square cardboard box which she hands to Mauricio. It's the Colombian version of a doggie bag. Taking a spoon, he loads it with rice and chicken. Not a bad idea, I reflect. But I haven't left enough to make it worthwhile.

When we leave, I pay. We pass a little cart on wheels from which an old lady is selling sweets, crisps and tobacco. Mauricio stops and buys two cigarettes. One he lights immediately, taking a deep draw; the other he puts away carefully in an inside pocket. It strikes me (what I should have seen before) that his worn shoes and thin coat are not simply the uniform of the Bohemian. No doubt poets in Colombia are even worse paid than in England. Mauricio is giving me the hospitality of his time and attention, an invaluable gift. I feel more grateful to him than ever.

Back at the hotel I make another fruitless attempt to call the *escuela de baile*. I'm determined to get some tuition in salsa, Colombian-style, while I'm in Bogotá but so far I'm getting nowhere. My room is chilly. It looks and feels centuries old. Near the door there is a hole in the plaster ceiling, and standing under it I can see right up through a tangle of ancient wooden beams into the rafters, and then to the curved, red clay tiles. There are chinks between the tiles and the sky shows through.

Mauricio has given me a copy of his last book of poems, *En la Raiz del Grito* (*At the Root of the Cry*). I settle down on the bed to read a sequence of prose poems called *Geografías*:

> My song inscribes vast geographies, burning chronicles.
> Land without memory, skilful in the trade of insomnia and
>   death.
> By a fire of thornbushes a barefoot people forge bronze statues
>   of silence.
> Secret dice encode their torment.
> I carve my verse on the wind, the sand sustains it.
> A rebel, taking my stand on dreams, facing death and his pale
>   banners.

The poems, written in the 1980s, are a surreal vision, beautiful but nightmarish, of Colombia's suffering during the worst years of the "drug wars" when citizens, especially those two vulnerable groups peasants and intellectuals, were caught in a three-cornered war between the government, left-wing guerrillas and the drug cartels with their private armies and wealth from the cocaine trade.

Things have quietened down now. The cities are safe and the drug wars, still flickering, have been pushed back to the forests and border zones. But every time I told anyone at home I was going to Colombia, their first response was "Aren't you afraid of being kidnapped?" In England, Colombia is a collection of images from movies: small planes bouncing onto makeshift runways to be loaded at breakneck speed with bulging sacks; shaky hands holding guns against the heads of gagged, sweating victims in the backs of cars. This cool room in its quiet, cloudy city seems to belong to another world. But then so does Mauricio, with his angular smile and deeply lined, humorous face.

A deep voice, an ocean in the sea shell of my breathing, cool spring water gushing out. Also the shriek of war, the broken bell of fear.

Early in the evening I meet Mauricio in a little café on the Avenida Jiménez. The yellow walls are lined with Van Gogh reproductions, the sound system plays English rock: it sounds like Coldplay. Mauricio drinks a *café tinto* – a very small, very black coffee; I have an orange juice. Then we set off.

La Candelaria looks wonderful under the chilly velvet-blue sky as the stars come out. Warm light floods out from the occasional restaurant. Two women talk on a high balcony above a wall covered in lush green vines. We're going, Mauricio tells me, to the former house of José Asunción Silva, a poet who lived in the late-nineteenth century. It's now a library and literary centre. We make our way along the small streets until we reach a white wall over which I can just see the tops of green, feathery trees, and then the pillared doorway of a square house, its frontage washed a rich, earthy red colour. From inside comes a hubbub of voices.

I plunge behind Mauricio into a series of rooms bathed in soft, golden light and full of people holding glasses and talking all at once. Clearly the party has already begun. Mauricio introduces me to a series of people ranging from plump professors in dark suits to gangly, sceptical-looking youths in baggy cardigans. Someone thrusts a glass into my hand. It contains a sweet liquor with an elusive scent a little like aniseed. Absinthe? The rim of the glass is crusted with white sugar. In between slapping friends on the back and sharing jokes too complicated for my rudimentary Spanish, Mauricio gives me snatches of Silva's life. About all I can retain is that he was a somewhat decadent poet, that he got into debt, and that he ended it all in the 1890s by committing suicide in this very house – a detail that doesn't seem to detract from anyone's enjoyment at this moment.

The large room set aside for the poetry-reading is crammed. I comment on the size of the audience. "A lot of people come to poetry-readings here," says Mauricio grimly, "but they don't buy books." Several people are already sitting on the platform under a large black-and-white photograph of Silva. A tall, thin man fusses with microphones, and a little, plump man in a worn, stained suit and greasy tie tackles one person after another, trying to persuade them to let him take their picture – for a price – with his Polaroid camera. We side-step the Polaroid and work our way along a corridor, emerging into a small, beautiful courtyard where metal tables are set out under a stone arcade. "We can listen here," says Mauricio. "The sound is being relayed from the main room."

The courtyard is open to the stars. In the middle are bushy green plants and a stone tank of water, where goldfish nose up and vanish into the depths. On the other side of the colonnade I can see the gently-lit, book-lined space of the library through its glass wall – an ideal place to read or write if I were staying here longer. The walls of the colonnade are lined with photographs of past Colombian poets. We sip our drinks. Mauricio lights a cigarette. He tells me the liquor is *panela*. It's made from unrefined sugar.

In the room behind us the poetry-reading has started, but we hear it only intermittently. Bursts of sound from the speakers in the courtyard come and go, separated by crackles and long silences. I catch odd words from the poems: "*Revolución … cerveza …* in your eyes I read philosophy…" A distraught man hurries past. "The recording isn't working," he calls to an unseen colleague. But we're too comfortable to care. The *panela* is good, the air is mild and the starry sky can be seen through the open roof.

Eventually we rouse ourselves and wander back towards the large room, hovering at the door to hear the last few poems. All this is part of a festival of Latin American poetry, and the poet reading at this moment is from Mexico. His composition seems to be more political diatribe than poem, but we join in the applause. After the reading there are more drinks and Mauricio introduces me to friends from the university, including a frizzy-haired woman writer in a rather severe dark blue suit, who asks us what we're going to do now the reading is over. When Mauricio tells her we're going to some bars, she brightens up and says she'll come too. The Polaroid man catches us in front of the picture of José Asunción Silva and we feebly resign ourselves to the inevitable. The camera flashes and the sticky product is handed to us thirty seconds later. I peer at it reluctantly. Mauricio looks brown, relaxed and cheerful. I look deathly pale, with an awful lopsided grin; my shirt collar has mysteriously disappeared somewhere inside my jacket, so that my neck appears abnormally long. Silva, of course, looks wonderful, serene and magisterial, his enlarged silvery daguerreotype looming over our shoulders from the wall behind us like some patriarchal deity, complete with mustachios and wise, dog-like eyes. I console myself with the thought that unlike him we're still alive. I may look like a scarecrow, but at least I haven't run out of money and topped myself. Not yet.

The crowd is thinning, so after more chatter and handshakes we head for the door to the street. At the top of the steps we're accosted by a plump, pale youth dressed in black. He has a round face, and in the middle of his broad forehead is an Egyptian *ankh* symbol, tattooed in blue. He's encumbered by a carrier bag bulging with books and papers; it swings about as he talks to us, waving his hands vigorously. He has a stammer and I can't understand a word he says. He rummages in the bag and produces a creased paperback which he opens in front of me, pointing urgently with a fat forefinger.

Mauricio explains. "He says he's a poetry-lover, and he wants you to read."

I take the book from the enthusiast's quivering hands and turn it over. It's a bilingual edition of Edgar Allan Poe, English and Spanish on facing pages. I scrutinize various scribbled notes inside the front cover. "What does he want me to read?"

"Here, here," pants the poetry-lover, scrabbling through the book until he finds the right page. "Here, please."

I gaze at the page. It's "The Raven", faced by a Spanish translation, "*El Cuervo*".

"Aloud," Mauricio prompts me. "He wants you to read aloud. It's because you're English."

Apologizing for my obtuseness, I take the book again and begin to read. How I long for the fruity, resonant voice of my favourite ham actor, Vincent Price, who recites the entire poem in that old Roger Corman horror movie *The Raven*! Still, I do my best to chant in a sufficiently incantatory manner:

"Once upon a midnight dreary, while I pondered weak and weary,
Over many a quaint and curious volume of forgotten lore…"

The poetry-lover, plastic bag haemorrhaging papers at his feet, clasps his hands, closes his eyes and sways to and fro in ecstasy at the music of an English voice reading the American lines. I plough on histrionically. The poem is badly printed and has words missing here and there, but I remember it well enough to replace them as I go along.

"Ah, distinctly I remember it was in the bleak December,
And each separate dying ember wrought its ghost upon the floor.
Eagerly I wished the morrow; – vainly I had sought to borrow
From my books surcease of sorrow – sorrow for the lost
    Lenore…"

By now we've drawn a small crowd of spectators. A figure in a navy-blue uniform hovers in the background: the janitor, hands spread wide as he tries to shoo us out into the street so he can lock up. We shuffle down the steps.

"For the rare and radiant maiden whom the angels named
    Lenore –
Nameless here for evermore!"

We've outstayed our welcome. I shake the enthusiast's hand – or at least his fingers, for he wears strange, dark blue wool mittens – and say goodnight as he stammers his thanks. His gratitude is humble and touching; he could not have seemed more delighted if Poe had dedicated the poem to him personally. Here at least is someone who buys books.

The frizzy-haired writer rejoins us, eager for her night out. Two or three other people tag along. Mauricio sets our course into the darkness down a precipitous cobbled street. After a few twists and turns we reach the Café Martí. The Cuban flags and photos on the walls indicate that it's dedicated to the Cuban national poet José Martí, a nineteenth-century prophet of freedom and independence. We settle down at a table in one corner, the only customers apart from a bulky man on a stool at the bar. A girl comes to take our order and we ask for beers all round.

Mauricio gets out his *célular* and punches some buttons. He listens for a while, then talks into the air briefly before snapping the phone shut. "I was trying to call the *brujo*," he explains. "He's got his voicemail on, so I left a message asking him to call me back."

Frizzy sits up, fascinated. "A *brujo*? Mauricio! Why are you calling a *brujo*?"

"Grevél had an important dream," Mauricio explains, as our beers arrive, "and he needs someone to interpret it for him. I know a wizard who understands things like that, so I'm trying to get hold of him."

"But I can interpret dreams!" Frizzy can hardly contain her excitement. "I can do a tarot-reading for him! I can read the twenty-two major cards. Grevél, tell me about your dream!"

But I don't want an amateur tarot-reading. I want someone who knows about *santería* and can recognize the gods and their symbols. I mutter something non-committal.

The sound system is playing excellent Cuban *son* music – the more leisurely, countrified predecessor to salsa. Mauricio notices that I'm listening and points behind me, towards the bar. "Have you seen the record collection?" he asks.

I turn round. I see now that the entire wall behind the bar is lined with shelves; and the shelves, divided into compartments, are filled solidly with vinyl LPs in their sleeves. There must be thousands of them.

"Come on," says Frizzy, hauling me up. "You have to talk to the owner."

I shake hands with the owner, a plump, grizzled man in shirt-sleeves, while Frizzy orders another beer. She explains that I'm an English writer and a salsa enthusiast. Or I think she does. The truth is she has a strong accent and talks fast, so actually I can't be sure what she's telling him. Whatever it is, he seems impressed. He starts pulling albums off the shelves to show me. He seems to have every Cuban dance record issued since the late 1950s. Of course I'm interested in hearing them, and he displays the discs to me, beaming with delight as he tilts them to and fro between his palms, inviting me to admire the perfect, unblemished sheen of each shimmering surface before he lays it reverently on the turntable and lowers the stylus. The trouble is, he can bear only to let me listen to a few bars of each before anticipation gets the better of him and he takes it off, anxious to put on something else even more spectacular. Tito Puente! Alfredo Gutierrez! Eddie Palmer! Anibal Velasquez!

I have an awful feeling that Frizzy has told him I'm a musicologist or a historian rather than just an ordinary salsa freak. I've heard of some of the artists, but I feel woefully unqualified to express the informed admiration he deserves. All I can do is run through my limited vocabulary of superlatives and hope for the best. "*¡Estupendo! ¡Increíble! ¡Fenomenal! ¡Fantástico!*" I bleat, as he pulls down one shiny cardboard sleeve after another, eyes gleaming, impatient to slide out the next slice of black treasure. It isn't only the artists he wants to show me. He has special prototype pressings. He has four-track albums played at 78 r.p.m., an early step in the direction of the long player. He has some of those floppy 45s that used to be given away free with magazines.

Frizzy perches on a bar stool, beaming, delighted to have brokered a true marriage of minds. Every so often she orders another beer from the girl, who's taken responsibility for the bar while her employer immerses himself in musical connoisseurship. The boss plays me Yma Sumac, the astonishing Peruvian soprano whose flawless voice soars bird-like into octaves almost beyond human hearing. He plays me *Ethel Smith's Cha Cha Cha Album*, an assemblage of Latin music played on the Hammond organ, *circa* 1958. He plays me *Panadeando* by Los Boby Soxers – surprisingly a male band, whose sleeve photograph shows a group of Hank Marvin look-alikes in cardigans, lounging on the bonnet of an American car.

Eventually I reach a point of overload where I feel I simply can't take in any more. I thank him profusely and tell him I must go back and talk to my friends. He acquiesces, but not before writing down a list of the more important but less-known artists he feels I must pursue when I get home. I fear he still thinks I'm writing a musical history. If so, he must have found me lamentably ignorant.

As I sit down at our table, Mauricio's *célular* rings. He talks for a while, then explains, "It was the *brujo*. He called me back. He's out of town right now and he says he's having trouble with his car. He thinks he can see you tomorrow; he's going to call us in the morning."

We finish our drinks and leave. Frizzy is talking enthusiastically to the company about – I think – my recondite conversation with the owner of the café. But her speech is now so slurred and her accent still so thick that I can barely understand a word. Out on the pavement in the chilly night air a debate takes place about where to go next. We wander downhill. Frizzy, who insists on leading the way, weaves delicately to and fro across the pavement, talking to us over her shoulder. I worry that she'll fall over, but Mauricio assures me she's adept at managing in this condition. He insists that we must go to the Café Habana. Others disagree. In the end, Mauricio and I leave the group and head for the Habana. Mauricio says his friend Mario will join us there.

We wander through a series of empty streets, then along a larger avenue to a strange, ugly redbrick shopping mall. It seems utterly deserted. We take a staircase which looks as if it belongs in a multi-storey car-park and cross a desolate space surrounded by closed, lightless shops. At the far side an empty escalator warbles. Stepping onto it we float up towards other silent, shadowy redbrick recesses. An odd and totally irrational thought strikes me. Has Mauricio brought me to this barren, hidden corner of the city to kill me? No, no. Of course not! Yet the harsh dim light and the sterile redbrick environment, the dark, closed shops are anything but reassuring. I don't know where I am. I could disappear here and no one would ever find me.

As we reach the top of the escalator I make out a dim red light in front of us. In the far corner of this uppermost concrete deck is a dark glass door, and over it the word *Habana* in red neon script. As we get closer I can also see a coloured sign advertising Cerveza Águila in coloured lights. It's the café. Mauricio opens the door. I'm aware of dim light, cigarette smoke, a few tables. The small counter at the back has an espresso machine and a lot of bottles. There are posters on the walls with photographs and political slogans which I don't understand. A good solid sound system is playing "Chan Chan" from *Buena Vista Social Club*.

Mario, a big chap with a moustache and light-coloured hair, is ensconced with four women at the only occupied table. He rises to greet us. I'm introduced and there's a flurry of names which I can't take in. The girls stand up each in turn to take my hand and offer their cheeks for a kiss. I'm introduced to a big, stocky girl with a long black plait and a thick accent. Then there's a thin, young woman with a dark, intelligent, quizzical face. There's a girl in a bright blue dress, with round eyes and broad, flat features. Last is a tall, curvaceous girl with a mass of dark curls and a deep green T-shirt. We order drinks. Everyone talks at once. Mostly I can't follow, and I don't try to. I just enjoy the ambience and treat the talk as music, another music weaving its way along in front of the salsa on the café's small PA system. But of course this can't last. Soon Mauricio is telling the girls that I've come to Colombia to dance salsa.

They look me over with interest. The girl in the green T-shirt begins a noisy discussion with the woman behind the bar about what music to put on. Back at the table, she tells the girl with the plait to dance with me. The café has a tiled floor and there's plenty of space beside the tables, so after a little verbal tug-of-war between the girls about who goes first, the girl with the plait gets up, we squeeze out between the tables and we dance.

I've been told that Colombian style is similar to Venezuelan, and so it turns out. My body seems to remember what Gustavo taught me and I do well enough, keeping to the rhythm, swaying to and fro, turning the big girl gently and then taking her into a *setenta* and out again, before returning to the drop-back step that's basic in this part of the world. The girl is solid and impassive: she drifts comfortably through the dance as if in her sleep, a vague smile on her creamy-complexioned face – but she seems to be enjoying it. I have to give her quite big pushes – almost *shunt* her, in fact – to get her to turn, but she seems to expect this and when I push, she moves – and in the right direction.

The music over, I thank her, she smiles, and we go back to our table amid a flutter of applause from the other girls. There are various comments, critical or complimentary – I'm not sure which, since the accents are so strong and everyone has long forgotten that my Spanish is patchy. They all talk at once and at great speed. The agreed outcome, however, is that I must now dance with the girl in blue. The woman behind the bar puts on a new track. As far as I can tell all the music in this bar is Cuban. In fact, recalling the previous bar with its dedication to the Cuban poet José Martí, it strikes me that perhaps Colombian salsa is mostly Cuban rather than Colombian. Though its steps, come to think of it, are Venezuelan.

But there's no time to ponder these subtleties because the girl in blue is getting up to dance. This time I'm a little more confident, and despite her stolid appearance this girl proves to be an adept dancer, spinning more quickly and able to follow my leads without needing more than a touch to send her in the right direction. None the less I feel I'm taking a kind of test where it's more important to avoid disasters than to perform riskily spectacular moves. I hold her against me briefly three-quarters of the way through the song and we circle on the spot, hips pressed gently together so that I can guide her as much with my body as with my hands. Then we separate again and continue as before: a few turns, a few 'open-out' steps, the odd curl in to the shoulder and out again with a right-hand turn.

We sit down and the talk continues. My partner tells me that the thin girl with the piercing eyes is an artist. The thin girl protests and tries to hush her, but the girl in blue tells me that she actually has the thin girl's portfolio with her. Why she should be in charge of someone else's artwork escapes me, but of course she's easily persuaded to get it out and show us. Girl in blue accordingly produces a large flat folder from under the table; thin girl reaches across the table and takes charge of it. Opening it up she displays a series of drawings – black ink and watercolour – showing strange faces emerging from masses of craggy rock. With long ears, pointed noses and sharp, cunning eyes, they have something devilish about them. Mostly coloured in red and blue, their sinuous forms, half human and half melting back into fractured planes of stone or torrents of lava, look like illustrations for Dante's *Inferno*, and I tell her so. She takes it as a compliment. It also strikes me that the shrewdly humorous intelligence of one or two of the faces gives them a distinct resemblance to Mauricio. I venture to say so, but she doesn't understand – or chooses not to react. It occurs to me that perhaps she's in love with Mauricio.

Mauricio has been watching the proceedings quizzically. He has resisted any invitation to dance (as has Mario). In fact, I get the impression that he doesn't dance at all. But who knows?

Suddenly I realize I'm very hungry. "Is there anywhere round here where we can get something to eat?" I ask Mauricio.

"Yes, but we'd have to go out to fetch it," he tells me. "Would you like something?"

I certainly would. No one else is hungry, so I give Mauricio some cash and he disappears, returning after ten minutes or so with a cardboard carton containing chicken in some kind of rich sauce and chips made from yucca – more chewy than potato but still delicious. I eat the chicken and share the chips, which are too plentiful, with Mauricio. The artist doesn't seem interested in dancing, but the tall, curvy girl in green certainly is. We get to our feet and there's an instant sense of connection: she's tall in her heels, almost as tall as I am, and she dances close to me, moving easily but firmly, swaying her hips with a smooth movement that feels very sexy. She looks into my eyes as we dance, but there's a sense that her consciousness is centred lower down so that her dancing has a very robust, physical tone about it. When I turn her she isn't feather-light like some of the best dancers, but the slight resistance and the need to push becomes a sensuous pleasure in itself, as if she's resisting just enough for us both to feel the pressure when I lead her.

It occurs to me that you can analyse the flavour of people's dancing as you would judge a wine. In her case it's full-blooded and just slightly rough; there's something distinctly Spanish about it but also a warmth and a lot of flavour. There's a lighter aftertaste which comes out in the way her smile suggests that she's sharing a joke with me. She looks amused and slightly challenging. When I hold her against me she stays there, her hips swaying firmly as we turn and move forward and back – for I find I can take her ahead and draw her backwards, as she gets the signals from the pressure of our bodies and adapts almost instantly – with, again, just that little resistance that presses us more firmly together before she goes with my move. I don't find her an especially pretty girl, but I feel a distinct spark that makes me enjoy the physical contact, and I sense her enjoying it too. I'm sorry when the dance ends, that magic circle of movement where we can play with these hot little energies while the music lasts. I thank her, squeeze her hand and give her a kiss on the cheek. She squeezes me back, seeming exhilarated. Now *that* was a real dance.

And so it goes. Some more talk, some more music, another dance or two, and then people start to mention work tomorrow and we say goodnight and drift down the echoing spaces of escalators and stairs and stroll out of the deserted mall, into an avenue of pale, ugly streetlamps where taxis wait in a line. Mauricio pulls a taxi door open, I get in while he speaks to the driver, and the car heads uphill towards my hotel.

In the morning I sit in the courtyard of the Hotel Platypus drinking coffee and looking at the strange orange flowers cascading down the stone walls on thin, black, shiny stems like electrical wires. Indeed, are they really wires? I get up and touch one to make sure. No, they are the stems of creepers, the weirdest I've ever seen.

I've danced in Bogotá but I still haven't had a lesson here, and time is running short. I want to call the Academia de Bailes Actual again, but all the hotel phones are in prolonged use, young travellers making complicated arrangements about flights to Medellin or raft trips on rivers. I go out and wander down towards the Avenida Jiménez. Plodding uphill towards me is a glimpse of the old, rural Colombia: a man and a woman, both wearing round felt hats and faded, patterned ponchos, leading two donkeys, one black and one white. The donkeys have home-made panniers, fashioned from cut-down plastic water-containers and square metal olive-oil cans, tied across their bony spines with pieces of rope.

I reach the business district. Here and there along the pavement are small stalls, often no more than a chair, an umbrella and a little table with six or more mobile phones in stands. In the chair, on which sits, usually, an old woman. A placard reads MINUTOS MÓVILES: here you can hire mobile phones by the minute. I show the old lady the number I want to call. She selects the phone for the network and keys in the number. Success! Someone answers, so she tells them someone wants to speak to them, and hands me the phone.

A woman's voice. I check: is that the *escuela de baile*? Yes. Can I arrange to have a private lesson in salsa? Today? Yes, surely. What time? Four o'clock this afternoon? Okay. Great. I have the address, so that's no problem. It's on the fourth floor, she tells me. Fine. She also says something else, which I can't catch. I thought I heard the word "sock", except that so far as I know nothing sounding like that exists in Spanish. Never mind. I hand the phone to the stallholder, who checks the time and asks me for the money.

I've arranged to meet a poet and musician, Fernando Linero, this morning near the city centre. Like Mauricio, he's involved in the International Poetry Festival. The plan is for me to meet Mauricio after I've spent time with Fernando, and for us to go on together to a poetry event across the city. I hope I can fit this in before my visit to the school of dance. Fernando Linero is supposed to be meeting me on a street corner, which is unfortunate because it starts to rain heavily. Wandering umbrella-sellers appear from nowhere and stroll up and down the street under their own umbrellas, shouting "*¡Paraguas-paraguas!*" But I have an umbrella back at the hotel and I'm not going to buy another one. I shelter under the cornice of a large building while people dash past holding plastic bags and newspapers over their heads. Eventually I hear a shout, and spot someone who must be Fernando waving at me from across the street. We go into a coffee shop.

Fernando is tall, dark and brooding, and he doesn't waste words. He lights a cigarette and we talk about ourselves and what we do. He has degrees in music and literature, but he's never had a steady job, he tells me. He couldn't bear to sit in an office, or go to work every day in the same place. "Freedom!" he exclaims, spreading his arms wide. He's a free man. But yes, he has a wife and children. He earns as best he can – as a session musician, and he plays in a band, though sadly they aren't doing any gigs this week. He's played trumpet and keyboards since he was a child, and now he writes songs and arranges music for his own band.

I've noticed that people talking about salsa bands will often tell you who the "arranger" is, something no one would think of saying about a pop group. The reason is partly that a salsa band, which may have sixteen or more members, takes a lot of co-ordination. It's also because the music is so complex. With three percussionists syncopating in different ways against one another, and often a brass section which has to inject precise phrases at crucial moments – in songs that can easily last ten minutes and evolve through several different "movements" – arrangement becomes crucial. Given the choice, many bands would rather lose a key vocalist than their arranger, who may be responsible for the entire sound of the group.

I ask Fernando which Colombian salsa *orquestas* are the best, the ones whose CDs I should get hold of. He tells me about Grupo Niche, Guayacán, Son de Cali, La 33 – all of them new to me. But he does better: he digs in his briefcase and produces two CDs he has made for me, compilations of his own favourite tracks. Wonderful!

Mauricio appears. He tells me we're going to a reading on the other side of the city, at one of the universities. He'll be among those performing, and he'd like me to choose some of the poems he'll read. He orders a coffee while I skim through *Geografías* and select five poems. Then we join the other poets, who are standing outside on the pavement in a noisy gaggle. We flag down some cabs. Mauricio, Fernando and some others get into the first. I follow in a second car, with a Mexican and an Argentinian, who fortunately know where we are going.

The taxi launches into the thick of the heavy lunchtime traffic. The driver doesn't hang about. Like all Colombian drivers, he goes straight ahead through the red traffic-lights, which warrant only a quick glance left and right to see if anything is imminently threatening to cross our path. We're on a dual carriageway leading out of the city centre. The traffic slows. Cars jockey for position. I can hear the wail of an ambulance coming up behind us, working its way through the clogged traffic. Our driver pulls over to let it by. The moment the ambulance has passed us, he floors the accelerator and we swerve out into its wake. Two other cabs try to do the same thing and we are nearly crushed between them. Our driver throws up a despairing hand and swears at his colleagues through the open windows. He slows down. The ambulance moves ahead, provoking a wave of manic driving as one car after another tries to get into its slipstream and take advantage of the swathe it cuts through the traffic.

Eventually we come to a complete halt. There's a demonstration, the driver tells us. It's blocking the way a few streets ahead. He'll go around it. Reversing a little, he turns down a side-street, then another. This certainly speeds things up, but after twenty minutes or so my companions start looking worried. When our taxi reaches the end of a cul-de-sac outside a factory yard and has to reverse, I'm worried too. It's clear the driver has lost his way.

It occurs to me that with the traffic as it is, and a *manifestación* blocking the main road back to town, I'm in danger of missing my dance class. This is my last full day in Bogotá and, much as I admire Mauricio's poetry, I'm determined that nothing is going to make me miss that class. I explain the situation to my companions, hand them some money and dive out of the cab. Fortunately I have my dancing shoes in my bag. I turn around, head for the largest street I can and hail a cab back into town.

I'm lucky. We get nearly to the city centre before the way is blocked again. I can see police and hear shouts, but I can't see the *manifestación*. I decide it'll be quicker to get out and walk, so I pay off the cab and make my way cautiously to the city centre. The protest has again moved on and I never see it.

The address of the Academia de Bailes Actual, which I copied from a folder at the hotel, is Cra 10 No. 18–44 Of. 401. For a stranger, addresses in Bogotá take some deciphering. Cra 10 means it's on Carrera 10, one of the big streets running north–south across the city centre. Of. is *Oficina*, so it's Office 401, which will be on the fourth floor. Number 18–44 will be forty-four metres from the corner of 18th Street. I find Carrera 10, a wide street with a junction so large that the traffic actually has to stop at the red lights. I walk along it until I get to Calle

18. Which way are the numbers on the buildings going? I walk back, scouting around until I find a couple of shops with numbers over the doors. The numbers are descending and these are in the twenties. That means if I walk back from this corner I should get to 44. I take another twenty or so paces and find myself outside a photocopying shop, its front open to the street, festooned with placards advertising cheap Xeroxing, passport photographs and mobile-phone hire. A cluster of tarnished metal numerals, inconspicuous on the grey stonework over the entrance, says 18:44.

The shop is busy. I make my way through to the back, where a plump janitor in a stained blue uniform sits in a little box reading a comic. "*¿Escuela de baile?*" I ask. He gestures towards the lift doors opposite. I get in, and the lift groans its way up to the fourth floor. The doors open on a dusty, partitioned space with two grey doors. One is the office of an insurance company. The other has a sign over it: ACADEMIA DE BAILES ACTUAL.

I knock nervously. The door is opened by a tiny woman with one of the sweetest smiles I've ever seen. She has a round, lined, elfin face, and hair dyed brown with orange highlights. I explain that I'm her four-o'clock student. Beaming, she invites me in. There's a small partitioned space with a couple of plastic chairs and a notice-board with some press cuttings on it. There's a little office desk. She sits down beside it and consults a big office diary. She's wearing red trousers, and a black Lycra top with decorative buckles on it. She opens a drawer and gets out a pair of bright red woolly socks, which she puts on. They clash with the red trousers.

Meanwhile, I sit on a plastic chair to change my shoes. I get out my white dance trainers. The teacher tells me I should dance in socks. (She calls them *medias* now – but perhaps I really did catch the word "sock" during that phone call?) She relents when I tell her I keep these trainers especially for dancing and never wear them in the street.

We go around the partition into the studio. It's a smallish room with lino on the floor, a battered gunmetal-grey electric fan in one corner, and a pair of speakers. The window looks out over the Bogotá commercial district. One wall is lined with mirrors, going just high enough to show my body and cut my head off. I guess six-foot-four Colombians are a rarity. We do some warming-up exercises and then move on to salsa. I've told the teacher I'm more used to the Cuban style than anything else, and that I want to learn the authentic Colombian way. And certainly what she teaches me now is unlike anything I've met before. The difference is in the footwork. The standard pattern I learned in England, the pattern I used in Cuba, and which Gustavo also used in Caracas, was "left-right-left (pause), right-left-right (pause)". My new teacher doesn't want me to do this. Instead of pausing, she wants me to give a tap with the foot I've just moved, before changing to the other foot. Effectively, this means stepping "left-right-left-left, right-left-right-right" and so on. I find it incredibly difficult. And there's a further refinement: each final toe-tap is completed by the lowering of the rest of the foot smoothly to the floor, as the opposite foot is lifted. She's a real perfectionist and she works me hard. She puts a CD on the sound system and I begin to get it, dancing side by side with her, my white shoes absurdly huge in the mirror alongside her dainty red woollen socks. Then she tells me it's time we danced as a couple, and I lose it all again. But she's good-humoured and patient and laughs a lot. Gradually it starts to come. And there's a further novelty. When I'm staying on the spot to turn her, she tells me, I should step "left-left-right-right" and so on. I find all this extremely challenging, since after the first few months of salsa the basic stepping is so ingrained you don't normally have to think much about it; you can almost let it do itself. Now I have to re-examine the whole way I move my feet. I keep tripping myself up.

But when it works I find that it gives a very smooth movement to the dance, a poised elegance quite different from the gusto and attack of the Cuban style. My teacher is a stickler for detail and precision. We practise for two hours while she gets me to take her through anticlockwise spins, *setentas*, and less familiar moves. She has to keep reminding me about the footwork but slowly it becomes easier, more natural. I notice that it's good when we're dancing to slower music: the extra tap helps me to keep time, and fills gaps in the music that might otherwise seem uncomfortably long. We dance around the room, and at moments I catch glimpses of us in the mirrored wall, an oddly-assorted couple: the long, pale, headless Englishman in his white shoes and the precise, petite, sharp-eyed Colombian in her red and black.

At the end of our two-hour class I am sweating, despite the whirring of the metal fan. My teacher, meanwhile, looks as fresh as the proverbial daisy; and indeed, when she beams up at me and asks if I'd like to come for another lesson tomorrow afternoon, she does look very much like a little, wrinkled, brown-petalled flower – a wallflower, perhaps, or some exotically-tinted pansy.

Sadly I have to tell her that I shan't be in Bogotá tomorrow afternoon. I'll be on the plane to Cali. She throws up her hands. Cali! Ah, she tells me, that's the place for music, for salsa! How good that I'm going there. But what a shame – she opens the desk drawer and gets out the big diary – she doesn't have a free lesson tomorrow morning. Too bad. I pay her, and as she sorts out change and writes the receipt I glance at her next pupils, two extremely cool-looking black dudes of about fifteen in white Nike gear, white baseball caps sideways on their heads, waiting on the plastic chairs by the partition. Judging by this sample of her clientèle, I've found the hippest dance teacher in Bogotá. I ask her her name, which I failed to catch earlier. "Victoria Laverde," she tells me, and she writes it down on a little card.

We shake hands and she wishes me *buen viaje* before disappearing into the studio for her next class. As I head for the door, the pin-board on the partition catches my attention again. It's covered with faded press cuttings and I stop to read one. "Victoria Laverde Tours America", the headline reads. Next to it is a picture of a gorgeous young woman, a kind of dusky, Latina Marilyn Monroe with a dazzling smile and billowing, silky skirts. I recognize that smile. It's my little dance teacher. Somehow she looks much taller in these pictures. It can't be just the high heels. I read more headlines. "Victoria Laverde Takes Latin America by Storm!" … "Victoria Laverde: The New Colombian Dance Sensation!" The cuttings date from the 1960s. There are pictures of her resplendent in silk couture gowns and on stage in sumptuous versions of Colombian traditional costume; paparazzi shots of her on the arm of a famous Mexican movie actor. Once – for how long? – she was the hottest Colombian dancer of her day, another Ginger Rogers. And I've just spent two hours dancing with her. Strange to think that in 1969 that would have made me the envy of every man in Latin America. Is she still famous? I don't know. I glance down at her name, written in blue biro on the little card which I'm still holding. At least I have her autograph.

I eat a wonderful and enormous steak pimiento in a nearby restaurant. It's the tenderest beef I've ever eaten, and to test it I put down the serrated knife and try cutting it with a spoon, which goes through easily. The sauce is hot and slightly green. The whole thing is exquisite. It's also, by British standards, inexpensive.

Later I walk up to the small café on Avenida Jiménez, where I'm to meet Mauricio. He's going to take me to Salome Pagana, a bar in the Zona Rosa nightclub district that is famous for its salsa music. I find him sitting over a *café tinto*, talking on his *célular*. He raises a hand to me mutely as I join him.

"That was the *brujo*," he says, snapping the phone shut. "He said he could see you tomorrow afternoon, but I told him that would be too late, right?"

"Right," I agree. My consultation will have to wait for another time and another city.

We wander out to find a taxi. Mario is working late and will join us at the club. The drive seems interminable: Zona Rosa is at the far north side of the city, and the taxi puts us down at last on a corner in a labyrinth of small, suburban roads. We can't see the club but we walk a couple of blocks and spot Mario coming towards us. He steers us around one more corner – and there it is, a strange, small beige building with a large orange sign.

The dimly-lit interior is painted deep red. There's a small dance floor at the centre, with tables at the sides and a bar at the back. The place is empty apart from us and a girl behind the bar, but the walls are thickly populated with photographs of the greats of Latin music and early rock 'n' roll – everyone from Tito Puente to Fats Domino. We settle down at a table and debate what to order, settling on a bottle of rum for Mario and Mauricio, and – since I haven't yet acquired the Colombian taste for drinking rum on every occasion – a Cuba Libre for me.

We chat, and listen to the music. Mauricio tells me that the owner of the club is a famous collector of salsa music, and certainly the record library behind the bar seems to cover even more wall space than the one in the Café Martí. It's a midweek evening and I wonder whether anyone else is going to come in, but eventually people start arriving in twos and threes. A young couple take to the dance floor, dancing stylishly with a lot of spins and turns through several songs. When they sit down they are clearly wrapped up in each other.

But I don't want to spend my last evening in Bogotá sitting down. I keep watching as new arrivals drift from the dark street into the mellow glow of Salome Pagana's interior. Finally I see what I'm looking for: a man accompanying two women. If he's a dancer I'm in luck, because he can't dance with both of them at once. The three of them come over and take a table on our side of the bar. They make themselves at home, they laugh, thy chat, they order drinks.

"Go on," says Mario. "Ask one of those women to dance!"

"Why don't *you*?" I counter. But it's clear to me that neither Mario nor Mauricio is going to ask anyone to dance. Never mind. I continue to watch the three at the other table, my game plan worked out neatly as a chess player's.

Sure enough, after a few minutes, a new, danceable salsa track comes onto the sound system, and the man – he's elegant and middle-aged, a suave-looking chap with silver-grey hair – gets up to dance with one of the women, leaving the other alone at the table.

Mario bounces up and down with excitement. "Go on!" he says, "Now's your chance! Go and ask her!"

But I'm not going to, not yet. That would look like pouncing. The lady would feel she'd been given no choice, no space. I calculate, rather, that if the man's any sort of a gentleman, he'll soon have to invite the second lady to dance. And when he does, it'll seem quite natural for me to go over and ask the first lady.

None the less, the waiting is a tense business. Salsa numbers take their time: instead of the three minutes occupied by a pop song, a salsa track can easily last seven, eight, ten minutes. Often it will begin with an introduction, a quiet, romantic passage during which people invite potential partners to dance, circle around, exchange a few words and get the "feel" of each other. Then the song itself will take off, the movement of the music becoming brisker and sharper, and the percussion will come in. The singer will sing several verses with increasing intensity, and when this seems to be approaching some sort of climax there may be a short instrumental passage, a percussion break or even (if the arranger is being really tricky) several beats of abrupt total silence, before all hell breaks loose and we are into the *montuno* – where a chorus sings a repeated phrase while the solo vocalist improvises responses. This is the heart of a salsa number, the focus of its excitement, the part where the dancers really let rip. Its chorus-and-response pattern comes from African music, where the dialogue can go on for a long time and is often intended to induce a kind of timeless trance in everyone who is involved. There's a peculiar intensity about the *montuno*: the chorus may be repeating a question over and over again ("Why don't you tell me the truth?" "Why has she broken my heart?") while the soloist invents more and more intense and extravagant responses. Or the chorus may be singing about partying and having a good time, while the soloist replies with jokes about himself and the band, or incitement to the dancers to burn up the dance floor. All this can go on for quite some time, eventually finishing usually with a short instrumental passage which brings the number to an end.

The grey-haired man and his partner finish their dance, sit down and resume their conversation with the other lady. I relax and keep them under observation. After a couple more tracks my patience is rewarded. The man gets up to dance with the other woman. I give them time to get onto the floor, then walk over and ask the first lady if she'd like to dance. She's petite and dark, in a black top and trousers, and she looks about thirty. She smiles, seeming perhaps a little surprised, but she accepts and gets up. We go onto the floor, where I catch an amused look from the other couple, surprised to see their companion joining them.

The dance goes quite well. I noticed during the lady's previous excursion onto the floor that she and her partner have quite a low-key style, with just a few turns and no complex moves, concentrating more on the subtle rhythmic interplay of their bodies than on elaborate pyrotechnics. This suits me fine; it doesn't challenge my repertoire of moves too much, and means that we can concentrate on just going with the music, letting the rhythm flow gently through our bodies, and I don't feel that as a total stranger I am imposing on or demanding too much from my unknown partner. She's pretty, and a precise, relaxed mover. Mostly I don't try to hold her close, though once I bring her gently against me and whisk us both around several times, just for variety and also to pay her the compliment of implying that I appreciate her attractiveness. Then I move her once again a little away from me, so it doesn't all feel too personal or too pressurized. She's responsive and lets me move her easily; she doesn't resist when I bring her close, and I sense that this will be fine as long as I don't overdo it. A dance can be as full of communication as a conversation, though much of it concerns things that you can't put into words. Surprisingly soon, the dance is over and I escort her back to her table. The other couple nod and smile as they too return.

Exhilarated and a bit breathless, I rejoin Mario and Mauricio and order another Cuba Libre. Honour has been satisfied. They pat me on the back and we all drink a toast, I'm not sure to what. The bar is still quiet and the clientèle thinly scattered, so I keep an eye on the neighbouring table and when, in due course, the man gets up to dance with his original partner, I wait a decent interval and then ask the other woman. She is a little older, blonde and not so slender as my first partner, but she's a more energetic dancer. She smiles a lot, so I'm emboldened to try a few gentle versions of the Cuban moves I know best: a *setenta*, a *sombrero* (crossing hands, then holding and raising them so that the lady spins round and we end with our arms over each other's shoulders before returning to the usual drop-back step). I can see the other couple watching us as we dance. I hope they won't think I'm doing too badly, for a foreigner. At least they smile when we finish and the man shakes hands with me. My partner goes straight to join her companions and they head back to their table.

I decide not to push my luck. It's getting late. With no more partners appearing, and the bar sparsely sprinkled with couples who seem more interested in talking, heads low over the tables, than in dancing, I feel it's time to go. Mario and Mauricio are a little bored now and they readily agree. We go out onto the street corner and stand on the dry grass and concrete waiting for a cab. Then we cruise back along the enormous yellow-lit dual carriageways, running the red lights, heading downhill towards the high walls, steep streets and bushy green trees of La Candelaria. When we pull up outside the hotel Mauricio insists that the cab wait, engine running, while I unlock the hotel door. It takes a tricky jiggle of the key, but by now I have the knack. I wave from inside the doorway, and the cab pulls away.

In the morning, I stroll down to meet Mauricio for the last time in the café on the Avenida Jiménez. There he is, his skinny figure hunched over the table in a grey-brown sweater, wiry curls clustering around his face, intense, dark eyes flashing up through his spectacles as he sees me at the door. The sound system is playing Pink Floyd. We have coffee, and Mauricio recommends a cake with hot jam on top. We talk about our work. Mauricio is writing a new collection of poems, as well as essays about popular culture in different parts of Colombia, and a novel for children about the first contact between the Spaniards and the Indians in his country.

He asks me which contemporary poets in English I like best. Among others I mention James Lasdun, and recommend his collection *Landscape with Chainsaw*. I translate it as best I can: *Paisaje con Motosierra*. Mauricio makes a wry face. "That title would have very dark implications in this country," he says. His words give me a sudden shock. Deforestation of the Colombian Amazon has been terrible and continues today, both as a result of corruption and the fact that some areas are beyond the government's control, ruled by guerrilla groups and drug gangs. I tell him I too am working on new poems. One thing I now want to do is to translate some of Mauricio's work, beginning with *Geografías*.

Time is getting on, and soon I'll have to get a cab to the airport. We leave the café together. As we come out we're greeted by rain, wind and bright sunshine: Bogotá's paradoxical weather, making me feel again that I could be in England. White clouds are drifting overhead. In front of us, at the top of the street, vast cool mountains tower above the little tiled houses, the line of a funicular traced diagonally across the thick green vegetation. The mists have lifted, and this clear view of the mountain is the first I've had. I thank Mauricio for all he's done for me. We embrace and go our separate ways. As I turn up the street to my hotel I realize that I never got round to taking a picture of him. At least I have that Polaroid.

CHAPTER FOUR
✳RUMBA CITY

It's early afternoon when the small plane lands at Palmaseca, the airport for Cali, after a flight through clear skies over a gently undulating, green surface of forests, mountains and fields. Cali is in the west of Colombia, not far from the Pacific, and the weather shows it. I emerge from the plane into hot sunshine so bright it makes me blink. Crossing the tarmac I breathe the rich, sappy aroma of lush vegetation simmering in tropical heat.

Awaiting my luggage, I read the advertising material on the carousel, most of it in English. I've heard that Cali is the salsa capital of Colombia, but these posters are all about its other speciality. "Gastric Bypass!" they proclaim. "Gastric Balloon! Stomach Stapling! Liposuction!" There are photographs, some of them pretty gruesome – a smorgasbord of yellow, red and white laid out in the pursuit of beauty. Cali is a centre for *cirugia plastica*, and North Americans come here because it's so much cheaper than in the USA. The emphasis here is on weight loss. There are before-and-after pictures of fat and thin women; phone numbers and addresses of clinics. I collect my bag and leave as soon as I can.

Out in the sun a friendly cab driver tells me the drive to the city should take about an hour. We roll along a highway through rich, intensely green farmland. Occasionally there's a small roadside building of corrugated iron and concrete, but mostly it's just wood fences, irrigation ditches, lush fields, clumps of palm trees and irregular herds of small, humped, brown-and-white cattle. It looks surprisingly close to paradise.

Every few minutes we pass a huge, slow truck coming the other way with one or two equally huge trailers, stacked high with immense tangles of woody brown branches. I ask the driver what it is.

"*Caña*," he replies. "For making sugar."

There's a strange, gassy whiff of something like bad eggs on the air. "That smell," I say. "What is it?"

"That's the processing plants. They're making the sugar cane into biodiesel," he tells me.

And soon we reach the cane fields themselves: great tousled plains of head-high green blades stretching for mile after mile. Far beyond them I can just make out the long, blue serrated edge of a mountain range, blotted here and there with white cloud.

Traffic builds up a little as we draw into the suburbs of Cali. Beautiful girls in designer jeans, with dark hair and long, long eyelashes, sail past on little motorbikes. Even their cycle helmets look *chic*. We drive along wide, tree-lined streets in the steady, warm sunshine and balmy air. There are clusters of high-rise buildings but the scale seems human. We work our way around to the hilly gardens and suburban streets on the city's northern edge.

As we slowly negotiate a hairpin bend and cruise down a residential street lined with flowering trees and high metal railings, the driver asks me, "Are you a singer?"

"No," I say, "but I'm here to dance, so I suppose that's musical. Why did you think I might be a singer?"

He shrugs, watching me in the rear-view mirror. "I don't know. Something about the face." He runs finger and thumb down his jawline, indicating a long face. "You look a bit like one of *Los Rolling Stones*."

"Must be my age," I say.

We pull up on a sloping street in front of a flight of steps up to a long, low brick building. "Here we are. Hotel Iguana."

I get out and pay, then haul my luggage up the tiled steps. As I reach the porch I can hear salsa music hammering from a superb sound system. All the windows are open and people are dancing inside. I ring the bell and a smiling woman lets me in. Right inside the door is a tiled lobby. In one corner is a high-quality portable CD player, and in the middle of the lobby a black couple are giving a white visitor a salsa lesson. Not too complicated: they're working on the basic forward-and-back step. The girl is dancing in partner-hold with the pupil, while the young man dances alongside giving advice and instructions. From the way the couple move I can see that I've struck gold. These guys can really dance.

I sign the register, produce my passport and take hold of my key – but I'm really not concentrating. All I want to do is ask one simple question. "Can I book a lesson with these people?"

"Sure, they come every day. Just speak to Carlos when they've finished the class."

The music alone is enough to make my feet move. Right now I don't bother about checking out my room. I just dance a few steps to a chair at the back of the lobby, where there's a roofed area opening onto a patio with some flowers, cacti and a dry pool that might once have been a jacuzzi. I dump my pack by the wall and settle back to watch with half an eye (I don't want to make that pupil self-conscious), trying to contain my excitement. When the lesson ends I walk over and introduce myself. The teachers shake my hand and tell me their names: Carlos Estacio and Maira Castillo. They're both poised, toned and stunningly good-looking. Carlos wears silky blue jogging bottoms, a white T-shirt with a blue Acrosalsa logo, and a light-blue baseball cap; Maira has nicely faded, figure-hugging jeans and an orange T-shirt. Her hair falls in thick black ringlets from a white headband. They are the absolute definition of cool. They're also extremely friendly and within a couple of minutes we've arranged a dance class for 3 p.m. tomorrow.

When they leave, I collect my luggage and go upstairs. My room, on the first floor, is the best I've had so far. I feel instantly at home. The wide window looks out through trees to a combination of restaurant and gym on the far side of the road: across a courtyard with some tables I can hear thumping music and catch a glimpse, through plate glass, of Lycra-clad bottoms oscillating on exercise bikes. Back here in the room there's a large, square bed with colourfully striped cotton sheets, and a solid, plain wooden table that invites me to make it into my desk. I take a shower and lie down on the bed. The cotton sheets are exquisite: cool without chilliness and just slightly rough against my skin. The air is a little below body temperature. Patterned shadows of leaves play on the ceiling. I grab a handful of sheet and roll over so I'm covered by a single layer. It's wonderfully comfortable. Something tells me I'm going to like Cali.

When I wake up, it's late afternoon and I decide to phone Rafael Quintero, my contact in Cali. Rafael is a friend of a friend of a friend, and I know nothing about him except that he's a musician. I borrow the hotel's *célular* and call his number. After a few rings it's picked up and I hear a tiny, high-pitched voice.

"*Hola,*" I say, "can I speak with your papa, please?"

A minuscule squeak: "*No está.*"

"*Entonces, ¿puedo hablar con tu mamá?*"

A tiny squeal: "*Mamiiiii…*"

A pause, and then a light, friendly female voice takes over. Yes, Rafael's been expecting me. He's out at the moment. Where am I? Can I call again at about eight?

Indeed I can. I can hardly wait to meet Rafael. I potter about, help myself to the hotel's free coffee and drink it sitting on the patio watching small birds flit in and out of a billowing vine covered with red flowers. A couple of backpackers loll in hammocks and collapsing armchairs at the edge of the patio, watching old *CSI Miami* videos on the TV. After a while I drift out and wander around the neighbourhood. I avoid the fake McDonald's and find a café where I can get a steak and a salad while the sun goes down. Then I go back and call Rafael again.

"*Papiiiii…*"

Rafael comes to the phone. A warm, decisive voice. "Welcome to Cali, Grevel! How was your journey? Where are you?"

Rafael, it turns out, has to see some people about work this evening, but he wants to recommend a club. It's called Zaperoco, and it's on Avenida Quinta – Fifth Avenue – between 16 and 17. It's completely safe, he says (that gives me pause – it hadn't occurred to me that it wouldn't be safe) and it's an excellent *rumba*.

"Rumba" in English means chiefly a variety of ballroom dancing. In Latin America it has other meanings. *Rumba* can be an Afro-Caribbean dance involving a lot of flirtation and explicit sexual moves, or a party, or just a seriously good time.

"I'll be there later," says Rafael. "Just hang on and I'll come and find you. I know what you look like because I've seen the picture on your website."

It's still only Wednesday – but Rafael says the *rumba* is good at Zaperoco, and he should know. It looks as if Cali is going to make up for the shortage of dancing in Bogotá. I go upstairs and think about what to wear, deciding on jeans and a white cotton shirt with deep blue stripes. I took the buttons off the cuffs a while ago to avoid the risk of their catching in women's hair when I'm dancing. And I have my white trainers. I've no idea what the facilities will be like and I don't want to have to change my shoes in a corner, so with some misgivings I decide to go out in them.

Outside, the night air is warm and clouds of moths swirl around the streetlamps. Cicadas are rasping like a whole orchestra of maracas. I stroll down the sloping pavement to cross the road – and suddenly I feel my feet dragging as if I've walked into mud. I look down and, sure enough, there's a large patch of mud running irregularly along the pavement. How did that get there? It hasn't been raining. The mud seems oddly heavy on my shoes. A few yards further on I find out why. An old man with a bucket of cement is mending the road by night. He has a trowel and he's carefully spreading cement over cracks in the carriageway. Wonderful! Now the soles of my best trainers are covered in cement. That's really going to help my dancing.

I turn into Avenida Sexta, Sixth Avenue, and find that I'm in clubland – a clubland of an intensity I've never seen before. Block after block is lined with dance clubs, and there's a different kind of music coming out of each one. I walk past velvet ropes protecting metal tables in the flicker of huge video screens and the thud of massive disco sound systems playing hip hop, rap, salsa, bachata, British rock, drum and bass, heavy metal, merengue and then salsa again. I brush off persuasive doormen. Lightshows swoop and wobble; floods of purplish ultra-violet spill out onto the pavement, making the Velcro strips on my trainers fluoresce weirdly.

The club isn't easy to find. I have to ask several times, but at last I spot a brick building with "Zaperoco" over the door in strawberry-red neon. It's already quite full. There's a long bar, dim red lighting, walls covered with framed posters and photos, lots of small tables. The dance floor is towards the back, under brick arches supported on pillars: a little Romanesque temple of dance. The tables are full, so I find a stool at the bar and order a beer. I've cleaned my shoes but I think I can still feel cement on them; I work at surreptitiously scraping off what's left on the rail under the stool.

The beer comes with a small wicker basket full of popcorn. Looking along the bar I see everyone has one of these. The barman doesn't ask for any money. I guess they keep a tab for each person.

I sip my drink and watch people coming in. They arrive in groups, six and eight at a time, middle-aged, young, and almost juvenile. Every group greets other groups with shouts, kisses and embraces. Soon all the tables are full; people stand about, lean on the bar, wander through onto the dance floor, which is already pretty crowded. The music is loud, but the hubbub of conversation around the bar is so raucous I can barely hear the music. Once I've finished my beer I thread my way between clusters of talking, gesticulating people to the edge of the dance floor. Quite a number of couples are already dancing. The style is similar to what I've seen in Venezuela: small, precise steps, continually dropping back, and neat little hand movements. In particular the style here favours circular movements of the hands: partners dance facing each other, holding both hands (left in right, right in left) and making little rhythmic movements with them as if polishing windows. The effect is almost cat-like. There are very few turns or spins. The dancers seem to play around in the music as if splashing about in shallow water. It's a nifty, elegant style that couldn't be further from the exuberant circling and spinning of the Cuban approach.

When the song ends, people stream back to the tables, only to surge forward again when the DJ puts on a new track. There are no obviously unpartnered women, but I notice a group of four girls dancing together and when the music changes I go over and ask one of them to dance. She's a slender girl in a shift-like dress, with long brown hair and a slim face that suggests some African ancestry. She giggles a bit. She seems very young, hardly more than a schoolgirl now that I'm close to her. Perhaps she *is* a schoolgirl? Anyway, she seems cheerful enough about dancing with me. I take her hands and we wiggle about. The hand movements, to my relief, seem to come naturally – a kind of instinctive co-ordination with the steps so long as I just allow them to happen. We make our way slowly around in a turn or two, and I raise her right arm with my left and gently turn her under it and around me, after which it's back to the dropping-back and the little hand movements. Two or three repeats of this and we are at the end of the music. I thank her, and she smiles sweetly and returns to her group of friends, who look as if they're eager to hear her report on her adventure.

I retreat to the edge of the dance floor and size up the chances of finding another partner. They don't look strong. Everyone here seems to be part of a group, and everyone seems to know everyone else. Occasionally I think I see an unaccompanied female or two arriving, but they always turn out to be part of a strung-out line of friends who find a table or a corner together and regroup. The noise level goes on rising. Waiters dive to and fro with trays, shouting to the bar as they deliver snacks and drinks to the tables. Some people join in with the tracks the DJ plays, clapping the *clave* or singing along with the songs at the tops of their voices.

To add zest to the proceedings, several young men have come equipped with cowbells. If you tried to bring one into a British club you'd never get it past the bouncers, but several people here are playing them, whacking them with sticks on the *one* of each bar, driving the music on with metallic gusto and then passing the cowbell over to friends so they can have a crack at it too.

The joint is certainly jumping. Rafael was right: it is an excellent *rumba*. The only problem is no one wants to *rumba* with *me*. I ask one woman after another, old and young, standing and sitting, with men or with other women, and they all turn me down. Some shake their heads politely. Others look apologetic and gesture towards their boyfriends or husbands. It becomes pretty clear that this is a place where people don't dance with strangers, at least not with *gringos*. And since everyone seems to know everyone else, I may be the only stranger here.

I keep watching the door for Rafael Quintero. It's a frustrating and one-sided business, since I have no idea what he looks like and will have to rely on his picking me out – though that should be easy enough. But every potential Rafael I see walks straight past me.

Then someone comes up behind and touches me on the elbow. I swing round to find a small dark man standing there. Rafael? He shakes hands and tells me his name. I don't catch it, but it's definitely not Rafael.

"*Hola, buenas noches,*" he says. "You're English? I've seen you dance. You dance well. Would you like to dance with my wife? She'd like to dance with you."

This strikes me as odd, but he's quite insistent so I get down from my stool and follow him to a nearby table, where he introduces me to his wife, a small dark woman who looks as if she's in her twenties. I take her gentle, limp hand and give a little bow, telling her how pleased I am to meet her.

"She will dance with you," says the husband.

His wife smiles – an apologetic, nervous smile. She doesn't move from her chair.

"Go on," says the husband. "Dance with him. Of course she will dance with you."

The lady shrinks. Her whole body posture speaks of embarrassment and nervousness.

My Spanish isn't good enough for subtleties. "I don't think she wants to dance with me," I say.

"Yes she does." He addresses her again. "You should dance with him."

"Look," I say, "the lady doesn't want to dance. It's fine, it's fine. No problem." I feel I should apologize to the wife. "I'm sorry," I say. "It's fine, we don't have to dance."

The husband begins again but I'm not putting up with any more. I bow, I say "*Gracias, gracias, señor, buena' noche' señora,*" I turn round and walk straight back to my seat at the bar. Is the man just a fool, or is he trying to drag me into some power game he's playing with his poor wife? Whatever it is, I don't want any part of it. What could be worse than partnering a woman who's dancing with me only because her husband forced her to?

Sitting up there at the bar I feel vulnerable. Zaperoco is a great club but it's not going to work for me – not tonight, anyway. It's after midnight and there's no sign of Rafael. I decide to leave. The barman tells me how much I owe, and when I've paid he writes something on a small piece of paper and hands it to me. I look at it as I go to the door. It says "*Pueden salir*" – "They can go out". Just outside the door in the suddenly cool and spacious night air are two doormen. They ask for my paper, check it and let me go. So that's how it works.

As I make my way uphill near the hotel I notice something twinkling at the edge of my vision. I look down to see an army of ants making its way up the pavement. They form a column about eight inches wide. Up the middle of it hurry ants – thousands and thousands of them – carrying neat, teardrop-shaped segments of green leaf. Down the outer edges of the column, in the opposite direction, empty-handed ants pour back to collect another load. The silently seething column proceeds for hundreds of yards. Where are the beautifully-cut slices of leaf coming from? I follow the bustling army back downhill. After about a hundred yards it disappears. I can't find it until I notice the same seething, twinkling movement on a tree-trunk at eye level. The indefatigable leaf-cutters are bringing their booty down from somewhere up in the branches.

Fascinated, I turn back and walk uphill alongside the vast army of little labourers. I pass the hotel. After two or three hundred yards the column makes a sharp right turn towards a wall. The ants straggle busily up the brickwork and crowd into a two-inch-square hole, a tiny army from an ancient world, little green shields on their backs tilting and jostling silently as they enter the city gate.

At eleven the following morning I'm having a coffee when the girl from the office comes and tells me there's a call for me. She hands me a cellphone.

It's Rafael. "Where were you?" he asks. "I went to Zaperoco but I couldn't find you."

"I was there," I tell him. "But I didn't see you so I left at around twelve-fifteen."

"Oh, you left too early," says Rafael. "I didn't get there until two. You should have stayed!"

Evidently my idea of timing doesn't match up to the demands of Cali's social life. When I left, the *rumba* had hardly even begun. Never mind: Rafael has plans for this evening. He explains in some detail, but I quickly get lost. There's something about dancing, something about his work, something about a theatre, something about a club. He's coming to pick me up in his car at around 8 p.m. At least this should guarantee that we're going to meet.

Meanwhile, I have my lesson with Carlos and Maira. They arrive at three on Carlos's motorbike. Carlos goes through to the office and comes back with the CD player. He asks me how much salsa I've done.

"This is Colombian salsa, but we're going to use Cuban music," he explains, putting a disc into the CD player. We start with a warm-up. Maira stands on one side of me and Carlos on the other so that I can copy what they do. We begin with the drop-back step and after a while change to the cross-over. Then it's cross-and-tap. Then we go on to a subtler version, where we give a little kick instead of tapping.

Next we move on to basic turns: I'm partnered with Maira, and we go over the anticlockwise spin and the waist spin. I think Carlos is taking me through these simple moves to see what I know and how clearly I can lead my partner. Maira is very pleasant to dance with. One distinct pleasure is that although she's shorter than I am, she's not actually *small*. This feels a bit unusual and makes me realize that recently I've almost invariably danced with women who are tiny compared with me. Maira is an elegant, athletic figure who's self-contained in a way that also makes her self-effacing: she dances beautifully with me while leaving the direction of the lesson entirely to Carlos. Yet she's far from being a doll or a robot. Her movements are fluid, her attention to me as we dance continuous and intelligent. But on a deeper level she's almost telepathically attentive to Carlos. She's doing with me – or letting me do with her – whatever Carlos needs, so that I can learn. It dawns on me that this is truly wonderful tuition, the best I've had since Geldys took me to pieces and rebuilt me in Havana.

Certainly Carlos is aware of the Havana connection. He's quite complimentary about certain things, and I feel it's a relief for him to be teaching someone who isn't an absolute beginner. But he's also sometimes amused at the way I move. He points out that Colombian salsa involves less body movement than Cuban, and fewer complicated turns. I should use smaller steps, and stay more upright. The Cuban tendency to lean forward a bit and push the chest out isn't part of the Colombian style.

Soon we move on to more complicated turns, including a satisfying move where I spin Maira clockwise and then back, turning myself in the opposite direction and passing her hand round behind my back. I then give her a neat push and we both turn in opposite directions, returning to partner-hold as we come face to face again. Or that's the theory. It takes a while to get it right, but the sheer neatness and apparent intricacy when it goes the way it should is an immense reward. It's one of those lovely, showy moves so plentiful in salsa, the ones that are liable to make people say "Wow!" And even when no one's watching, the wow factor is its own reward. Before the end of the lesson I'm so hot – with nervousness as well as exertion – that looking down I'm startled to see drops of sweat from my forehead splashing onto the tiled floor.

The lesson is thoroughly enjoyable but I'm not altogether sorry when it's five o'clock and time to stop. I get bottles of *jugo* from the fridge in the kitchen and we drink our tropical juices in the shade of the patio, chatting lazily while we feel the heat bounce off the stone paving around the defunct jacuzzi. We agree to meet the next day for another class. I have just about three hours before Rafael arrives to claim me. I haul myself upstairs, take a shower and collapse onto the bed.

A few minutes after eight I hear a car horn. I go out into the deafening racket of cicadas to see a big beige car standing below in the street. I hurry down and Rafael, beaming, gets out of the driving seat to greet me. He's tall, with a round, handsome, tanned face, and looks to be in his forties. He's wearing jeans and a striped green T-shirt. He seems genuinely delighted to see me, and I tell him how grateful I am for his willingness to show me around Cali. I climb into the passenger seat and Rafael introduces me as best he can to two women who are sitting in the back. We shake hands awkwardly between seat-backs as Rafael starts the car. It's an automatic, and an extremely smooth ride. My feeling of surprise at its gentle, purring movement makes me realize how long it is since I've sat in a car that was anything other than a wreck. Rafael tells me it's a Chevrolet.

The two ladies in the back are both attractive and dark-haired. The older of the two is Rafael's wife, Noelba; the younger is Lucero, a friend of my friend Maria in England. Noelba is lovely in every way. The impression I had of her on the telephone was accurate. Not only is she pretty, but she radiates kindness and a sort of gentle warmth. And strangely, although she's certainly Colombian, I sense something *English* about her manner. Is it a kind of quiet openness, something subtly different from the slightly self-regarding and defensive edge that a lot of Latin American women have alongside their wonderful warmth and intensity? I'm not sure, but it makes her very easy to talk to. I ask about the children who answered the phone when I called, and tell her a little about my travels so far.

The other woman, Lucero, is a slender, smouldering beauty with big dark eyes and long hair. She's perhaps thirty years old. She's very quiet, but I coax her into talking about herself. It turns out she's a painter. I tell her I'd love to see some of her work, but she says that's impossible at present: all her pictures are at the framer's. (What, *all* of them? Maybe she's just shy about showing them.) She tells me she's painted a lot of murals around Cali, in schools and hospitals. I resolve to get her email address before the evening is over; and not just to see her murals.

Meanwhile the car is heading along a broad boulevard towards the suburbs. I notice Rafael pays slightly more attention to red traffic-lights than the taxi drivers do. He definitely checks his speed a little as we approach them and has a good look to see if anything is coming. There's no question of stopping, of course, and it would probably be suicide to do so.

We pull in outside a large building surrounded by metal barriers, security guards and police. Someone checks Rafael's security pass and then waves us into a parking area fenced off with plastic tape. Leaving the car, we make our way between two groups of hefty doormen and into the building through what look like the fire doors. A corridor leads us upwards and we come out into a large theatre. We're down in the stalls. Behind us there are balconies, rows of plush velvet seats, and hundreds of people sitting in groups or wandering about. There are electric cables taped to the floor, men standing about wearing enormous headphones, people carrying fluffy boom microphones. Dotted around the auditorium, and at the sides of the stage, there are TV cameras.

Rafael scans the crowd, hails two men and hurries over to confer with them. They hasten off backstage. Noelba leads us up the sloping floor to some seats behind a velvet-topped rail, where we can watch the proceedings without being dazzled by lights or hit by a microphone. As we go she explains it's a telethon, a fundraising evening for local charities.

"So is Rafael's band going to play?" I ask.

"No, no, it isn't a band, it's a team of dancers. Rafael is the manager of a professional salsa dance company called Swing Latino. They're doing the main spot this evening."

At last I understand what's going on. Not that recognizing this as a telethon would have been difficult. At one side of the stage, a little oasis of artificial clarity amid the chaos: two tall, slender female presenters in long, low-cut black dresses are relentlessly beaming, twinkling and flashing meaningless wide-eyed smiles at the cameras while they exchange time-filling banter with a male presenter in a black tie and suit. Over centre stage a long black panel displays, in lights, the amount pledged so far. The panel needs to be long because Colombian pesos are worth so little that any significant donation has to be in millions. The total raised so far already runs into ten figures. Even the presenters get confused trying to articulate the enormous strings of numerals.

"And Claudia, this is so wonderful, I have a call here from Cali Telecommunications saying that they're pledging two million five hundred thousand pesos."

"Fantastic, Dolores, so that brings our total pledged so far in tonight's telethon to two hundred and seventy thousand ... no, sorry, to – er – two thousand seven hundred..."

"Wait a minute, Claudia, let's check that, yes, it's – um –"

And then, in chorus, "Two thousand seven hundred and sixty million, one hundred and twenty thousand pesos!"

There's a strong sense of civic pride. The presenters keep repeating a slogan: "If you're for Cali, I'm with you!" Everyone knows that Cali is the finest city in Colombia, with the best climate, the most beautiful women and, of course, the finest *rumba*. The presenters stand aside for a middle-aged pop diva, the mixers bring up a surging backing track and she launches into a power ballad about Cali. Noelba turns and smiles ruefully at me, as if apologizing for subjecting me to all this; but I must admit I'm enjoying all this Cali kitsch. The diva holds her final sobbing notes, tearful with sincerity and gratitude for the shouts of the audience. The male presenter half-carries her from the stage, exhausted by the passion of her performance, while Claudia and Dolores announce more donations before turning coy and flirtatious to giggle and flutter their eyelashes at the cameras as they introduce the podgy, leather-jacketed, vintage male rock singer who's next on stage. Noelba smiles philosophically and sighs.

"No," I say, "this is great. I'm enjoying it." Still, I'm not sorry when the singer goes off, the stage is cleared and the lights go down as the PA announces Cali's own world-beating dance troupe, three times crowned World Champions at the International Salsa Congress in Las Vegas. It's Rafael's company, Swing Latino, and they are clearly the serious act – the only really important act – of the evening. The audience finally focuses, and there's a huge sense of expectation as the music starts up and the dancers swagger onstage.

There are eighteen dancers – nine couples – and they're dressed like rainbows in extravagant multicoloured gauze and satin costumes with enormous ruffled sleeves that fan out as they bow and spin. The girls have split skirts with layers that shake and float out in coloured clouds when they turn or wiggle their hips. When there are seventeen dancers working the stage to pounding salsa music, a lithe figure in red comes spinning into the centre of the stage. The PA announces him as the leader and founder of the troupe, "Luís Eduardo Hernandez, *conocido como* El Mulato".

El Mulato is a dark, muscular guy with a round face and close-cut blond hair. He grabs a partner and the rest of the troupe fans out around him. He struts across the stage, every inch the *guapo* style gangster: he has a cheeky, challenging bearing that suggests he could take on the whole world and flip it behind him with one hand. He turns his partner back over his knee in a spectacularly low dip so that her head almost touches the stage, and then the whole company dives into a dizzying dance routine, a tearing pattern of criss-cross movement to some of the fastest salsa music I've ever heard. The men change partners every few bars, with the girls hurled from one male to another, spinning so fast they're reduced to a vertical flicker of colour. Men throw girls between their legs and catch them behind, tossing them forwards again over their heads so that they somersault in the air before landing lightly on their feet. Many of the moves look lethally dangerous, jolting gasps of admiration from the audience. It's impossible to see how some of these moves can be performed, let alone survived without concussion or fractures. But it all moves ahead with hypnotic, perfectly choreographed precision. And then, still in full action, the dancers begin to peel off and leave the stage, though as soon as the last girl has glittered out of sight, the first is re-entering from the other side of the stage in a different costume. This time the troupe are in red and black: red trousers and black vests for the men, red halter tops and skirts with a waist-high split for the girls. And the show continues.

The moves are based on salsa, and unlike the televised dance competitions in the UK, where so-called "salsa" is often unrecognizable as having any relation to the way real people actually dance on Friday night in a genuine club, here you can recognize all the basic salsa patterns in the company's routines. It's just that it's taken to a degree of elaboration, speed and accuracy you'd never see except in a competition or on a stage, and it has a whole layer of acrobatics added on top. Yet it's all completely in the spirit of salsa. It has the tension and magnetism between the couples, the feeling that they're relating to each other and not just drawing a picture for the audience, and it retains (albeit at lightning speed) the traditional basic salsa footwork and arm movements. I can feel the rhythm in my own body as I watch them. It makes me want to get up and dance.

Soon the company introduces (more announcements over the PA) their new up-and-coming star, a fifteen-year-old boy in a black and gold lamé suit and gold shoes, who does a featured spot, mamboing at astonishing speed, turning momentarily into a revved-up, shimmering version of Michael Jackson, then throwing himself into breakdance and hip hop before returning to high-speed salsa. He dances weightless on the points of his golden toes, seizing partners from the line of rainbow-clad beauties behind him and then returning them to their places before spinning himself to a black and gold blur.

The whole performance lasts around a quarter of an hour but it's packed with so much variety and action that it seems longer. Not that I want it to stop. Watching it is addictive. The audience is reluctant to let Swing Latino leave the stage – but they do. Then it's back to more donations and "If you're for Cali, I'm with you!"

I realize that Rafael is standing behind our seats. He seems pretty pleased with it all. "What do you think?" he asks me. I can only run through my limited repertoire of superlatives, but I mean them all.

"We may as well go now," he says. "Where would you like to go? Do you want to try Zaperoco again? Or we could go to Tin Tin Deo. That's the *alternative* salsa club – you have the expression *alternative* in English? Like ... different, underground, unofficial? Tin Tin Deo is the place where the *Bohemians* go to dance."

This sounds good to me, and I tell Rafael so. We thread our way to the car through a mob of police, security guards and technicians. Rafael drives us back into town along the river, which meanders among trees and tall streetlamps. We park on a bleak road running through an industrial estate. A brick building, reddish in the white sodium street lighting, towers over us. It looks like a factory. There's a neon sign: TIN TIN DEO. I have no idea what the name means. We go up a tight staircase, just room for one person at a time, and surface into a crowd, jammed together in the dark.

Gradually my eyes adjust. It's a big space, maybe part of a former warehouse. The walls are black, the lights red and orange. There are posters and amateur murals: tropical scenes, flame-like dancers, pictures of Che Guevara. On the wall by the staircase someone has written *LA CULTURA DE LA RUMBA* in large red letters. It's all splendidly chaotic. The culture of *rumba* is alive and well here, and no mistake. People spill, overflow and jostle everywhere. Drinkers stand talking in groups between dancing couples. Oddballs in baggy jeans and loose white shirt-tails gyrate, with or without partners, to the music pounding from the big black speakers. People wave and shout to each other across the room, over other people's heads. It reminds me of an enormous students' union bar during happy hour – and I guess many of those present are in fact students. We sit down at a table equipped with a mixture of sagging armchairs and precarious, upright metal ones. Behind us a group of young men are clustered around a cowbell which one of them is smacking enthusiastically right on the *one* of every bar. Elsewhere in the room people are intermittently clapping the *clave*. The whole room seems to levitate on the rhythm.

Rafael says he'll get drinks. Everyone seems to take it for granted that we'll have rum. So he disappears and we chat in shouted fragments until he comes back. A waiter follows, bringing a squat, round bottle and a supply of thimble-size plastic cups. There's also a large plastic tumbler full of ice, with a pair of tongs. Everyone takes an ice cube, puts it into their plastic thimble, and tips rum over it.

While we drink, Rafael gives me a commentary on the music. Besides well-known salsa tracks, mainly Cuban, we have tracks which he says are typical of Pacific Coast music, with a lot of African influence because the slaves were kept mainly near the coast. There are songs dominated by marimbas, and some in three-four time instead of the four-four of salsa. A few songs sound almost like calypsos. Rafael is keen to point out these distinctions, because the music is typical of Cali and the Pacific coast. It's something you wouldn't find in Bogotá. He also opens my eyes to things I've completely missed about familiar songs. One well-known track, to which I've danced weekly in Manchester, turns out to be Joe Arroyo's "Rebelión"; Rafael explains that it's about a slave revolt at Cartagena. I listen carefully and though I can't follow the lyrics properly, sure enough I can now pick out individual words like *negros* and *esclavitud*, "slavery"; and the chorus, which is "*No le pegue a la negra*" – "Don't hit the black woman". It's a revelation. The song becomes both more aggressive and more celebratory. Listening to the track with this new understanding, I sense that next time I dance to it I'll be far more deeply moved, knowing that the music carrying me and my partner is a piece of hard, painful history as well as a great dance tune.

And that reminds me: I'd like to do some dancing. Soon after "Rebelión" comes "Chapeando" by Los Van Van. I simply can't resist this, so I ask Noelba if she'd like to dance. She seems keen, so we get up and launch ourselves into it – no complicated moves, just dancing to and fro, swimming in the music, the occasional turn, separating briefly for a "shine", a little individual footwork and then back to join hands and dance on to the end of the track. Now Rafael gets up to dance with Noelba so I invite Lucero to dance with me. She's a wonderful, willowy follower, extremely elegant in her tight jeans and black T-shirt. Again it seems the key to Colombian style is simplicity: not to be perpetually twisting ourselves into elaborate knots but rather to maintain a sort of floating precision with small steps and a lot of sensitivity to the music. The floor is so crowded anyway that elaborate moves are impossible; you'd hit someone in the eye or kick them in the shins. So we undulate and do little turns and float from side to side, and it feels as if there's an invisible elastic band connecting the middle of her body with mine, with the rhythm of the music alternately tensing and relaxing it.

We sit and sip our drinks for a little while. Tin Tin Deo seems so much more relaxed than Zaperoco that I don't feel any hesitation in asking other women for a dance. I ask a slight, brown-skinned girl and, with a little encouragement from the friends sitting with her, she accepts. It all goes well enough, and from then on the pattern is established: a dance with Noelba, one with Lucero, and then an invitation to some other nearby woman. A break to cool off and have a drink, then begin again.

It's getting on for 2 a.m. when we start to think about leaving. Rafael tells me he has a treat for me tomorrow: he's going to take me to Juanchito for the afternoon. He's got something special to show me there; did he say something about children? I can't follow all of it, but never mind. Tomorrow is Sunday and he's going to pick me up around noon, which suits me fine because I have Carlos and Maira scheduled for a lesson at ten.

We fight our way to the stairs and go out from the hot soup of the club atmosphere into the cool night. As we make for the car I notice a steamy cloud pouring from the air-conditioning units into the black emptiness of the sky. I suddenly feel very tired.

I'm awakened at 6 a.m., as usual, by music thumping from the gym across the road, and a stentorian female voice exhorting its victims, through a microphone, to burn calories. The fact that it's Sunday doesn't seem to make any difference. I try putting a pillow over my head but it does little to diminish the sound, so I grope my way downstairs, take a bottle of water and a bottle of mango juice from the fridge, then sit in the courtyard watching little brown birds flit around in the recesses of the creeper-covered walls.

By ten I'm feeling better and am positively happy to see Carlos and Maira climbing off their *moto* and coming up the steps to the door. Today we work on extending my repertoire a bit further. I don't do too badly, and when Carlos puts on "Cambiaré Por Ti," a hit by the famous local band Guayacán, we end up dancing just for the fun of it. It's always the same: no matter how tired I think I am, if the right salsa track comes along the energy seems to be inexhaustible.

We finish at twelve but Rafael hasn't shown up yet, so I have time to shower and change. The sun outside is so hot that the tiled floor of my room stings the soles of my feet when I step into a patch of light. I've just pulled on a new shirt when I hear Rafael's car in the street below. I join him in the upholstered, air-conditioned comfort of his Chevrolet and we take the dusty, concrete highway out of town. We pass long, heavily-built single-decker buses painted in bright stripes. They look like recycled North American school buses. Buildings thin out; the landscape opens into farmland and cane fields. We pass a horse-drawn cart driven by an old man and woman wearing battered straw hats. The wooden cart is filled with an enormous mass of flowers of all colours, like a float from some Arcadian carnival.

Rafael explains that he's taking me to Juanchito, a Cali suburb, to watch a children's dance competition. Juanchito, he tells me, is completely dance crazy. There are five hundred *salsotecas* there and the music never stops. The kids in Juanchito learn to dance before they can walk.

The sun blazes down onto the rich, ragged green vistas of countryside: palm trees, bamboo fences, wandering chickens, the rough blue edge of mountains in the distance. There's a muffled vibration of thunder. A few miles to our right a colossal slate-grey cloud has given way at the bottom and a solid column of granite-coloured water is pouring down onto the fields, edged with neon-white crackles of lightning.

Something reminds me that I still haven't found anyone to consult about that dream. I ask Rafael if he knows of anyone.

"Certainly," he says. "When are you going back to Bogotá?"

"I'm not," I tell him. "I'm flying direct from Cali to Panama City."

"Ah, that's such a pity. There's a really powerful Cuban *santero* in Bogotá. He would definitely be able to tell you."

Damn. That could have been interesting. "So he's Cuban? How come he's in Bogotá?"

"It's a long story. But he's one of the most powerful Cuban *santeros* alive. I know someone who knows him. You've been to Cuba, haven't you? Did you know that when Fidel Castro fell ill, all the *santeros* in Cuba met together and performed a ritual to preserve his life? They say they put so much energy into their magic that some of them died as a result."

"So did this *santero* from Bogotá go over for the ceremony?"

"He couldn't. Not physically, anyway. Maybe he found some other way to be there."

I'm still pondering this when Rafael asks if I've had lunch. He wants to eat too, so we look for somewhere to stop. Every so often we pass a shack of corrugated iron or breeze blocks with a metal Coca-Cola sign. Rafael peers at these and drives on. Eventually he pulls in on the dusty grass verge beside a littered space with a small concrete building. There are some tables under a roof of tattered palm-thatch on bamboo poles. Hens peck about in the dust. A small black dog runs to and fro. There's a stack of old tyres by the wall, and next to it an array of plastic buckets for sale. I follow Rafael into the shade under the thatched canopy. I can smell food. At the far end of the roofed area, out in the sun near a collection of old oil drums, several rusty iron grilles rest on stacks of bricks: primitive barbecue apparatus. There are heaps of charcoal and ash on the ground.

A plump woman in jeans, a bulging T-shirt and an apron comes out of the concrete hut and asks us what we'd like. Or so I assume – her accent is so strong I can't understand a word. Rafael orders two beers, which arrive in cold, slippery bottles dewed with condensation. Rafael uses a corner of his shirt to wipe the mouth of his bottle very thoroughly so I do the same, while he engages the lady in a discussion about food.

Soon an old man in a blue cotton shirt arrives with a plate of greenish-grey soup, which he sets carefully in front of Rafael. Rafael sips from a spoon and considers, then nods. We'll have another helping, he tells the old man; and chicken too. After a few minutes our host returns and places a second dish in front of me. It contains the same greenish-grey liquid, but this time, jutting grotesquely above the oily surface, are the scaly yellow feet of the chicken. Rafael looks at this with distaste, shakes his head wearily and asks the old man to remove the feet. The plate is taken away and returned footless. It's followed by a plate of barbecued chicken, which Rafael dismembers, shovelling chunks of shreddy white flesh into my soup. I try it. It's not bad. There's a big piece of yucca submerged in the soup, hard but good-tasting. Also some smooth, round, chewy things.

"Beans?" I ask Rafael.

"*Platano*", he tells me. Banana.

Soon we're back on the road, passing ploughed fields and cane crops. The first sign that we're nearing Juanchito is the appearance of motels – long, low, white concrete buildings strung out along the highway. Some have archways and verandas, a kitsch imitation of *hacienda* architecture. Others have outline drawings of nude women traced on the white concrete and coloured in. It's not hard to guess what the motels are there for. One even has a larger-than-lifesize cast of the Venus de Milo on the archway over its gate. A placard at one side reads MOTEL VENUS: *Tarifa 5 horas $15,000*. Fifteen thousand pesos is about eight US dollars. Four pounds. I wonder what sort of room you get for your hourly eighty pence.

After the motels come the *salsotecas*. These are more adventurous in their architecture. We pass one called Changó: it's circular, with a conical, thatched roof so it looks like an enlarged version of an African village hut. Another has a metal replica of the Eiffel Tower poised over its entrance. The clubs stream past, one every few hundred yards. Beyond them the unbroken landscape of cane fields stretches to the horizon, with only the occasional shack of corrugated iron and breeze blocks, or a few humped brown cattle to punctuate the green monotony.

Eventually a somewhat larger building looms up. It seems very new, and the outside is clad with metal panels. It looks like a high-tech factory or some kind of state-of-the-art crop-storage facility.

"Citrón," Rafael announces. We pull over, through a gateway in the low brick wall and into the extensive car-park. Stepping out into the shimmering heat, I see the club's logo splashed in lime-green neon across the gleaming, silvery surface. We join a small queue at the entrance. Rafael shows our tickets to a pair of plump, motherly ladies and spends a minute or two chatting with them about their children. They seem straight from an English PTA, and I remember we're here to watch a competition for children. I guess the people who organize these things are the same kind of people who run kids' events the world over.

Citrón, however, is something else. I've been in many clubs and discos before, but I've never seen anything like this. The design and the level of luxury surpass anything I've ever encountered. There's a gallery running around above our heads, like the balcony at a cinema. The carpeted floors are raked, sloping gently down to the dance floor. Above the dance floor, where the screen would be if this were a cinema, there's a wall covered with a vast bank of monitors, which slowly and continuously fade from one pure colour to another. Sometimes the entire wall is cerulean blue; sometimes it's a rich orange or deep red; sometimes the monitors break up into different patterns so that the wall is chequered or striped. And always, every two minutes or so, the whole wall fades back to lime green. *Citrón* means "lime" and *everything* here is lime green. The dance floor is edged all the way round with a curving strip of lime-green neon. The spotless carpets are lime green. All the way from the dance floor to the rear wall are curved lime green sofas, each with a glass table in front of it. The walls, naturally, are lime green. So, probably, is the ceiling, but it's invisible behind the rigs full of coloured lights projecting swirling patterns onto the floor, in colours that harmonize with the reds, blues and greens of the monitors. The whole place looks pristine. It's astonishing.

People wander around in groups or sit here and there on the sofas. Evidently most have yet to arrive. Like the telethon, this is a public event: microphone booms, cables and TV cameras are all over the place. Rafael goes over to talk to a bald man holding a clipboard.

Gradually the place fills up, the trickle of newcomers swelling to a flood. Rafael returns and we ensconce ourselves on a sofa at the edge of the dance floor. The music gets louder, the club more crowded. Rafael disappears again. I watch the hypnotic coloured monitors and listen to the music. It's "A Cali" by Guayacán:

> En Cali mira se sabe gozar...
> In Cali, look, they know how to enjoy themselves –
> If you go to Juanchito it'll be beautiful,

If the music's hot we won't look at the time…
The women of Cali have such tasty salsa
Because they know how to move their hips…
Come to Cali and see!

I've never known anywhere with so much local pride. And it's all about having a good time.

Rafael is certainly entering into the spirit of *rumba*. He emerges from the crowd accompanied by two of the most beautiful girls I've ever seen. He introduces them as Carmen and Susana, *primas bailarinas* from Tex-Tropical, another local salsa dance company. Carmen is black; her skin is like satin, the colour of dark chocolate. She wears jeans and a short-sleeved gold top. Susana is white and petite, dressed in a miniskirt with glittery high-heeled sandals; her skin is the colour of very milky coffee. Both have perfect breasts, and plunging necklines that show them to full advantage. Both are absolutely charming. Rafael has evidently recruited them for the afternoon, though quite how I don't know: is it his natural charm, or has it something to do with the fact that he's the manager of Swing Latino? The girls settle between us on the lime-green sofa and Rafael cranes around to find a waiter. He orders a bottle of rum and some Cokes. We chat with the girls until the waiter returns with a fat-bellied bottle, four tumblers of Coke and ice, and four tiny glasses. Rafael fills these from the bottle and we all clink them – "*¡Salud!*" – before drinking.

Meanwhile lights have come on and an MC with a clip-on microphone is rattling off details for the benefit of the TV audience. I notice that the next sofa to our left is occupied by two men and two women, all equipped with pads and pencils: evidently the competition judges. A spotlight swings onto their table and the cameras turn their way as the MC reels off their credentials. I'm listening with half my attention when, amidst the rapid torrent of Spanish, I distinguish the words "…*el eminente poeta y critica cultural inglés, Grebél Liiindop…*" Susana nudges me and the next moment I'm doused in the white glare of a spotlight and the cameras are on *me*. I'm on Colombian TV! I sit up and gaze into the cameras, trying to look alert, friendly, poetic and critical all at once. I hope to God they're not expecting me to say anything. Fortunately they aren't, and after a few seconds the lights and cameras swing away in pursuit of other prey. They leave me, though, wondering if by any chance I'm expected to participate in the judging. Fortunately I've got a pencil and paper on me. I get them out just in case.

The child contestants troop out onto the dance floor. None of them looks much higher than my waist. They seem to be six or seven years old, and they're an astonishing sight. The little girls, who are of every ethnic shade, glitter with make-up, their eyes hooded with eyeshadow in lavish blue, mauve or slate, their lips glutinous with strawberry-coloured lip-gloss. They wear spangled dresses, handkerchief skirts starred with sequins, gauzy tops, high-heeled gold and silver shoes. The boys are mostly black, and have their hair dyed a startling gold-blond. They wear gold-and-black tuxedos, or silk waistcoats with striped trousers, and shiny, pointed two-tone shoes: black-and-white, red-and-white, blue-and-white. All the children stream off again, and the first of the individual competing couples is announced.

The dancing is astonishing: if anything, it's even more athletic and frenetic than the work of the adult dancers I saw yesterday. The little girls flash smiles, flutter their false eyelashes, pout and grimace through their mask-like make-up in imitation of adult sexiness and allure. They do the splits, they cartwheel across the boys' knees or backs. The boys spin them at dizzying speed by their skinny little arms, toss them around their necks or roll them over their backs. Their self-confidence, as they hurl their tiny partners between their legs or twirl them in the air and catch them on their shoulders, is daunting. I wonder what kind of kids these are: are they already obsessed, succeed-or-die professionals, or are they tense little nervous wrecks, drilled by pushy parents? Or are they, as Cali's self-image would no doubt have it, enthusiastic little dance-crazy good-timers, who love it all so much that they compete for the sheer joy of it?

There's one dreadful moment when a boy is throwing his partner, a little girl in blue chiffon, over his shoulders. Fumbling his catch, he drops her. There's a thud as she hits the floor in sitting position – and a stifled gasp of shock from the audience. For a microsecond the tiny girl's face registers absolute horror. Then it moulds itself back into the compulsory smile. But the sense of trauma doesn't evaporate so quickly. That this couple are out of the competition goes without saying. The girl isn't obviously injured, but who knows? The real pain, we all know, must be in what that boy will be feeling, what his partner will feel about him, what his parents and her parents will be feeling, thinking, saying… It's all just too dreadful to contemplate. They finish their performance, grimly flawless, and go off amid loud, sympathetic applause.

The dozen or so couples are whittled down to four, and a final dance-off secures trophies for the best two. Fortunately I'm not asked to judge, but I've compared notes throughout with Carmen and Susana, and we're pleased to find that we've identified the first and second prize-winners right from the first heat. They were, in fact, the first and last couples to dance; it occurs to me that maybe they were deliberately scheduled in those positions if they're known to be the best.

After the children's competition, there's a short display by Swing Latino's adult dancers. Their muscular expertise is something of a relief after the brittle brilliance of those terrifyingly talented *niños*. Then the show is over, the technicians start packing up, and the floor is turned over to the rest of us. I ask Susana if she'd like to dance; she accepts, so we launch ourselves into the gathering crowd that's rapidly filling the lime-green loop around the shiny floor. Susana is a joy to dance with: she's feather-light and she spins with the precision of an angel dancing on the point of a needle. She may be a *prima bailarina* but, wonderfully, she's not at all intimidating. Her dancing is easy and relaxed, she smiles and laughs a lot, and she doesn't seem to expect me to introduce lots of intricate moves. I drop in some of my Cuban moves, suitably toned down to fit the stylish precision of the Colombian ambience, and she seems amused and delighted. The dancing is very much a mutual activity, a shared game. When the music stops, we go back to the table and sip some more rum.

Rafael, meanwhile, is making his way into the crowd with Carmen, ready to dance to the next song. When they return, we sip our drinks some more and I ask Carmen to dance. She is more buxom than Susana, a little heavier, or maybe just a little *firmer*, to dance with. Susana's dancing is a sparkling champagne, Carmen's a full-bodied red. I have to push her firmly when I want her to spin; but once pushed, she certainly goes. Her movements are elegant and powerful, and her hip movements are superb: we spend a lot of time just pacing from side to side, or revolving together in partner-hold, simply communicating with the sway of our hips. There's an earthy, physical chunkiness about the way Carmen moves that's delightful. Again I find myself laughing from the sheer joy of the movement.

And so it goes. Rafael and I take it in turns to dance with Carmen and Susana. Every so often one of them goes off to dance with someone else, or one of us will ask a nearby lady for a dance. In between we sip rum and Coke, listen to the music and talk – as far as my defective Spanish and the surrounding noise allow. Susana tells me she works in some kind of business, as an *ejecutiva de ventas*. A sales executive? The term sounds vaguely familiar but I don't know what it is. Never mind. We talk about poetry. I suddenly find I'm unusually vehement on the subject and detect that the rum is making its presence felt. It occurs to me that I'm dependent on Rafael's driving to get me back into Cali, and I wonder how the rum is affecting him. Well, no point worrying about that.

As we dance and return and dance again, we change places on the sofa. In due course Rafael is at the far end, with Susana sitting between him and me. His arm rests along the back of the sofa behind her, and I notice that he's gradually extending it around her shoulders, a manoeuvre I remember well from my adolescent days. At the same time Susana is edging along the sofa towards me. I take this as my cue to act the perfect gentleman. It occurs to me that I'd very much like to see Susana again. Right now I ask her for the next dance; she agrees at once. When we get back to our table I ask both her and Carmen if they'd like to exchange email addresses so we can keep in touch. They seem delighted with the idea and write the addresses out carefully. They tell me I must be sure to write when I get back to England.

It's now about four in the afternoon and the bottle is empty. Rafael is suggesting that it's time we left. There are farewells, kisses and elaborate goodbyes all round, and while Rafael is buttonholing one of the competition judges I grab a few surreptitious words with Susana.

"I'm flying to Panama City the day after tomorrow," I say. "Would you like to have dinner with me tomorrow? It'll be my last evening in

Cali." I feel it's a long shot, and I don't quite know why I'm trying it. It's almost as if I feel I'd blame myself if I *didn't* make some attempt to go on a date with a girl as lovely as Susana. And after all, it would be wonderful to spend my last evening in Colombia with her.

To my amazement she smiles and says, "*Sí.*" She sounds quite decisive.

"Do you read your email?" I ask. "Make sure you read it tomorrow. I'll invite you. Okay?"

She agrees. We kiss again and I join Rafael. As we make our way through the crowd it occurs to me that another half-conscious motivation is at work. The truth is that Rafael has brought out my competitive instincts. What a *coup* it would be if I could have a date with Susana!

As we get near the door, Rafael's brisk tread slows a little. He hesitates. He notices someone he knows and turns aside for a chat. When he's finished talking he turns as if to make for the exit again, then stops and hovers to and fro. Finally he grabs my elbow. "Why are we leaving?" he asks rhetorically. "We don't have to leave. Let's stay." And he sets off back to our sofa, our table, and the girls. In our absence another couple have taken our places. Rafael evicts them with surprising ease and we rejoin Carmen and Susana. I shrug my shoulders and do my best to make it clear to them that I'm not sure why we're back. Carmen suggests ordering another bottle of rum, but Rafael raises his palms fastidiously. He thinks we've had enough. Five minutes later he decides we really do need another bottle. It duly arrives, and we all raise our glass thimbles in a toast.

From there on, the day disintegrates into a mass of coloured fragments like a dropped jigsaw. I remember it being seven o'clock and I remember it being nine, not necessarily in that order. I remember some people behind us passing a cowbell and stick to our table. We all had a go: Susana was best at keeping time, and Rafael was less good than I was. I remember Rafael explaining to me, with much complex logic, why the *culo* was the most beautiful part of a woman's body. His theory had something to do with geometry and perfect curves. Had I been more *compos mentis* I might have countered by putting a case for breasts on similar grounds, but I couldn't muster the energy or the words so I went along with him. I remember us all dancing frantically to house music, in the middle of an enormous crowd, waving our arms in the air and yelling:

> Put your hands up!
> Put your hands up!
> Put your hands up!
> Put your hands up!
> Left! Left! Right! Right!
> *¡Izquierda! ¡Izquierda! ¡Derecha! ¡Derecha!*

And I remember us dancing to salsa music that actually did sound like 33 r.p.m. played at 78.

Finally the crowd thins, the music stops, the big overhead lights come on. It really is time to leave. Susana and Carmen are insistent that I email them. I remind Susana to check her email tomorrow, because we're going to have dinner. We join the stream of people heading for the car-park. My legs are aching. I've never danced so long or so hard in my life. As we get out into the warm, fragrant night air, Rafael is ecstatic. He slaps me on the back. Don't I agree now that Cali is the world capital of salsa? Have I ever had a night out like that? Isn't Cali culture truly the culture of *rumba*? Intensely and sincerely, I agree. My Spanish superlatives have long since been exhausted but I use them all again. *Estupendo. Halucinante.*

The journey home is better than I would have expected, though the driving is perhaps a little impulsive at times. I won't say we don't find ourselves at one point going the wrong way up a dual carriageway, or that we don't briefly get lost. Or indeed that, sailing as usual through a red traffic-light, we don't miss a taxi by a few feet – though you could say it misses *us*. But we get back intact, with Tito Puente blaring on the car stereo, and Rafael pulls the car up outside the hotel without actually hitting the wall, and we embrace, and we agree that it's been an utterly unforgettable afternoon. Night. Day. Whatever.

I don't feel too bad the following morning. Rum must agree with me. I have a lesson booked with Carlos and Maira at ten; before they arrive I manage to get enough time on the hotel computer to email Susana.

Hola Susana,

¡Que noche fantástica! Hope you're well and not too tired. Would you like to have dinner tonight? Maybe at Casa Vieja at 7.30? If you prefer a different place or time just email me. Anywhere, any time will be fine for me.

Hasta la tarde,
Besos.

I send it off, wondering what response I'll get. Then it's time for my lesson.

I check my email soon after midday: nothing. I suppose Susana is at work. I check again at five. Still nothing. Nor at six. Nor, finally, at seven. Well, that's it. I guess Rafael and I are about quits now.

Never mind. The Casa Vieja is still the best restaurant I've found in Cali. I stroll down there and eat an exquisite dish of grilled pork covered in a rich fruit sauce. Then I walk back through the neon-lit darkness to my hotel. At the side of the patio two tanned girls, an American and a Canadian, are watching a movie on TV. The American is curled up on a sofa; the Canadian sprawls in a hammock, one bare brown foot, toes spread, poised elegantly over the side. A cadaverous, intelligent face presents itself on the screen in an eighteenth-century wig. It's John Malkovich. I find a chair and settle down to watch *Dangerous Liaisons* until bedtime.

CHAPTER FIVE
✳GAUGUIN AND THE GODDESS

At Panama City it finally happens. This time they really *have* lost my luggage. I stand by the almost empty carousel watching a couple of lopsided cardboard boxes tied with string orbit sluggishly again and again. Then I go off to find the nearest official, a stolid brown lady in a dark blue uniform who stands behind a little counter in the corner. She calls a man, who tells me to wait two minutes and goes off across the hall. The lady brings out a telephone from under the counter and makes some calls. Twenty minutes later the man returns. "Still not arrived?" he asks me. Indeed not, I tell him. I wonder what he's been doing for the last twenty minutes. Not chasing my baggage, that's for sure.

The lady makes another call. She asks me a string of questions about my rucksack: colour, size, make, distinguishing marks. She enters it all on her computer and prints out a sheet of paper for me. It contains a list of phone numbers, a code for my rucksack, and an apology in Spanish. With this and my hand luggage, feeling oddly weightless, I make for immigration, customs and the exit.

A driver from the hotel is waiting for me, holding a cardboard sign with my name on it – an honour I've never had before. He introduces himself as Carlos. I apologize for my lateness and explain what's happened. I ask him to wait a little longer while I change some money.

"What kind of money do you have?" he asks me.

"US dollars."

"That's what we use here. We call them *bolívares* but they're just *dólares*. You don't need to change anything."

"Really? There's no separate currency?"

"No. There are the small coins, *la moneda*, but the notes are US dollars."

This degree of US dominance is something I hadn't known about. I wonder how on earth the Panamanian economy works. I've noticed that the advertisements around the airport are in English and that most of them seem to be aimed at urging visitors to buy real estate in Panama. The favourite image is Panama City's waterfront, a glittering rampart of featureless glass towers, and the general message is that you should hurry to buy some land and build some more glass towers right now. I wonder what all this is doing to Panama City and its environment.

As we launch onto the highway into the city, Carlos turns on the radio, which is playing excellent salsa.

"*Buena música*," I tell him, pointing to the speaker.

"You like salsa?"

"That's why I'm here."

Carlos digs under the dashboard with one hand and produces a sheaf of discs. "You know this?" he asks me. "And this?" Pressing his knees against the lower rim of the steering wheel to keep us on track, he slides a CD out of a plastic wallet and into the slot on the dashboard. The radio cuts out and the new music begins, a warm, grainy voice punching lyrics across an intricate backing of piano and violin. "Oscar D'León!" Carlos tells me. But already he's fumbling in the wallet for another CD. He presses a button and grabs the first disc as it ejects. Controlling the wheel with his knees again, he slides the disc into the wallet and inserts the new one. "Grupo Niche!" he shouts.

And so it goes on. We dodge in and out of the traffic, cutting in behind lorries and overtaking long, sturdily-built buses painted in all colours of the rainbow, while Carlos introduces me to his favourite salsa artists. He keeps the wallet on his knees so he can flip the discs in and out as he drives. Occasionally he has to grab the wheel fast and a disc ends up between his teeth.

"Is there anywhere I can buy cheap CDs in Panama?" I ask.

"Only from the men at the *semáforos*."

Sure enough, as we turn onto the Via España and pull up at the traffic-lights, a man strolls towards us, pacing carefully like a tightrope walker along the white lines, flipping through an album of plastic pockets to display the photocopied sleeve art of some fifty bootleg discs. I wave him on and tell Carlos I'll stick to browsing in the shops. "And where should I go to dance?" I ask him.

"Bohío Florencia," Carlos says without hesitation. "The best *rumba* in Panama. We passed it a few blocks back. Ask anyone, they'll know where it is."

I check in at the hotel. It's a small, yellow-plastered building with a wooden porch that makes it look like an old *hacienda*. The lady at reception hears the tale of woe about my luggage and promises to call the airport for me. I'm delighted to leave the problem with her. I find I have a cool, dark room at the back with no view – the window faces a blank wall across a narrow gap between buildings – but it has a large comfortable bed, a bathroom and a ceiling fan which I switch on at once because the humidity is oppressive. I take a shower and then, having no choice, put on the same grubby clothes. Except for my socks: I simply can't bear to put them back on. While I dress, I swear never, *ever*, to fly anywhere again without a complete change of clothes in my hand luggage.

I ask at reception for advice about where to buy some cheap clothes, and am told there's a store a few blocks away on the other side of the Via España. I set off to look for it.

The view outside, once I'm on the main street, is dispiriting. The Via España itself is a six-lane highway jammed with fuming traffic. As far as I can see in either direction stretches a landscape of tacky urban sprawl: used-car lots, McDonald's and Blockbuster; cracked cement paving, piles of rubbish, manholes with missing covers. Tilting poles of wood or metal line the avenue, festooned with sagging bundles of electrical cable from which traffic-lights dangle at crazy angles over the intersections.

Three or four blocks along España I find the clothes shop. A sprawling department store, it seems to specialize in end-of-line remnants. I settle for a T-shirt in an odd shade of orange and a collared shirt, also orange, with blue stripes, plus some socks and underpants. I ask about jeans but the assistant says they don't sell them. That seems odd. Still, I reckon I can make my jeans last a little longer. I plod back through the diesel haze and sauna-like humidity to my hotel, where after another shower I lie down on the bed, feeling I've done a heavy morning's work.

But I need to eat. The hotel doesn't serve food, so I go to reception, where a beautiful young lady with sparkling eyes and looks that seem somehow French (she introduces herself as Virginia) directs me to a good restaurant – "*muy sabroso*" – around the corner. I wander out again, shoulder-to-shoulder with the quivering, roaring diesel trucks and the scarred yellow taxis, and a few blocks away on a quieter, more prosperous-looking street I find it. It has a terrace under a red-and-white striped awning, so I can watch the street life while I eat.

I order a steak and a local beer. The traffic here isn't as ferocious as on the main road. People, many of them Chinese in appearance, hurry past carrying parcels and coloured plastic bags. Despite the serenely oscillating fans on the terrace, it's oppressively hot and humid. The sky has been overcast all day and now it's sheeted with thick cloud on a spectrum from dirty yellow to purple-black. I cut into my steak. In the sky there's a sudden hiss followed by a deep continuous rumble. People in the street start running, or dive into doorways. The awning overhead rattles and thrums, and after a moment water starts pouring in sheets over its edge onto the pavement. It's a tropical downpour. The street is awash with water. At first it just courses along the gutters, but within a minute or so it's spreading like a tide across the entire roadway. Soon the tarmac is inches deep in water and cars are ploughing through it like motor launches, their wakes washing over the pavement and slapping at the base of the café terrace.

Two tables ahead of me a tall, curly-haired man ducks in under the awning and lodges a large rucksack beside a table. He shakes the water out of his eyes and gives me a wry smile. The rain continues, its muffled roar accompanied by the irregular thudding of distant thunder. I eat my steak (a good one), watching the procession of passing umbrellas. By the time I've finished my meal the rain is slackening and then, as if someone had turned off a tap, abruptly it stops. I pay the bill and leave my table, grinning at the tall backpacker as I pass.

"Excuse me," he says, "you look like a fellow-traveller. I wonder if you know of an inexpensive hotel around here?"

I do, of course, and I give him directions. His formal English has the trace of an accent, so I ask where he's from.

"I'm from France." He offers his hand. "Frédéric." I introduce myself and perch on one of the metal chairs at his table.

Fred, it seems, has just arrived in Panama and suffered a disappointment. He's a devotee of couchsurfing – something new to me. Apparently there's a website where you enter your profile. Then you search for people – fellow couchsurfers – who live in the area you want to visit, and see if any of them will put you up for a night or two. And away you go.

Unfortunately, in Panama Fred's couch has failed to catch a wave. In fact, it's sunk without trace. Someone in Panama City invited him, but when he called the man's mobile, the response was strangely hesitant. It didn't take Fred long to realize that his prospective host had forgotten he was coming, and wasn't pleased to find he had an impending house guest. Fred put an end to the embarrassing conversation and was hunting for a hotel when the downpour started. Noting Fred's critical Gallic eye assessing the curious orange shade of my T-shirt, I explain about my lost luggage. We shake hands, with a certain shared satisfaction over these small tribulations of the traveller's life, and I leave.

As I walk back, I stop noticing the ugliness of the cityscape; my attention has been grabbed by the buses. I've never seen anything like them. As they plough past in the heavy traffic or stop, fuming and rumbling, at the traffic-lights, I get plenty of time to admire them, and it's time well spent, for Panama's buses are exuberant works of art. They're long, ribbed single-deckers – clearly, in fact, decommissioned yellow school buses from the USA. But they're no longer yellow, and they're school buses transformed, decorated with florid extravagance and loving ingenuity. Every bus has its unique style. Stripes and curlicues of peacock blue, vermilion and silver run along above the windows; around the windscreens are angels' wings, sprays of roses, wreaths of rich green leaves. Jokes and Spanish mottoes, too idiomatic for me to comprehend, run along the bumpers and over the radiators. The side panels carry grand decorative schemes: Asterix dashing along full tilt, moustaches flying; a winged horse soaring through the clouds with a square-jawed classical hero on its back; idyllic landscapes of forest and coastline in clear sunlight; or a group of well-endowed girls in bikinis. Each bus has its own name, inscribed in flowing calligraphy or chunky graffiti-style capitals on a painted scroll or a slab of notched stone: *Fantomas*, *Sin Vengüenza* (Shameless), *Jesus Cristo*, *Tifoon*, *El Impenitente*, *Ca$hmoney*.

And on the back panel of each bus is a lovingly airbrushed portrait of some special person, all glistening highlights and dark, syrupy shadows: a boxer; a Panamanian pop star; the driver's daughter. One bus has a glaring Clint Eastwood, battered stetson on head, framed by the vertical barrels of two six-shooters. Another has the anguished, blood-bedewed face of Christ under his crown of thorns. And at the next set of traffic-lights a quivering, diesel-hot rear panel treats me to the flawless, shimmering smile of Beyoncé.

There's no news yet of my luggage. But at least I can look for some classes. I find a copy of the Panama *Paginas Amarillas – Yellow Pages –* and search for dance teachers. I find Escuelas de Baile and note down half a dozen numbers, one of them – Alina's Dance Academy – chosen simply because the name is English. Then I start calling them. One number doesn't answer. On another I get voicemail, so I leave a message. Next is Alina's Dance Academy, but I'm not sure I can read my own writing so I go back to check *Paginas Amarillas*. I'm running my eye down under Escuelas de Baile when the column alongside catches my eye. It's headed Esotérica. Under the heading is a display advertisement:

OGUN YEMAYA
Articles Religious, also for Santeros and Babalawos, on Sale
Santos' Tools, Cascarilla
Baths for Good Luck, Candles, Soaps
Matters of Ifa, Energy of the Santos
Business with Magician Santos
Consultation of Cards and Babalawo

There's a lot about this that I don't understand, but I remember from my visits to Ernesto in Havana that Ogun is the god of metal and Yemaya is the beautiful sea-goddess. Cascarilla is a medicinal herb with magical properties. Ifa is an alternative name for *santería*. Well, I still want to ask someone about the meaning of my Bogotá dream, and it strikes me that this might be just the place to go. I write down the phone number. Then I finally get down to calling Alina's Dance Academy.

Making phone calls in Spanish to unknown people is one of the things I dread. Invariably I have a sinking feeling in my stomach, and a fear that I'm going to be unintelligible, or will simply dry up. So I feel deeply nervous as I listen to the ringing tone and wait.

Finally a young woman's voice greets me: *¿Allo?* I explain that I'm an English visitor and would like some lessons in the local style of salsa. The woman asks me if I'd like one hour or two, and suggests eleven the following morning. Intrigued by the school's name, I ask if she speaks English. She says she doesn't. I tell her the name Alina's Dance Academy had made me think she would. She laughs, a sweet light laugh, and says well, yes, it does bring the occasional foreigner.

"And where are you?" I ask.

"Find a taxi," she instructs me, "and ask for Supernoventaynueve, Chanis. When you get there, call me from a *cabina telefónica*. I'll come and find you."

Stumblingly, I repeat "Supernoventaynueve" until I get it right. Then with a huge sense of relief I finish the call. At least I now have a lesson booked. But Supernoventaynueve? What on earth is that? I try to translate it. Super new…? No – super ninety-nine… God knows. I go back to my room and spread out my map. I see there's a district called Chanis not far away. That gives me confidence. But Super… Well, I just hope the taxi driver understands it better than I do.

I remember the club Carlos recommended: Bohío Florencia. I ask the young man at the desk if he knows it. He pulls out the phone book and gives me the address. And the phone number.

I brace myself, groan silently, sort out some essential phrases and punch in the number. A miracle: it's answered instantly! I ask if the club is open tonight. From eight o'clock, the man tells me. *¡Estupendo!* And there are classes? Yes, from eight-thirty. I put the handset down with a sense of achievement. Things are starting to come together.

Strolling through to the patio at the back of the hotel to get a coffee, I recognize a curly-headed figure hunched over a computer in the lobby. It's Fred, my French acquaintance from lunchtime, who has followed my suggestion and taken a room here. Or half a room, since he's sharing with another backpacker. We shake hands and agree to meet when he's finished sending his email. I flick through a glossy bilingual magazine all about property investment in Panama until Fred logs off. Then we wander out onto the patio, where a dishevelled green parrot waddles to and fro on his wooden perch, shouting hoarsely. We help ourselves to coffee from the permanently simmering urn and sit down.

Fred, it turns out, is a mathematician. He used to work for a chemical company but became bored and disillusioned, and spoke his mind too often for the management's comfort. A friend on the managerial rung above kindly arranged for him to be sacked – which Fred tells me is a good thing in France, because you get benefits you wouldn't receive if you left voluntarily. Here there's a brief detour on the subject of the French social-security system: Fred tells me it's the best in Europe but unlikely to last, now that the French have elected "a fascist dwarf" (Fred's words) as President. Indeed, Fred predicts that on his return to France he may well find himself demonstrating on the streets for the first time in twenty-five years. I tell him I've been out on the streets over Iraq after a similar interval. Predictably, we get onto Bush and Blair. We finish our coffee and Fred tells me he has some beer in the fridge. He fetches two cans of Balboa, the local brew named after the conquistador who grabbed Panama for Spain in 1510. I tell Fred about the friendly hooker in Caracas who identified Blair as a psychopath, and we drink a toast to her sound judgement.

Fred resumes his story. Having succeeded in getting sacked, he discovered couchsurfing, flew to New York and then decided to travel around Central America. And here he is. I like Fred. He has a wry sense of humour and a sceptical twinkle in his blue eyes. He says he's worried that he may be an Anglophile because wherever he goes he seems to get on best with English travellers. I agree that this sounds pretty serious. To redress the balance we talk a bit about French culture. It turns out we're both interested in painting. We mention a few obvious names and converge on Gauguin.

Something stirs at the back of my mind. That TV documentary a couple of years ago. Didn't the presenter say that Gauguin once lived in Panama? I ask Fred if he knows anything about this. He doesn't, but admits sombrely that a BBC documentary is bound to be a better source on Gauguin's life than any French production. We agree on a little project. I will search the internet to discover whether Gauguin was ever in Panama, and if so, where he lived. Then, if there is such a place, we'll visit the house together.

But I'm hungry. Fred, who seems to have an instinct for these things, has already found a place where they serve good roast chicken to take out. Following his tip, I cross the street and find a bleak metal counter under white strip lighting, where a Chinese girl stands in front of a price list and a stack of beer crates. I ask her for a *cuarto pollo asado* and a can of Balboa. She takes my money – less than three dollars – and gives me a can and a ticket. Then she points out to the street. I look round, puzzled, but don't move, and she stabs her finger insistently in the same direction. I turn around and notice, on the pavement, a middle-aged Chinese man standing by a bench and what looks like a battered metal wardrobe with black smoke pouring out. I take him my ticket. He opens one silvery door, reaches inside, and from the fuming inferno produces a potato wrapped in foil, followed by a roast chicken quarter. He drops them onto the wooden bench, grabs a cleaver and slams it down – *bang! bang!* – on the potato, cutting it neatly into four. Then the cleaver slams down on the chicken – *bang! bang! bang! bang!* He flips the whole ensemble into a styrofoam box and hands it to me. I take it back to the hotel and eat it on the patio. It's some of the best chicken I've ever tasted.

At around seven-thirty, I put on my striped orange shirt (there's still no sign of my luggage) and go out to stand under the sodium lights on the Via España, waving at speeding taxis until finally one pulls in, rolls down the window and tells me it'll be two dollars. I sit on a torn seat packed with lumps of wire while the driver races along past the concrete shopping malls and the dumpsters full of rubbish and the glass-box buildings stretching up out of sight.

After a few minutes we pull off the road onto a sloping piece of waste ground. Cars stand around, parked at odd angles. Downhill I can see a red neon arrow pointing to a doorway. "Bohío Florencia?" I ask the driver. He confirms it, so I pay him and walk down the slope. A barn-like building looms up in the darkness. At the door a couple of men stand behind a battered table, taking money. They tell me it's three dollars; I pay and go in. The place is, in fact, like two barns – or perhaps two big industrial sheds – pushed together with no dividing wall. One of these large spaces is roofed with thatch, the other with corrugated iron. There's a tiled floor, and a bar in one corner selling canned beer and Coke for a dollar a time. It's a real down 'n' dirty neighbourhood dance hall and it's seething with people. Air-conditioning is provided by big metal fans in cages standing in the corners, but the atmosphere still feels like hot cotton wool. Floor-standing speakers the size of fridges are pumping out salsa music. I don't recognize it, but it's truly excellent. I can't wait to dance.

Threading my way around the edge of the dance floor I equip myself with a beer and stand to watch the dancers. They're all ages: kids who look about twelve, young people in their teens and twenties, older people – though there are more middle-aged women than men. The men and younger women wear jeans, the older women dresses or loose skirts. One side of the hall is lined with old wooden chairs occupied mainly by older women, talking volubly despite the bludgeoning noise from the speakers. I walk in front of one speaker and the music is so loud I can feel the bass notes cutting into my diaphragm. There's what I can only describe as a curious *ceramic* quality to the sensation: it feels like being hit in the stomach with broken plates. Instinctively I clench the muscles above my jaw to try to protect my inner ear, and move away fast.

I watch the dancers. Their style is definitely not Colombian – none of those neat little drop-back steps. They're not circling around like Cubans, either. Many of the moves look familiar – but there's something different too. There's a kind of *angularity*, and the men are dancing pretty much on the spot, sending the girls across in front of them in an almost linear style. It's that linearity that finally gives me the clue, and then it all comes into focus. They're dancing "New York" style! Rather than doing South American or Caribbean salsa, these people are dancing the way they dance in New York or Los Angeles. It's a style often taught in the UK, but not one I've learned. In New York style, the dancers move to and fro on a single axis ("as if they're on tramlines" is how I've heard it described in England). When the men send the girls across in front of them to begin a move, they don't swing them around and back, they just step neatly out of the way and push the girl across from one side to the other so she moves in a straight line. Then they swivel onto the same track and move there, to and fro, until it's time to step off the track again and shunt her back. It's a tight, neat, self-conscious style, with the men looking very cool and controlled and the women stepping like catwalk models.

Not that the dancers here look particularly suave. This is a pretty rough-and-ready version of the New York style, and some of the dancers are clearly novices, but there's no doubt at all that this is what they're doing, or aiming at. I suppose in a country where the currency is the US dollar I should have expected it, but still it's a surprise. All my Cuban practice isn't going to help me here. I'm going to have to learn yet another kind of salsa!

And I can start right away, because a man with a microphone is announcing that the salsa class will begin in five minutes. I join a queue to pay another dollar to a man behind a table and receive a paper wristband as receipt. The man looks at me curiously. I sometimes forget that as a tall, pale *gringo* I stand out a mile in these places. Looking around, I can't see another *gringo* anywhere, just a crowd of shortish, brown-skinned people, slight or stocky but undeniably Latin. This definitely isn't a tourist place.

When we've all paid, the more experienced dancers move to the sides of the floor to chat or fetch drinks from the bar. The rest – forty or fifty of us, at a rough estimate – form two lines facing the front of the room. The instructor, a young man in jeans and check shirt, climbs onto a long, metal-legged Formica table. He holds a cordless microphone. Music starts up, a little quieter than before, and he shouts out instructions to begin the "warm-up", dancing on the tabletop so we can see him. There must be a small camera rigged up somewhere in the corrugated iron roof, because a grainy image of him from a high perspective appears on a makeshift screen behind him. That way, we can all more or less see what he's doing. We dance in long lines on the tiles: forward and back, cross-over, left and right turns which I find hard to match (I always seem to be late or spinning in the wrong direction). Poised, athletic, cat-like, the instructor dances on his table, urging us on. After five minutes or so of this he tells us to separate, men in the right-hand half of the room and women on the left. We start going through the basics of some moves, while he gives instructions to the two halves of the room – men and women – in turn: cross-body, *sombrero*, some other turns which I find hard to get hold of. He doesn't spend very long on each stage and I feel a bit lost, but I soldier on none the less.

Then the two halves of the room are mixed together again and we're told to get into pairs. I find myself dancing with a plump brown girl with very red lipstick and runnels of sweat pouring down her face. We have to do a move that involves holding crossed hands (left over right, is it, or right over left? I've always had trouble distinguishing visually between left and right.) I do my best but I can't help feeling sorry for my partner, who has to dance not just with a *gringo* (no doubt a frightening prospect in itself) but with an incompetent *gringo* at that. She does her best, and sometimes corrects my hand position while we pace to and fro and rivers of sweat trickle through her sticky, cranberry-coloured lipstick, down her neck and on into her ample cleavage. But I really don't do very well and it's a relief when the class finishes. I thank her and she takes refuge in a gaggle of her friends over by the cement wall. I take a deep breath, dig a dollar out of my pocket and head for the bar.

Once I've relaxed a bit and fortified myself with another drink, my spirits start to lift. The music is excellent, and lots of women are sitting around the edges of the hall. It occurs to me that I may be able to adapt some of my Cuban moves enough to fit in with the prevailing New York style. Calculating that the older women are likely to be made of sterner stuff than the younger ones, and less alarmed by the idea of dancing with a *gringo*, I locate a group of cheerful middle-aged ladies chatting and watching the dancing, and ask one of them if she'd like to dance.

She agrees, I take her into partner-hold, and everything starts off fine. We go to and fro, backwards and forwards, and every so often I turn the two of us. But when I try to take her into a *setenta* it simply doesn't work. There seem to be arms and elbows everywhere. I manage to turn her around and get her back into partner-hold but it's a struggle. She laughs happily but it's clear she has no idea what I'm doing. I try one or two other moves but they all feel awkward and I sense I'm imposing something, rather than leading her through something she can both follow and contribute to.

After taking her back to her seat – still all smiles and perfectly uncritical, so far as I can see – I decide to try again and ask a black lady. She has marvellous hip movements, undulating with the music in a way that delights me so much I keep finding myself on the edge of laughter. This time I keep the moves to a minimum and we do better, but even so on the few occasions I try a turn it doesn't really work and feels as if I'm pushing against some sort of grain. After a third dance with similar effects I decide enough is enough. I head out of the noise towards a cluster of taxis parked on the patch of waste ground. I just hope Alina's Dance Academy can sort me out tomorrow.

At 10.30 the following morning I stand on the corner of Brasil and España to hail an eastbound taxi. When one stops I ask for "Supernoventaynueve, Chanis". The driver seems to know it all right, and we're soon in Chanis. We turn a corner and I see a large red "99" looming up, on the roof of a concrete supermarket. The whole sign comes into view and then I understand. Supernoventaynueve is simply Super99 – a grocery chain. Meeting someone outside the Super99 is the Panamanian equivalent of meeting them in front of Tesco. I pay the driver and step out into the blazing heat. By the supermarket entrance there's a row of phone booths. I find the number and call the dance school. The same young woman's voice answers, a gentle, musical tone. "I'm here," I tell her. "I'm in the phone booth."

"What do you look like?" she asks.

"I'm tall and I'm wearing jeans and a white T-shirt."

"Okay," she says, "I'll come and get you. I've got black hair and I'm wearing black trousers and a red top."

I stand by the row of phone boxes and wonder what she'll be like. Cars come and go. On the corner a man is selling from a flat diesel truck piled with a mountain of pineapples. I see a slender figure in red and black heading towards me across the forecourt, her dark face lit up by a brilliant smile. She's pretty – indeed, beautiful – and she has dimples. She's black – in reality a light coffee-colour tinged with gold – and she has the high cheekbones of a model. It's an intelligent, humorous face, and I find myself beaming in response to her lovely smile.

She holds out her hand. "*Hola*", she says. "*¿Como estás? Soy Alina.*"

"*Encantado*," I reply. "*Soy Grevel.*"

Alina waits for a pause in the succession of buses and diesel trucks, and leads me carefully across the road. We walk in the scorching heat up a small road into an industrial estate. There are low metal buildings with signs advertising car body repairs and furniture making. She stops in front of a white door with a mirrored glass panel, unlocks the door and we go in.

Alina's Dance Academy is a small, cool studio with a polished floor, an air-conditioning unit, and a large mirror covering half of one wall. There's a water-cooler and a stereo system in one corner with speakers up near the ceiling, and a board with some press cuttings: I can see a magazine feature, with a picture of Alina, all about the health benefits of dance. At one end, beyond a half-open door, there's a little office with a desk and some chairs.

Alina asks me again what I want to learn with her. I'm able to be more specific this time. I tell her I've danced Cuban salsa, and recently I've learnt to cope with the Venezuelan and Colombian styles, but I've just realized people here dance what I'd call New York style, so now I need to learn that. Alina understands at once. What I need to learn, she says, is the *estilo línear*: the linear style. She knows about Cuban salsa and how different it is. So we start with the inevitable "warm-up" – uncomfortably, for me, in front of the floor-to-ceiling mirror. Alina puts on a CD and we dance side by side, with me imitating what she does. We do the usual forward-and-back, drop-back, side-step, cross-over in front and behind, and some left and right turns. The music is wonderful – it's "Ay Amor" by Guayacán, a Cali band. No particular problems come up, though looking into the mirror I see myself disconcertingly huge and untidy beside the petite figure of Alina with her flawless poise and economical movements. Alina appraises me as we dance. "Okay," she says when the track finishes, "you have a good sense of rhythm. That's the most important thing."

We leave the mirror and start work on the *estilo línear*. Alina shows me how with this "linear style" I can actually use the strips of wood in the floor to keep a check on the straight linear pathway where my partner and I should move. We begin by taking up the partner-hold (backs straight, my right hand between her shoulder blades, her left hand on my right shoulder and my left hand holding her right, poised just below shoulder level) and moving forward and back. We go to and fro on the same line, a smooth fluid movement that floats along without the energetic chest, shoulder and hip movements of the Cuban style. Then Alina shows me the cross-body movement: not a swinging arc like the Cuban version, but taking two steps backward, getting myself out of the lady's path so she can slide past me on the same track as before, after which I turn ninety degrees and follow her. We end up going to and fro on the same track again, only by now we're facing the opposite way. All very neat and tidy.

The cool geometry of the *estilo línear* makes me realize how earthy and vigorous the Cuban style is. There's a hint of *possession* about it, a feeling of becoming different people, different *creatures* almost, as the music drives you one way or another. Its African roots and its links with the sorcery of *santería* are very apparent. *Estilo línear*, the style of New York and Panama, on the other hand, is a *cool* style. The erotic and physical energies are there, but diffused, hinted at, played with. We know they're there, but we're not going to let them take over. We're urban and streetwise and poised. We're *in control*.

When we have the cross-body sorted out, Alina teaches me the *sambuca*. There are two kinds: *sambuca de mujer* and *sambuca de hombre*. This is what I've learned before, Cuban-style, as a "reverse-arm": holding both my partner's hands and raising her left hand above her head to turn her clockwise, so that her right arm ends up behind her back, then spinning her round again to extricate her. *Sambuca de hombre* involves doing the same thing to myself, turning clockwise so my own left arm ends up locked behind my back, my hand still holding the lady's right. The difficulty here, I find, is to spin fast enough to turn a full one hundred and eighty degrees: in this linear style the lady can't help me by moving round. I have to make a complete turn so I can continue dancing, on the same old linear track, before turning back again at the same dizzying speed.

Despite a drink of cold water at half-time, I'm sweating profusely and very tired by the end of a two-hour lesson. We go into the office and I pay Alina the princely sum of twenty dollars (ten pounds). She gets a little pad from her desk drawer and fills out, in neat curly writing, a specially printed receipt decorated with a drawing of a little dancing couple. We shake hands and I kiss her on both cheeks. I book to return the tomorrow at the same time. Then it's out from the cool air-conditioning into the overcast, humid glare of suburban Panama. It's been a good morning.

And it's still good when I walk into the hotel. The boy at reception calls me over and tells me my luggage has been delivered. It's in the corridor outside my room, sealed into a transparent plastic sack with a lime-green label reading EQUIPAJE PRIORITARIO. Thank God, I have my white trainers back. *Prioritario* indeed!

I shower and change my shirt, then fetch a coffee from the percolator on the patio. Logging on to the computer, I start looking for "gauguin + panama". Plenty of results come up, all saying that Gauguin was briefly in Panama in 1887. Typically improvident, he ran out of money and ended up working as a labourer digging the Panama Canal. But where did he live?

After working through eleven pages, I find a reference to a place called Taboga. I ask Google for "gauguin + taboga". The results are few but illuminating. It turns out that Taboga is an island – Isla Taboga – off the coast of Panama, near the entrance to the canal. Gauguin fell ill with fever while labouring for the Panama Canal Company and was sent to the company hospital on the island – which is said to be very beautiful. My spirits rise. Can we get there? Yes, we can: it's thirty minutes by boat from Panama City. One website mentions the ruins of Gauguin's house. Great. It looks as if Fred and I have an appointment on Taboga Island. Before I rush off to see if he's in the hotel, I want to know if that Gauguin documentary is available on DVD. The BBC Shop website tells me: "Your search for Gauguin returned no results. The closest match was penguin." Well, you can't win 'em all.

I knock on Fred's door. He emerges, rubbing his mass of curls with a towel, and I tell him the good news. We instantly commit ourselves to getting to Taboga Island and finding Gauguin's house, or what's left of it. Fred suggests lunch. It seems he's found a good pizza place a few blocks away, so we set off. It's a cheap restaurant bustling with lunchtime customers. The proprietor, another Chinese cook (perhaps, like many Chinese Panamanians, a descendant of one of Gauguin's fellow canal-workers), greets Fred like an old friend. We choose from a large, oil-stained menu of pizza toppings ("What on earth are *honghi*?" I ask Fred. "*Champignons*," he replies) and watch in fascination as the maestro, beaming and blinking at us with the delight of a seasoned performer, grabs a lump of dough from a shelf, flips it sideways between his palms and then tosses it into the air. He catches it and twirls it on his fingers as it grows thinner and wider, a wobbling weightless elastic disc spinning faster and faster until he slaps it down, a perfect circle just the right thickness, onto a board dusted with flour. He adds the toppings and slides it into a blazing, blackened oven fired from an array of butane cylinders interlinked with rubber tubes. The heat of the oven is overpowering despite the rotating ceiling fans. A bluish TV screen on a shelf bombards us with grainy midday news. Outside I can hear the lunchtime downpour starting up. Damn – I forgot to bring my umbrella.

Every morning I go to Alina's studio for my lesson. In the afternoons I lie on my bed, reading Borges, translating Mauricio's poems (Bogotá already seems far in the past) or simply sleeping. And I wander around the city. After forty-eight hours I've decided that Panama City is the most soulless place I've experienced. Its combination of shoddy concrete strip-mall development and bank architecture – polished towers of steel and mirrored glass designed to repel the approach of anything more human than an electronic money-transfer – is truly repellent. The financial district of Panama looks as if it was designed by, and for, some robot replacement for the human race: Transformers, perhaps, or the machines from Arnold Schwarzenegger's *Terminator* movies. Enormous flights of granite steps lead to black glass sliding doors in featureless glass walls, which rise like cliffs into the sky. I never see anyone go in or out.

Fred, meanwhile, researches ways of reaching Taboga Island. A ferry leaves every morning around eight and returns at five. Given the Panama City traffic, we'll need to get a taxi well before seven if we're to be in time. So we go to bed pretty early by our usual standards, and 6.45 the next morning finds us standing by the Via España waving at taxis as the torrent of traffic thunders past.

At length we're heading south across the city and down the Causeway, a long raised highway running straight out to sea, linking a series of small islands. The driver tells us the Causeway was built from rocks blasted out when they dug the canal. Sometimes it's just a road running on a high stone platform; sometimes it widens out and has hotels and marinas, even a wooded island or two. Reaching the quay, we leave the taxi for a café where we drink milky Nescafé in the cool sunshine, gazing out over the hazy water while we wait for the boat. Few other people seem to be waiting: a couple of tourists, two or three locals; no one else.

The ferry churns in at last, looking very much like the Mersey ferries of my Liverpool childhood as it edges into place, squashing and grinding against the large rubber tyres hung along the quayside. We go to sit on the breezy upper deck. From here the shores of Panama look remarkably green, the glassy ramparts of the city a brief anomaly in a ragged belt of tropical forest. The ferry pulls out, and we can see a deep bay with some white buildings at one side: the entrance to the Panama Canal.

Fred is keen to remind me that the canal was conceived and begun by a Frenchman, Ferdinand de Lesseps. The Americans took over only when de Lesseps ran out of money. I've noticed that many people are keen to claim the canal: several I met in Colombia reminded me pointedly that Panama used to be part of Colombia until US troops levered it off as a separate nation in 1903. Afterwards the Americans held onto it for nearly a century: it became Panama's property only in 2000. Fred writes a postcard to a friend, sending the English palindrome "A man, a plan, a canal – Panama!" The man in question is, of course, de Lesseps.

Once the ferry is well out into the bay, a strange sight reveals itself. All the way to the horizon, the sea is thickly dotted with ships. We're surrounded by them: oil tankers, cargo ships, passenger vessels – everywhere you look there's a ship, and others beyond it. They're all waiting their turn to get into the canal. We glide under a huge overhanging cliff of smeared, rusting metal: the battered, red-and-green-painted bows of a ship named – and I tilt my head back to squint up at cream-painted letters sliding past against the sky – *Sunlight Venture*. One colossal, taut, matt-brown anchor-chain runs from a port dizzyingly high above us to disappear into the murky water of the bay. A cream rail edges the deck but there's no sign of life. She looks spookily deserted. We slide out from *Sunlight Venture*'s shadow and soon see which of several islands in the bay we're headed for. Isla Taboga is a wooded cone with pastel-coloured buildings around its base.

The ferry feels its way in, reversing, churning the water to foam. We make our way down the wooden gangplank and along the pier, morning sunlight glinting between the planks from the sea below. A sandy beach stretches away on both sides. Ahead of us is a small stone sea wall and above it a cluster of low buildings, their blue, white and yellow walls overgrown with flowering vines. I can see scarlet and purple bougainvillaea. Taking a deep breath, I realize how long it is since I've been surrounded by anything but concrete and heavy traffic.

We have breakfast – coffee, omelettes, pancakes with syrup – under a trellis festooned with vines covered in white and yellow flowers. Then we stroll through the village. We don't meet anyone and there's nothing to indicate Gauguin's residence. The village street turns uphill and fades into a broad track of red earth running between small orchards. Fred's eyes light up. "I always prefer to go upwards," he says. I feel the same, so we walk on. The track – sometimes earthy, sometimes stony – leads us into bushy scrub and then forest. The sloping hillsides are covered with trees netted in vines. The track climbs and climbs. A lizard flicks from a stone and threads itself into the undergrowth. A shimmering, sky-blue butterfly as big as both my hands floats past at head height. There are strange seed pods scattered on the earth. I pick one of them up: a perfect, heart-shaped box in two halves, flat on one side and rounded on the other. It's brown, with a furry texture like stiff velvet. I carry it until I notice a burning sensation in my palm. The velvet surface of the pod is in fact a myriad tiny needles a millimetre or so long. A good many are now embedded in my hand – a reminder about messing with things you don't understand in a tropical forest. I chuck the pod away and pass the time by easing filaments out of my skin as we plod on up the track.

"Is it possible Gauguin would have made the effort to come up here?" Fred asks.

"Not if I know anything about him," I say. "He'd have been in the village having a drink. Or in bed groaning with fever. How far should we go?"

"It would be nice to get to the top of the island," says Fred.

So we go on. The sun has imperceptibly grown hotter and hotter. The track twists and turns, offering little shade. "These sandals are not good for walking on stones," says Fred, pausing to remove something sharp. Although we're now high up, the humidity is at Panama City level: our clothes are saturated, and sweat is streaming down our faces, arms, legs, backs. We're now – though neither of us admits it – looking for an excuse to stop climbing and turn back, when a sudden bend in the path brings us out above the forest and we find ourselves in clear sunshine beside a flat white rock. We're on a headland from which the ground falls steeply away, dropping hundreds of feet to the sea. A dazzling surface of ocean spreads out below us, sunlight blazing from a wrinkled silver surface dotted with ships. Somewhere behind us is the summit of the island but we shan't go there. We sit and gaze at the vista for several minutes, enjoying the breeze that floods up the cliff from the sea and dries the sweat on our faces. Then we head back down the stony track.

"This would be a good place for a mountain bike," says Fred as we stride along, jolting our knees and ankles. He tells me he cycles everywhere in France, even in Paris.

"If you cycle in Paris you're a braver man than I am," is my response.

"I drive only once a year," Fred explains, "and that is when I fetch my year's purchase of wine from the *négotiant en vins*. Then I borrow my brother's car, and I drive through the Paris streets slowly and carefully. Not to shake too much the bottles, you understand." Fred is evidently particular about his wine. "When I am with friends in England," he tells me, "sometimes they offer me wine. I refuse it. They are surprised – they say, 'But you are French, surely you like wine?'" Fred gazes into the distance, a wry curl on his lip. "Yes, I say to them, I like wine. That is why I do not drink this stuff you offer me."

On the way down we notice something we missed earlier: a track leading off into the forest at one side, with a hand-painted wooden sign: *SENDERO DE LAS CRUCES*. We decide to take a look. The Path of the Crosses leads downhill and then over to a small clearing amongst the trees. In the middle of the clearing is a miniature shrine: a little roof on blue-painted metal poles some four feet high and under it a long block of concrete, also painted bright blue, making a kind of altar. On the altar are three crudely-made wooden crosses, painted white, each with two pieces of white lace or gauze tied to its arms. They hang down like long empty sleeves. Between the crosses someone has placed two clay pots of scarlet geraniums. There's a bank of raised earth like a seat facing the shrine, where we sit for a while. The wind stirs the rags of white lace that hang from the arms of the crosses. It's very quiet. The place is distinctly eerie. The shrine is brightly painted and clean, but there's something disturbing about it. I'm uncomfortable – and it's a relief when we get up and retrace out steps to the main path.

We reach the village once more and wander between the pink and blue and cream houses with their patched plaster walls and deeply grained, weather-worn wooden doors. Up a small flight of steps is the police station: two dark windows without glass and a blue-painted door. There's a faded poster with a blurred photograph of a small child, vanished without trace several months before. A tinny bell tolls somewhere. Children in brown-and-white school uniform straggle past us on their way home for lunch.

We find a sign announcing a restaurant and make our way up a twisting brick staircase to a roofed patio overlooking the beach. A round-faced, wrinkled elderly man in a blue cotton shirt puts down his newspaper and rises to welcome us. With elegant gestures he ushers us to a table near the railing where we can look down over a purple-flowered vine to the sea. Placing bottles of cold beer and mineral water on the checked plastic tablecloth, he asks what we'd like to eat. After a leisurely debate, using English, French and Spanish to arrive at the probable identity of various fish, we order grilled red snapper.

When we've eaten, we remember that we're supposed to be looking for traces of Gauguin. The afternoon is getting on. I ask the restaurateur if he can help us. He's delighted; he tells us that he'll be only too glad to be our guide. He puts his paper away, entrusts the restaurant to a small boy from the kitchen, and we set off down the stairs to the village street. As we go I ask if he can tell me the meaning of the three crosses in the forest.

"An aeroplane came down there," he says. He doesn't elaborate.

"What, recently?"

"No, many years ago."

"How long? Twenty years?"

"Much more."

"Fifty years?"

"More."

And that's all I can learn. We walk on silently, take a lane that slants uphill and cross the square in front of a small white church. Along the street ahead I spot a cluster of bright primary colours. It's a mural; in fact, it's a hand-painted copy of a Gauguin on the wall of a building: two life-size, heavy-limbed Tahitian beauties relaxing on golden sand, one with her melancholy gaze fixed on the ground, the other, a flower in her hair, looking expectantly out at the viewer. Facing the mural across the street is the windowless shell of a building – a dilapidated, roofless structure like a stone barn, its wooden lintels split and worm-eaten, its floors cracked and grass-grown. In front is a stone block with a metal plate confirming that this is where Gauguin stayed.

Someone is moving about inside. We peer in, just in time to see a man in a T-shirt, jeans and a yellow hard hat swing a hammer at a wall and bring down an avalanche of old plaster. Another man steps into view and attacks the cracked concrete floor with a pickaxe.

Our guide cries out as if the pick were aimed at his own heart. He's almost in tears. "This is terrible!" he exclaims. "How can they do this? It's a disgrace. It's a desecration. This is a historic building!" Agitated, he hobbles in to confront the workmen. Amid the swirling dust a conversation ensues. When he rejoins us, blue shirt powdered with fragments of plaster, he's smiling again. "It's all right," he tells me. "They're not demolishing the building, they're renovating it. It's going to be turned into a museum as a monument to Gauguin. And there will be a restaurant serving French food!"

I ask the man in charge if I can photograph the work in progress. To my surprise he refuses. Perhaps he doesn't want the world to see the building in its current state of disrepair. We take a closer look at the small plaque in front of the door. Placed by the Ministry of Culture, it commemorates Gauguin's visit in 1887 "to enjoy the beauty and the colours of Taboga Island". It doesn't mention that the place was a fever hospital. I wonder whether diners at the future French restaurant will be given this information. Probably not.

We walk back with our friend to his restaurant and take our leave. We've done what we came to do. The Gauguin connection is established. The heat is fading, so we decide to explore the higher levels of the village, a maze of tiny lanes straggling terrace by terrace up the hillside among small garden patches, orchards, chicken runs. Flowering vines are everywhere – pink, scarlet, purple, blue – billowing over wooden fences and down the sides of concrete watercourses. Plastered stone houses give way to wooden shacks perched on the muddy, crumbling banks of a ravine. On the wooden porch of one shack a little girl in school uniform lies on a blanket doing her homework, carefully writing in a lined exercise book with murmured advice from her mother, who sits in a chair nearby.

A damp earthy track leads towards the edge of the forest. We reach a wooden hut with the usual rail and porch, from whose shadowy recess the cavernous white mask of a horse's skull glowers at us. The hut seems deserted. Pinned to the door is an official form on green paper. I can't read much of it but I can make out the words *mosquito* and *dengue*. I *think* the form says the house has been certified free from mosquitoes and dengue fever. But I'm not sure. We decide we've come far enough.

We walk back along the hillside, down concrete paths between orchards. As we pick our way around some rusty oil drums we hear a faint music, which focuses itself to high notes of intense and gentle clarity. Someone is singing. It's a recording, playing somewhere behind a split and blistered wooden door in a patched wall of plaster and stones. A perfect soprano voice, singing Gounod's "Ave Maria". We stop without a word and stand motionless, until the lovely voice reaches the end. Afterwards it's a long time before we can bear to break the silence. We walk down to the beach and lie there until we see the afternoon ferry returning from Panama City.

We settle on the top deck and talk to a young couple sitting opposite. It turns out they live in London, but they're Venezuelan, from Caracas.

"That city gets worse every time I go there," says Paolo. "My mother still lives there but I hate going to see her because of the way Caracas has deteriorated. The traffic, the crime… It's unrecognizable from how it was even ten years ago."

I tell him about my brush with the police.

"Yes," he says. "Typical. All these guys bear grudges. You were lucky. These are the same bastards who take people to the police station, put a bag over their heads and beat them half to death."

We talk about salsa and he recommends classic artists I should look for. Oscar D'León above all. Ruben Blades, Hector Lavoe. I can buy them all in Panama City, easily. And the Fania All Stars. Fania, he says, was the New York record label that made salsa famous. They put out these amazing live recordings. Any time you see Fania All Stars on a disc, buy it!

In the morning I'm back at Alina's studio for my lesson. We're now working on moves that involve what she calls *deplazamiento lateral* – "lateral displacement". This sounds very technical, but what it actually involves is my taking a step diagonally to my right, then side-stepping to and fro while guiding my partner with one hand. I can take her from side to side, moving in the opposite direction to me, so that she passes to and fro in front of me; or I can spin her in a whole variety of ways before rejoining her on the basic to-and-fro "track" of the dance. It's complicated and I have to practise over and over, helped on by Alina's seemingly inexhaustible patience and her excellent music.

When we pause for a drink of water I ask Alina about her own background. Did she study dance or go to ballet school? She sighs. "*¡Ojalá!*" If only! No, she says, she has no formal training, she had to do it all by herself. She watched people dance, she studied videos, she went to Puerto Rico to learn what she could, and she practised, practised, practised!

She tells me she was born in Calidonia, one of Panama's very poorest districts. Her father is a musician: he played trumpet, saxophone and keyboards all his life – but his great ambition was to be in the Government Band. To do this he needed a qualification, so having at the age of forty managed to get into music college, he put himself through it, got his qualification and auditioned. He's now played saxophone in the band for twenty years. I sense that determination runs in Alina's family.

We talk a bit about my travels. Alina wants to know if my wife dances. I tell her yes, and she asks, "*¿Por qué no trajiste a tu esposa?*"

Where have I heard that before? The phrase has an odd familiarity. It sets off a series of echoes, each one activating another like falling dominoes. Caracas. The bar at the Hotel Gavial. The *fiesta*. Aïda turning to me and asking, over the pounding disco music, "*¿Por que no tra–*"

I'm so absent for a moment that Alina has to ask me again. "*¿Por que no trajiste a tu esposa?* Why didn't you bring your wife with you?*"

I can't really explain to Alina why I'm laughing, or why I'm so thoughtful for some time afterwards.

I dial the number of the Babalawo. A man answers. I say I'd like to see the Babalawo. He tells me to wait. Another man comes to the phone. "You can see the Babalawo at his house if you wish," he says.

So I say yes, I'll come over. I'd like the Babalawo to interpret a dream. Can he do that?

"Sure he can." The man suggests four o'clock and gives me an address. It sounds like "Dorado Lake".

"Lake?" I query. "*¿Como* 'Lake' *en inglés?*"

"*Sí.*"

Around 3 p.m. I go out onto the Via España and flag down a taxi. I give the driver the address at Dorado Lake. "Dorado," he says, slowly and thoughtfully. I don't find that reassuring. Still, he seems to know where he's going. There's a pretty young woman in the back, and I chat with her as we go. After a few minutes we're under the shadow of a large concrete building. "Which entrance do you need?" the driver asks me.

I have no idea, of course. We drive on a little and I spot a sign reading *Centro Comercial El Dorado*. He's brought me to the El Dorado shopping mall. I'm pretty sure this is wrong. I show the driver the written address. The phone number is also there, so he gets out of the car and goes to a pay-phone.

While he's hunched in the callbox I ask the young lady where she's going. She says the driver is going to drop her off for work later; right now she's just passing the time riding with him.

"Where do you work?" I ask her.

"In the casino."

I've seen a large casino, lit up at night, not far from where we are now. I ask her if that's the one she works in.

"Oh, not just that casino," she says. "No casino in particular, just any of them."

I kick myself for my slowness. Of course she's not a croupier or a cashier; she's a hooker.

The driver comes back. "It's the other side of the city," he says. "It's a new development, I never heard of it."

And off we go. We crawl across Panama's congested and fuming labyrinth under the scorching afternoon sun, emerging onto a wide road between a series of new housing estates. They're walled and gated and look opulent. We pass high, cream-coloured walls with wrought-iron gates and a security lodge. A big sign in florid cursive writing reads DORADO LAKE. The driver pulls in by the lodge and gives my name and the number to the security guard.

I'm bemused. I'd expected to find the Babalawo in a back street somewhere – instead of which we're in the stockbroker belt, surrounded by sprinkled lawns and stuccoed Spanish-style bungalows, with four-by-fours on the driveways. We find the house – a cream-coloured bungalow like all the others – and as I press the doorbell I feel that all this is a dream. A set of chimes burbles softly in the background, and the door is opened by a young woman in jeans and a white blouse who invites me in.

I step into a large lobby, furnished in a style of slightly kitsch luxury, perfectly matching the exterior of the house. There's a thick, pale green carpet. The lighting is dim and the air is fragrant with perfume or incense. There are oil paintings in knobbly gold frames. A large Buddha meditates on a low, circular glass table. The sound of a TV emanates from a half-open door at the back. The only sign that we're in a *santero*'s house is a large terracotta tray on the floor by the front door holding bowls, fruit, an irregular-shaped object which is probably Eleggua, and a candle burning in a tall glass.

The Babalawo comes forward to greet me. He's around forty, a solid, muscly, smiling man in loose trousers and a sleeveless vest, both brilliantly white. On his head he wears a white cap like a tam-o'-shanter. He shakes my hand warmly, invites me to sit down and returns to a table where he resumes talking earnestly to an elderly lady. There are several sofas, each with a multitude of cushions, so I do my best to relax. I'm not alone for long: a young woman and her mother soon arrive and join me on the sofa. A girl comes in with a baby, which is passed from hand to hand and cooed over. I hold the baby and admire it. The Babalawo finishes his consultation with the elderly woman and leaves the room. From time to time the young woman in jeans wanders in and chats to the others. I get the impression she's the Babalawo's wife, but I'm not sure. I chat a little with the women. Time goes by. It's very warm. I'm sleepy. The girl on the sofa has already fallen asleep.

After more than an hour, when everyone on the sofa is practically comatose, the Babalawo reappears and invites me to follow him. We go through the room with the TV into what looks like a utility room with a bare concrete floor. In one corner stands a stone-carved statue of St Francis of Assisi about four feet high, with a long necklace of coloured beads draped around the neck. In front of it are lighted candles and dishes piled with fruit and vegetables. The Babalawo asks me to sit on an upright chair at the far end of the room. On the floor nearby are several objects familiar from Ernesto's house in Havana. Two fist-size lumps of cement with cowrie-shell eyes and mouths are instantly recognizable as my old friend Eleggua. Ogun is also at hand, in the form of two huge pots the size of buckets, bristling with machetes, knives and other rusty iron objects. Lighted candles are everywhere – on the floor, on shelves, on tables. Directly in front of me is a round wooden platter two feet across. The Babalawo hands me a lined school exercise book and a biro and asks me to write my name. While I'm doing this, a second man in white, much older and wearing glasses, arrives and the two of them sit in chairs facing me. They confer in murmurs. I guess the older man is a senior *santero*, perhaps the younger man's teacher.

Turning their attention to me, they ask me why I've come and I tell them about my dream. It's still clear in my memory and I find it easy enough to relate in Spanish. The younger man checks details as I go, and confirms that he's understood me. There's a very odd sensation that sometimes he's stating details virtually at the same moment as I am. In fact, I have a strong impression that he knows what I'm going to say before I've said it.

I finish my story of the cats, the lady in blue and the three kisses, and without a word the Babalawo hands me two pebbles, black and white, and starts rubbing a chain rapidly between his hands. It's just like the one Ernesto used. As he rubs the chain round and round in his hands he chants my name over and over again, like a mantra: "*Lindoplindoplindoplindoplindop…*" He taps my hands open to see which holds which pebble, and drapes the doubled chain across the wooden platter.

Then he starts telling me things, things I now recognize as standard *santero*-speak. I have many good friends; but some who pretend to be my friends cherish enmity for me. I should wear white to sleep in. I should take care of my legs and watch out when lifting heavy weights. I should get my blood pressure checked.

He stops to see if I've understood all this. I query something, and he evidently decides my Spanish isn't good enough. We begin a farcical series of experiments. First the Babalawo sends for his wife. She translates into English a little, then decides her English isn't adequate. Producing a cellphone she dials a number, then holds the phone near the Babalawo's face as he talks. She hands the phone to me, and I hear a man's voice on the other end, translating. After a minute or two this method is discarded. Another call on the cellphone follows and a youngish man comes into the room. He shakes hands all round and says he's come to interpret for me. Henceforth my side of the consultation is all in English.

We finally get to the dream. You have a gift, says the Babalawo. You can see spirits and other things most people can't see. There are many spirits around you right now. But your gift isn't fully developed. It's important for you to remember your dreams and interpret them. The dream you had in Bogotá is a gift from Ochún, goddess of the moon, of the river and of copper. She granted you a vision of herself. The black cats are troubles which will surround you – but they won't harm you. That's why they were playful. The three kisses were three tests Ochún put you through. She loves you very much. Whatever you want, she'll give it to you if you ask her. You should pray to her often. Have a glass of water with her name on it. Offer it to her and change the water every three days. You can put flowers in the water. Burn incense for her. Also you should offer her five eggs, five candles and five *ñames*.

I'm not sure what a *ñame* is, but I'm guessing it's a yam. My interpreter gets up and goes over to one of the shrines, returning with a thing like a slightly hairy black potato. Boil it, he says, mash it and make it into five balls. Put them on a plate for Ochún, then next day take them in your hands and pass them – not touching – over your head and upper body. He demonstrates. Take them to a hill or a wood and leave them.

Finally the Babalawo advises me to buy a statue of Ochún. He indicates something about eight inches high. Several shops in Panama sell copper statues of her; he mentions their names, which I don't manage to retain.

And that's it. I shake hands with all three men and thank them. I'm content. I trust the imagery of dreams, and I knew that a *santero* would identify that lady, just as an art historian would identify a saint in a medieval painting by clothing, posture, the objects she might have in her hands. I leave the utility room and am heading for the front door when I realize no one has mentioned payment. I turn back to the Babalawo. "May I pay for your advice?" I ask. "I'd like to give something."

The Babalawo makes a graceful gesture with his hands. "*Lo que quiere*," he says. "Whatever you wish." He shows me back into the utility room, gestures towards the statue of St Francis, and goes out, leaving me alone. In a bowl in front of the saint's statue I see a number of dollar bills, folded among some dry objects which might be bones or desiccated plants, I can't tell which. I take out some money, fold it and cross myself with it, and put it into the dish under the bones, plants, whatever. Then I go back to the hall.

The young man has already called a taxi for me. He escorts me out. He speaks to the driver, then turns to me. "Have a good journey. This is a safe taxi. He says it's two dollars. Don't let him charge you a cent more."

Next day, after my lesson with Alina, I explore the waterfront district of Casco Viejo, one of the oldest and poorest parts of the city. It's much like Havana but if anything more dilapidated, the architecture less lovely, the balconies plain and cast from concrete. There's a thin concrete sea wall, a poor imitation of Havana's Malecón. The streets are dirtier and the people look poorer. Here and there are two-storey houses built entirely of wood, and between the planks you can glimpse daylight.

Crossing a street, I notice a sign saying *Esotérica* over the door of a dark, grubby blue building. Maybe they sell statues of Ochún? It's worth a try. The interior is dim but spotlessly clean, and it's highly ordered: the walls are covered with little brass-handled wooden drawers labelled with the names of herbs. Behind the long counter are several little old ladies neatly dressed in matching overalls. One of them is already smiling in welcome.

"*Buenas tardes*," I say, "Do you have a statue of Ochún?"

"No statue," she says, "but we have a picture." She shows me a glass-topped section of the counter. It contains hundred of little Catholic religious pictures the size of cigarette cards: saints, angels, Madonnas and Sacred Hearts by the score. She reaches in and hands me a card. It's laminated in plastic and shows a gold-crowned Madonna in a blue robe, her feet on a crescent moon, floating in the sky above three men rowing a boat in stormy water. On the reverse are the words of a prayer, headed "*A Nuestra Señora de la Caridad de Cobre*" – "To Our Lady of Charity of Copper".

"This is Ochún?"

"*Sí.*"

I buy it for twenty-five cents and she puts it into a tiny red plastic bag for me, which I pocket before going outside. A bus passes, its back panel painted with a male *santería* deity in gold crown and cloak. It stops at the corner and I get my camera out to photograph it. An old gentleman passing shakes his head. "*Peligroso,*" he warns me. I agree. I feel unsafe on these streets. Avoiding groups of sullen-looking men who stand around on the pavements, I walk to a nearby square where the tourist area begins and get into the first cab I see.

Back at the hotel, Virginia calls me as I pass reception. "My boyfriend's father-in-law would like to talk to you," she says.

I'm puzzled. I don't know her boyfriend, let alone his father-in-law.

"You're interested in salsa, aren't you? He'd like to meet you. He knows all about salsa. You might even have heard of him."

"What's his name?" I ask.

"Francisco Buckley – but his nickname is 'Bush'."

This rings a bell. Wait a minute. Yes. This guy has written the definitive history of Panamanian salsa: *De la Salsa en Panamá y Algo Más*, by Francisco Buckley "Bush". It's on my shelf at home. Incredible.

"I'd love to meet him," I say. "When can he see me?"

"He says you could have coffee with him tomorrow morning in the Minimax. It's a cafeteria on the corner opposite, across Via España."

So the following morning at nine I dodge the traffic across España, find the Minimax and ask at the counter for El Señor Buckley. The response is puzzled, but then the lady in the white overall guesses who I mean. "*Señor Booosh! Sí, par' acá.*"

A tall dark man is waving from across the room. I hurry to join him. Bush is a thoughtful, sensitive-looking man in his sixties, with a high, wrinkled forehead. He shakes my hand warmly and introduces me to his friend Roberto Gyemant, who's grasping a copy of the music magazine *Wax Poetics*: he has an article in the latest number, a special issue devoted to hip hop. Roberto, who's in his thirties, tells me he's currently writing a history of salsa from the '50s to the great days of the Fania record label in 1970s New York. Both men are bilingual, so we speak English.

Bush is delightful. His face combines a scholar's acuteness with a musician's passion. Delighted to hear I have his book on Panamanian salsa, he tells me he's writing another, in fact two more: one to bring the salsa story up to date; and alongside it, a book on the Chombo tradition – the almost forgotten music of black Panamanians of Antillean (Caribbean island) backgrounds. The last people who played it, Bush says, are now in their nineties, and he's interviewing them before it's too late. It's part of his own heritage: his forebears came from Barbados and Jamaica. Panamanian music is of endless fascination, he says; Greeks, Chinese, Cubans, Antilleans and others have all come here to work on the canal, railways or banana plantations, bringing their music, traditions and food with them.

Bush's own contribution to Panamanian music is important: his band, Bush y sus Magníficos, was famous in the '60s and '70s, and he played percussion for Hector Lavoe, one of the all-time great salsa singers. His three sons are now salsa musicians in turn: one teaches percussion at the university and plays *timbales*; another is an aero engineer and plays congas; the third, a lawyer, plays keyboards. Their band is playing tonight at Platea in the old town, and Bush hints that he'll probably step in and lend a hand with the percussion. We talk about music, and history, and my travels, for half the morning before going our separate ways.

The hotel staff know I'm fascinated by Panama's wonderful buses, and Carlos, the hotel taxi driver, claims to know who puts the artwork on them. He wonders whether I'd like to go and see them in action.

I certainly would. So we take a highway out of the city. As we go, Carlos explains that the buses are decorated in two ways: *plástico* and *pintura*. *Plástico* means computer-cut vinyl stick-on decals. The really fine stuff, though, is *pintura*: hand-painted airbrush artwork. So we're heading for one of the airbrush studios. We take a side-road through a hummocky grass-grown territory of scrapyards – paddocks full of rusting lorry carcasses and disintegrating gas tankers. We fetch up at a high gate fastened with a rusty chain. Inside is a large field with several buses dotted about. Carlos shakes the chain and shouts. A muscular man in a green T-shirt strolls down the field towards us, an enquiring look on his face.

Carlos somehow explains our presence and the man unlocks the gate. He introduces himself as Enrique and ushers us in. We've struck gold: he and his assistant, a young man in his late teens, have several buses in the process of transformation. One of them is at the preliminary stage, its windows masked with taped newspaper while the assistant, in goggles and breathing-mask, stands on a ladder spraying it all over, covering its school-bus yellow with a basic coat of white. Next, says Enrique, bands of red and other colours are sprayed on. Over these comes the customized artwork – different for each bus. Give Enrique a picture of your girlfriend or your favourite saint or film star, and he'll put it onto a panel with loving care in radiant colours. We're standing right next to a partly finished bus, decorated as richly as a medieval manuscript. Enrique shows me how he draws the outlines in by hand, using a thin brush with black paint. Then he airbrushes in the colours one by one, delicately. His speciality is fantasy: dragons, witches, battleaxe-wielding warriors. He says he's been painting buses since he was fourteen. But it's a dying art: it's hard to make money from it now and the local authorities are planning – incredibly – to prohibit coloured decoration on buses in two years' time and switch to standardized white.

"Why on earth are they doing that?" I ask. Enrique frowns darkly. All to do with politics, he says. But they won't find it easy. The drivers own their buses, and they won't take kindly to having all the character taken out of their decoration.

It seems crazy. Panama should be promoting these buses as a tourist attraction, on a par with Cuba's classic cars. I ask Enrique if I can take his picture. He agrees readily and beckons me round to the other side of the bus, where the artwork is finished. He squares up proudly beside a panel showing a buxom female warrior in steel bikini, fur cloak and horned Viking helmet. I photograph him, an unsung hero of Panamanian art. It strikes me that if Gauguin had been here a century later, he'd have made a wonderful bus painter.

That evening I get into the hotel minibus with Roberto, Virginia, Virginia's boyfriend and a group of others and head for Platea, a club by the waterfront in Casco Viejo. The old town looks less menacing by night, the streetlamps bringing out a certain picturesqueness. Platea is a dimly-lit space with mellow brick walls, tables and a small stage. After ordering drinks, we sit and talk while the band sets up and the DJ plays classic salsa tracks. Bush arrives, beaming and debonair, his furrowed, scholarly forehead looking higher than ever. Towering over the table, he shakes hands all round. He shows me the percussion instrument he's brought: it's a *güiro*, a hollow brown thing a foot or so long, shaped like a teardrop with the point cut off. One side is ridged, so that when scraped with a stick it emits a resonant, satisfying *ttrrriskkk* sound.

"What's it made of?" I ask.

"This one is fibreglass," says Bush. "It's supposed to be a gourd: they fall off the tree, people cut the end off and dry them, and you get this shell. Personally I prefer the real ones, but this sounds good enough." I run the stick over it. It's a good noise. By now the musicians are setting up. Bush introduces me to one of his sons, who'll play congas; another is busy checking the sound from the keyboard. The band – Andy y su Charanga – has six members: two percussionists, bass guitar, flute, keyboards and lead vocalist. The instrumentalists act as chorus when required.

When the place is crowded and expectation high, the *charanga* launches into its music. It's a rich, punchy sound, solid and driving but also mellow: having flute instead of trumpet means it avoids that sharp edginess which can become strident, and instead goes for a richer, softer tone over which the rawness and intensity are injected by the singer. Andy – if that's the vocalist's name – is Cuban and cheeky, and he's a star. Dressed in white from his long-toed winkle-pickers to his huge jacket with wide lapels and embroidery, he stomps and dances, shakes his finger at the audience, shouts, challenges and incites. He spins in front of the microphone until the white skirts of his coat fly out horizontally on the air. He swaggers to and fro, thrusting out his chest like a gamecock in the inimitable Cuban style. Very soon people are dancing, though the space in front of the band is pretty small. And here, everyone is dancing Cuban style (just as well, because it's flexible enough to allow couples to avoid collision). Virginia looks ravishing this evening, in a short, diaphanous black dress, her hair lustrous against her honeyed skin. I invite her to dance, and once out on the floor we're soon moving fast and lightly. I'm not sure what kind of steps she's doing, but she's such a good follower that we dance some kind of salsa without any problems. Dancing to a live band adds another dimension: there's a sense of spontaneously expressing the music – even at moments exchanging glances with the singer or musicians so the electricity flows both ways at once. It's wholly delightful.

After a while Bush goes up to join the band and adds his *güiro* to the percussion, sharpening the sound a little. I dance with Virginia again, several times; with a Swiss girl who's there with her boyfriend; and then (urged on by surreptitious pantomime gestures and grimaces from her elderly friend) I ask a plump Panamanian lady at the next table, who happily gets up with me.

And so it goes. We order more Balboa and more cocktails. We change partners. We dance until we're all dead on our feet. And then, as it's Panamanian Independence Day tomorrow, the Cuban singer starts to sing what I guess are patriotic anthems. People stand up and sway, arms in the air. Others hold flaming cigarette lighters aloft in the club's dim recesses. I haven't a clue what we're singing about but I croon along with the rest. Someone drapes a Panamanian flag over the microphone. We all feel very good and very happy and know we're in the right place. And when it's finally over and we're tired with applauding, we wander out onto the cobbles, and opposite is the lovely neoclassical façade of a gutted colonial building – a mere shell, fragile as a stage set, white in the moonlight with the sparkling ocean visible through its empty windows.

❋

It's my last day in Panama. Around three in the afternoon I'm resting in my room when there's a knock on the door. There's a phone call from Bush.

"I'm listening to some very good music here," he says. "You can probably hear it right now." I certainly can; in fact, it's easier to hear the music than to make out what Bush is saying. "You've got to come over here now," he insists. "It's behind the TVN station, a place called Papo's. Virginia will tell you how to find it."

Virginia does, and in ten minutes I find my way to a restaurant called Don Papo. Inside, I see Bush at a table with half a dozen people. The place is small and bright with white walls, a bar at the back decorated in red and pale green, and several TV screens all showing different channels: horse-racing, news, a movie. It's fairly full; people sit at small tables or stand about talking. Next to the door is a small stage, empty apart from a lot of microphone stands and instruments. The band must be taking a break.

Bush welcomes me to his table and makes the introductions. I shake hands all round but forget the names. It doesn't matter: half a dozen smiling faces, some brown, some black, four middle-aged men, two women – one young, slim and beautiful, one older and solider – all friendly. There's a forest of glasses and bottles on he table. Bush orders a bottle of rum.

When it arrives, with a tub of ice, Bush tells me, "Now, this is what we do. Grab a handful of ice." I do it, and he follows suit. "Now we add the rum." He splashes a good shot into his glass and hands me the bottle. I trickle rum over my ice. We both add Pepsi. Bush fills his glass to the top with milk from a small carafe, stirring the whole concoction with a straw. I decide to forgo the milk, but the iced rum and Pepsi tastes good.

Bush gestures around the restaurant and says, "This is where the old people come to dance. Well, I'm saying 'old' – what I mean is, everyone here is over fifty. Some a lot more. You'll see a very different kind of salsa here, just straight dancing. No acrobatics!" He's right:

this is a middle-aged venue, and none the worse for that.

Two more friends of Bush's arrive, a big man resplendent in a wonderful black-and-gold shirt, and his wife. Bush introduces the man as Benito Guardia. He takes my hand in his enormous warm palm and greets me in courtly, American-accented English. Bush explains that Benito is a pianist of genius: he's played every kind of music – in orchestras, small bands, trios, as well as solo in hotels and restaurants. Benito pours himself the same milky cocktail as Bush, but with ginger ale instead of Pepsi, stirring it with his index finger.

The band assembles, picking up instruments and tapping microphones. They launch into a salsa number. There are six members, on keyboards, bass guitar, tenor sax, trumpet, congas and *timbales* – small, deep drums on a stand, played with sticks. The conga player takes lead vocals. They have a very precise, chunky, solid sound that is both rich and satisfying. The percussion, with the bright, hard *timbal*-playing, is excellent. Quite a number of people get up to dance. As Bush said, the dancing is simple: just to and fro, sometimes round and round, the occasional simple turn of a lady clockwise and back or vice versa; but it has subtlety and it's keyed to expressing the feel of the music. It's the easy, matured dancing of people who've had a lifetime for the music to sink into their bones and permeate their lives. They float and sway in it comfortably, knowing they're among friends.

The brass players punch in their phrases with perfect accuracy, and I find it hard to believe when Bush tells me, "It's a *descarga*, a jam session. These people don't rehearse together, they just come along to see who'll show up. It's on Sunday afternoons normally, but today is Independence Day so they're here now." Watching carefully, I can see that the music is co-ordinated by an almost invisible system of nods, glances, or the occasional raised finger counting in a change in the music. After a while Bush gets up to join the percussion section.

I sip my rum and Pepsi, entranced by the music but occasionally distracted by the TV screen on the wall to my right, silently showing an incredibly depressing blue-grey-tinted horror movie in which Halle Berry and Penélope Cruz are slashed, beaten, set on fire, drenched in blood, imprisoned behind bars – a nightmare of abject misery in bizarre contrast to the hot, sunny energy of the music.

There's a break; then Benito Guardia gets up from our table to play. Settling in at the keyboard, he spreads his hands over the keys to play a chord or two and a small arpeggio. The sound is magical: there's a fluidity, resonance, depth and ease about the notes he coaxes out of that electronic keyboard that's instantly recognizable as mastery. You can tell from those few notes that he thinks and breathes through the keys. The rest of the band make their way to the platform. A quick collective glance around, a nod, and they're off.

Benito leads the band into a cha-cha-cha, where his playing moves effortlessly between *legato* and percussive; then there's a salsa number, where he floats the whole band on the raft of a rocking *montuno*. With Bush's encouragement I get up and dance with Benito's wife. The emphasis is on rhythm, on keeping together and moving gently, collecting our bodies *around* the music, no big steps or elaborate movements, just letting ourselves enjoy that physical flow. She smiles at me a lot.

And so the time passes. A bit of talk, introductions to friends as they come and go, superb music and a little dancing, and, as an undercurrent, the trickle of Pepsi and milk over ice cubes. Around seven I decide I must leave: I have to say goodbye to Alina, and I'm going to do it at the weekly gathering of her dance class in a bar near the El Dorado shopping mall. Bush is heading off to yet another gathering of musicians. After the goodbyes we move towards the door, detained by many last-minute chats with friends and much consulting of cellphones. When we emerge onto the street it's dark. Bush gives me a lift back to the hotel in his comfortable American car.

After picking up my dancing shoes – I've managed without them so far – I go out again and flag down yet another taxi. I find the club where I'm to meet Alina and her class on the upper level of the mall. It's a dimly-lit place with a small circular dance floor, and a DJ playing salsa tracks. Alina and most of her students are already there: a dozen or so young people and a few middle-aged ones, including a stocky humorous man who dances nimbly and beautifully, as so many heavy men do. Alina makes introductions and everyone greets me with graceful, natural courtesy.

Alina's "class" isn't a formal affair. All that happens is that we dance in couples, with Alina sometimes dancing, sometimes watching and occasionally giving a bit of advice or demonstrating something. What she mostly does is swap people around, so that everyone dances with everyone else. She's very systematic about this. At one point, between tracks, when seven girls are sitting together at one side of the bar, Alina laughingly instructs me, "*Baila con* ella, *baila con* ella, *baila con* ella…" pointing to each in turn. And sure enough I'm to dance with *her*, dance with *her*, dance with *her*, just as instructed. There's a slender dark girl who doesn't speak a word of English, a small blonde who tells me (in a wonderfully abrasive Britney Spears voice) that she's Panamanian but used to live in Los Angeles – and many others, too many girls to remember. By the end of the evening I've danced with every woman there and at least have confidence that I know enough *estilo línear* to get me through an entire track without embarrassment.

But the greatest pleasure is dancing with Alina herself, with her lovely smile, her intense, classically chiselled features, her weightless movements. And finally I can't resist asking her for a dance Cuban-style. We whirl around and I throw her into all my most dramatic movements, the ones least like the tight discipline of the New York style. She follows them beautifully, laughing at the surprises I create by twirling her round behind me or suddenly dipping her nearly to the floor. Then we kiss and embrace, and after I've shaken hands with all the men and kissed my way around all the women, Alina and I go out of the club to say goodbye. We hug very warmly. Pressing her slim, graceful body against me I feel truly sad to leave her. I don't know if I'll ever be back in Panama, but I'll certainly never forget Alina.

Afterwards I stand at the roadside a long time before a taxi stops. It's very battered; the driver looks about eighteen and there are two teenage girls in the car, eating ice-cream out of tubs. I ask for "*La esquina de España y Brasil*", the nearest intersection to my hotel. We turn off onto the almost empty freeway. The young driver has an open tub of ice-cream on his lap. Steadying the wheel with his knees, he accelerates until we're doing around 80 kph. Then he takes both hands off the wheel, picks up his ice-cream and starts eating it with a plastic spoon. When we come to a bend he puts down the spoon, turns the wheel a little and waits until he can let go again. We stop at traffic-lights and I hear him say something to the girls, including the word *esquina* ("corner"). They all laugh. Did I say something funny? Heaven knows. The lights change and we head up the long straight Via España towards the city centre, while the driver lets go of the wheel, picks up his ice-cream and digs in contentedly.

CHAPTER SIX
✳ SALSA IN FIVE MINUTES

I don't see what Puerto Rico looks like from the air, because I'm engrossed in filling in my Visa Waiver Form. I've known that Puerto Rico had some sort of connection with the USA, but it seems that in practice it's simply part of the States. The flight attendant has handed me a long green form from the Department of Homeland (*sic*) Security and I'm busy ticking boxes. Am I mad or a drug abuser, the form asks. Am I seeking entry to engage in criminal or immoral activities? Am I now or have I ever been involved in espionage, sabotage, terrorism or genocide? The logic of these questions baffles me but I dutifully tick the "no" boxes and hope for the best. I wonder if the cluster of Latin American stamps in my passport will attract unwelcome attention, but the man at immigration nods it through without hesitation, the US stamp thumping down on the page right next to the puce blur of the Cuban one.

Out in the blazing morning heat I find a taxi and we head into the capital, San Juan. We pass blocks of flats that look as if they're built from pastel-coloured Lego, then drive alongside the sea, its dark green waves smashing into a line of low boulders. The driver, a skinny man with a moustache, has 1960s New York boogaloo-style salsa on the CD player. He tells me he was born in New York and came to Puerto Rico in his teens. People come and go all the time, he says. And if I'm interested in music there's a festival in the streets this weekend.

It sounds too good to be true – and it gets better. When I sign in at the hotel, a tall, narrow building hidden in a maze of streets at the heart of the old town, the pretty, dark girl at reception tells me they often have live salsa music downstairs.

"Downstairs?"

"Yes, in the Nuyorican Café. It's right under the hotel. We have the best salsa band in Puerto Rico playing the day after tomorrow.

The bandleader owns this hotel: you'll see him in here later if you're around."

"That's unbelievable," I say. "I'm actually in Puerto Rico because of salsa. And by the way, is there anyone around who gives dance lessons?"

"There's a group of Germans having a lesson in the café right now. If you ask their guide he'll fix up for you to talk to the teacher." She peers over my shoulder. "Yes, he's coming up the stairs now. Just ask him."

Carried onward by this unstoppable flow of good luck, I introduce myself to Uli, the German guide. "Well," he says, "my group will finish their lesson in half an hour. You could talk to the teacher then."

I haul my pack up two flights of stairs and let myself into my room. It's a white cube with a single big, colourful abstract painting over the double bed. I open the wooden shutters and look down onto a narrow alleyway. There's a tiny bar opposite with chairs on the cobbles and a faded photograph of Hector Lavoe on the wall over the red neon Grolsch sign. The strains of "El Cantante" float up to my window.

After a quick wash I head downstairs, taking my trainers just in case I can have a lesson right away. The café is right next to the hotel entrance. The door swings open into a dark, cavernous space full of upturned tables and stacked chairs. The walls are timber-clad, covered with old posters and painted with the weirdly contorted figures of dancers. Some lights are on at the far end, where bags and shoes are scattered about and a black girl in a T-shirt and jogging pants is up on a stage, showing a series of moves to a dozen people standing on the café's tiled floor. I sit on a table and watch them step, turn, spin and lose their balance as the teacher calls out instructions, clapping and counting: "*Dos-tres-cuatro, seis-siete-ocho…*" The students are a mixed bunch, mostly in their twenties, tall and pale, in tracksuits, shorts or jeans. One pretty, slender blonde girl wears a denim miniskirt. They follow the moves with fierce determination.

When the lesson ends, the teacher goes to a corner for a much-needed drink from a bottle of water in her bag. After a decent interval I go and introduce myself. She tells me her name is Norma. She has a round, powerfully expressive, almost pugnacious face and a chunky, voluptuous body which I realize, when we shake hands, is all muscle. She says she can give me a lesson tomorrow, right after she takes the German group. So that's settled.

Returning to the hotel foyer I meet a ruddy, fair-haired giant of a man who introduces himself as Juanra Fernandez. He has huge hands, a broad grin and a ponytail, and he looks archetypally North American. However, he tells me he's a *puertorriqueño*. He's the man who runs the hotel and the resident salsa band, Las Estrellas del Comborican.

Juanra radiates enthusiasm. "Come and hear us," he urges. "We're trying to get back to the real roots of salsa, the hard stuff, the kind of salsa the Fania All Stars used to play. You know the word *rabia*? We like to play with *rabia* – a bit of madness, a bit of passion. You need to hear our singer, Wilfredo Otero. He's still young but he's a genius. He comes from the country, he grew up with the music and he was improvising *décimas* when he was five years old. And this week we've got a real salsa hero, Herman Oliveras. He's a classic salsa artist. You have to hear him!"

Décimas are intricately rhymed ten-line verses, and singers often make them up as they go along. Sometimes two will compete by arguing in *décimas*, throwing improvised verses at each other. I tell Juanra I'll be there.

At present I decide to explore Old San Juan. The architecture is Spanish colonial, not unlike Havana's, though tidier and less varied: tall, pastel-coloured buildings with balconies overlooking the narrow streets. Every street is jammed with cars, which move at less than walking-pace. I follow Calle San Francisco down to the high stone rampart of the city wall. An arched gateway opens onto a wide blue vista of sea. I step through and find myself on the Paseo del Morro, a zigzag walkway alongside the ocean. The white stone fortifications tower above me, overflowed by an occasional billow of purple bougainvillaea. Neat little feral cats, white and tortoiseshell, watch from the rocks on the seaward side. I walk until the sun sets, around 6 p.m., dropping into the palm-fringed sea with a great splurge of gold clouds. The ramparts still radiate the day's stored heat; I can feel it against my face as I walk back in the dark.

I eat a lobster at a pavement café and return to the hotel, which is also an art gallery: the stairs are hung with paintings, and the lobby extends into a long gallery with bays, each displaying more paintings. The current exhibition shows large semi-abstract nudes by two Puerto Rican woman artists. They're pleasant enough, though they don't really grab me.

I'm wandering along the lobby examining them when I notice, at the far end, a tall, slender figure pacing slowly and deliberately along the chequered marble floor – arms outstretched, prowling cat-like, placing one foot precisely in front of the other. I watch, transfixed, until he stops in front of me and extends a hand. He wears jeans, a bright scarlet vest over a short-sleeved dark red shirt, and enormous wraparound sunglasses.

"Morgan Isaac," he announces.

"Are you a dancer?" I ask.

"No, I'm a couturier. I am planning out the use of this place for showing my next collection in a month's time." He takes in the lobby with a sweeping gesture. "It's a marvellous space. Varied, articulated. I shall sit different groups of people in each of these bays, and the models will come through *here*" – indicating the corridor. "There are many places I could hold my show, but no other has my father's name on it." He points to the metal plate on a nearby door. It reads *Domingo Lopez de la Victoria*. "In the 1970s this building was an arts centre. It was full of crazy Bohemians – poets, painters, musicians, film-makers – all the avant-garde of San Juan. My father had a studio here – he was a painter – and I used to hang out with him when I was a kid. When they made it into a hotel they put a plate on each door with the name of one of those original artists. For me, holding the show here will bring all of my life together, you understand?"

We stroll along the lobby. Morgan Isaac is fervent and intense. He fans his long fingers out eloquently, telling me of his plans. He has a high domed head, shaved close. A little leather bag on a long strap – is it Gucci? – dangles from one shoulder.

"I thought at first you must be a dancer," I tell him.

"I've been a dancer. I've also been a painter. I express myself in many ways. Now it's clothes. My parents always wore good clothes; my mother wore couture all the time, my father wore tailored suits. His tailor and his shoemaker would come to our house to measure him." Morgan sighs. "Now all the money is in the hands of people with no taste. But I am going to change all that. I'm going to launch a range of beautiful clothes that will be marketed internationally. England, Spain, France, Italy! The United States! The world is in the hands of punks these days. Of course," – he winks conspiratorially – "I was a punk. So were you. But now punk is something you buy in a shop, along with a book telling you how to be a punk. So we punks must do something different!"

We've reached the end of the lobby. "You have a few minutes?" Morgan asks. "Then we can walk together. I'm free until nine o'clock."

I suggest a coffee and we go out into the street. It's cool and dark outside and there's little traffic. As we walk, Morgan points to a fine colonial building, its decorative glassed-in balcony jutting over the street. "My father restored that building," he says. "After painting, he went in for architecture. He brought craftsmen from Europe to restore old buildings in San Juan, so the work would be as authentic as possible. And he was a modernist! My father built a house in New York, very geometrical, very elegant. *Architectural Review* wrote a feature about it in the 1960s: they called us 'the family that lives in the twenty-first century'! But later my parents divorced. My mother ran a nightclub, a disco. She had Led Zeppelin playing there when they'd just released their first album. I used to hang out at the club or go with her to collect the takings. I spent half the year with my dad in Madrid or Puerto Rico, and half the year in New York with my mother."

We reach a small square. At the centre are half a dozen tables and chairs made from black-and-white stone slabs. It takes me a moment to realize that the slabs are giant dominoes: four-foot rectangles of black with big white dots.

"This is where the domino players used to meet," says Morgan. "Look at it now! It's full of people eating fast food." He's right: the people seated on the marvellous Toytown furniture are eating from styrofoam boxes surrounded with crumpled paper. A pallid light floods over the small square from the window of Burger King.

We stroll on to the spacious Plaza de Armas, where I buy coffees from a kiosk and we find a small table under an awning. "This is where the intelligentsia, the political people, the Bohemians, used to come," Morgan tells me. He points to an elegant Art Deco hotel across the plaza. "My father restored that, too," he says. "It was an independent hotel then; now it's run by Howard Johnson. Everything is owned by a chain. But my couture show – that will be independent, individual. And *all* the top people will be there. Politicians, the Church, the arts, business – not only from Puerto Rico but from all the countries where my clothes will be sold. They won't all get on together, of course, so it's good that the gallery has different spaces. I can keep them apart!" He sips his coffee. "Did I tell you that I'm to be confirmed as a Catholic the day before my show? I think that will be very appropriate. My sponsor will be a *very* important Italian who has many links to the Church."

"Nothing but the best," I comment, and he beams at me appreciatively, a hint of complicity in his eyes as if we shared a secret.

"I'm half Jewish," he confides, "and my mother is a rabbi. I study the Cabbala. A friend once told me I was the best-balanced person he had ever met. This is what I aim for. And I have achieved it. All I have to do is to continue. If you are seeking the path, you are already on the path, as the Cabbala says."

I tell Morgan a little about my own journey. I keep it brief and he listens politely, but I can feel his attention ebbing away. The truth is that only Morgan and his own doings can hold his interest for more than a moment. I ask whether he's been to Panama.

He responds decisively. "I think Panama's a bit too… *Third World*. I'm not comfortable with that. To tell you the truth I'm not really very Latin American. About the most retro I can go is here, San Juan. I prefer New York or European cities. Don't misunderstand me – I *approve* of Latin American cities, I think they have the right to *exist*. But I don't want to go there."

A plump man with a black ponytail joins us; Morgan talks to him for a few minutes in Spanish. "An old friend," he tells me when the man leaves. "He pioneered the use of computers in art." He removes from his coffee cup the plastic straw supplied for stirring. "I recycle these," he tells me. "I try to recycle everything. I haven't yet found a way to recycle all the things I find discarded in the street, but if I could I would do it. I'm working on it." He frowns. "What time is it?"

"Ten o'clock," I tell him.

"I was supposed to be picked up in a car at nine to go to my mother's. Never mind, too late. Well, I think perhaps I won't go to my mother's tonight after all."

We stroll back along the street. A girl carrying a bulging bag greets Morgan with delight.

"A choreographer," he tells me when we walk on. "She planned several of my shows." A car pulls up and a woman winds down the window. Morgan goes over to kiss her. "A famous writer," he tells me on his return. "Also she is involved with politics." He grows thoughtful. "This is why I missed my nine-o'clock lift," he says. "God must have meant me to be here at this moment to meet these people, these old friends. God is never late."

Suddenly he stops. "Wait," he says. He walks back ten yards and bends down to pick something up from the pavement. He returns to show me a six-inch length of pink satin ribbon, which he ties carefully to a brass ring on the strap of his bag.

"Next year I shall take part in London Fashion Week," he tells me as we reach the hotel. "You can help me. You don't know people in the fashion business? Never mind. You are *there*. In the UK! We'll keep in touch."

Someone has recommended a club called Rumba up at the top of the hill, near the El Morro fortress. At eleven I set out from the hotel, disappointed to find that it's started to rain, a heavy drizzle. I walk past bars and restaurants until I hear the muffled sound of music, which I follow to what seems an anonymous building – until I spot the word *Rumba* painted vertically on a side window. Going in, I find a bar with a fair number of young people standing about. I buy a drink and walk through to the other room at the back. It's a bleak, cavernous space – a courtyard which has been roofed over in recent times. The brick walls are bare, apart from a few posters and an enormous speckled mirror on one wall, tilted forward so that it looks down on us from a great height. The music is controlled by an immensely fat man in a check shirt who sits in a corner frowning over a laptop, which evidently serves as his DJ deck.

I stand and watch for a couple of numbers to see what's going on. Several couples are dancing, in a variety of styles: one pair seem to be dancing Venezuelan, others are doing Cuban, others again some kind of hybrid between Cuban and New York. It doesn't seem intimidating. When the music pauses I scan the sparse clientèle for a partner and approach a tall, skeletally thin girl, her altitude accentuated by very high heels and a kind of leotard. We dance a restrained version of Cuban, which seems to go well enough. When it ends, I thank her and look around for another partner. But there are few unpartnered women, and the laptop artist for some reason clears the floor by putting on an extremely slow cha-cha-cha. I give up and leave.

Next day I have breakfast at a workmen's café across the street and prepare for my first lesson with Norma. But where are my dancing shoes? Mentally I run over yesterday's events. Of course: I must have left them in the Nuyorican Café when I went down to meet Norma. I hurry down and find a boy sweeping the floor. "Yeah," he says in English, "I found them when we were opening up last night. I didn't know whose they were so I mixed them in the trash. Sorry."

Uli the German guide has come in after me. "He *mixed them in the trash?*" he repeats, aghast. "In Germany, we would keep them for six months!"

Anyhow, my shoes are gone and the lesson begins in an hour. Uli says there's a shop selling trainers half a dozen blocks away. Swearing under my breath I hurry off to find it. I'm a little concerned, because my requirements are pretty specific. I want white ones, but more importantly they mustn't have much grip because I need to spin, and they have to be size 12. Does anyone in Puerto Rico wear shoes that big? I find the shop and explain what I need. After trying a variety, I end up with a lightweight pair of dazzlingly white Pumas. They're better than the ones I lost – and a fraction of the price.

I get back to the café just as Norma is finishing her lesson with the Germans. I'm sweating as if I'd already danced for an hour but she's as cool as ever. Once the class has left, we practise some basic steps on the chequered floor and I soon realize that I'm facing a new challenge. "You want to learn *estilo puertorriqueño*?" Norma asks. "Then you dance on two."

Dancing "on two" is something I've heard about but never tried. What it comes down to is that you take your first step on the *second* beat of the bar. And so on. In Cuban style the count is "one-two-three ... five-six-seven", but when you dance "on two" it goes "two-three-four ... six-seven-eight". Otherwise the moves are in the linear or New York style just as in Panama. But doing everything one beat later feels tricky. We practise the basic steps with music, and I find I have to listen in a completely different way, finding a different emphasis within the music. Somehow the "on two" rhythm is more natural, but less obvious. If that makes any sense. And while it's easy enough to begin on the correct beat, keeping to it and remembering to hit it again after turning or making a complicated move is much harder. All my instincts are to find the *one*, which has been the key rhythmical landmark in all the styles of salsa I've danced before.

Still, it starts to come. We dance to instructional CDs where the beats are counted aloud over the music, working on the cross-body move, Norma showing me how to take a small step back on the "six" so as to stay in exactly the same position, rather than following the woman as she moves across. Lacking Alina's weightless quality, Norma is physically much more solid. Chunky and voluptuous, she wears a low-cut black T-shirt, tightly stretched over her full, round breasts. She has a cheeky, humorous face with wonderfully flexible features, easily assuming a mask of disdain, bafflement or hilarity as the occasion demands. She expects me to give her a good push when I lead her, and I enjoy doing it. We work on comparatively simple turns where I break back, lift our hands, turn her, turn myself and rejoin her. It works as long as I can keep to the new rhythm and avoid slipping back onto the *one*. By the end of the lesson I feel I'm getting the hang of it, though I'm still far away from being able to dance "on two" in a disco. Well, I suppose it may come. We agree to meet at the same time tomorrow.

The following morning I'm sitting in the lobby looking at the local paper when a beautiful young woman with black curly hair comes in. (By the way, are *all* Puerto Rican women beautiful? So far I haven't seen one who isn't. Last night I went into the grocer's shop on the corner for a can of beer and a packet of banana chips, and noticed, pinned up behind the counter, a photograph of Miss Teenage Puerto Rico International 2006. The gorgeous girl in the picture looked very much like the woman serving me, so I asked, *"¿Ella es su hija?"* and was proudly told, yes, that was her daughter. The mother looked pretty good too. But I digress.)

The girl at reception asks the new arrival "How's your dengue?" Registering this, I put the paper down.

"Not so bad today," says the newcomer. "Two nights ago my temperature was still up, but it was down last night."

Since they're right beside me, I feel I can join the conversation. "You have *dengue?*" I ask.

They both nod. "There's a lot of it about," says the receptionist.

"But I'm getting better," says the newcomer.

"A few days ago her temperature was a hundred and five," adds the other cheerfully. "And she was delirious. You should have heard the nonsense she talked."

They walk off. I return to my newspaper. Dengue? Isn't that sometimes fatal? Wow. I turn to page two and there's a story about it. The epidemic of dengue that's been raging in Puerto Rico for five months is settling down. Epidemic? Five months? No one told me there was an epidemic of dengue here. I suppose it's just as well, or I might not have come. I scrutinize various mosquito bites on my wrists and ankles. I feel okay so far, but who knows? Too late to worry now, though, anyway.

Thinking of dengue reminds me of Taboga Island. Ever since my visit there with Fred, a question has been floating at the back of my mind. My hotel offers free internet access so I cross the lobby, sit down, and call up Google to try and find out about that eerie little shrine with the three crosses on the mountain. The restaurateur said something about an aeroplane, "many years ago". I type in "plane crash taboga island". After various irrelevant entries I find a site called planecrashinfo.com. Sure enough, there it is:

June 09 1946, 10.30 a.m. Taboga Island, Panama. USAAF, Douglas DC 4. Aboard: 23. Fatalities: 23. Crashed into a summit after flying below the prescribed altitude.

So that's it. No wonder the place felt so melancholy.

I remember that Fred mentioned that he was writing a blog; I wonder what he has to say about the island? I look up www.toolaba. com (it's a pun – "*tout là-bas*" in French means "way over there") and find not only Taboga Island but myself as well:

I met Grevel on the terrace of the Café del Prado [writes Fred, in French]. He was lamenting the loss of his luggage, I the telephonic disappearance of a couchsurfer… Grevel made on me at once the impression of the long-term traveller. Tall, white hair, earring, the air of those who feel themselves at ease everywhere and at home nowhere. The guests of the whole world … It was easy to tell that he was English. Though tempered by kindness and intelligence, I recognized that little cold flame which I often see gleaming deep in the eyes of our best enemies: that which lights up an infallible sense of humour, and the unconscious certainty of being the issue of the only civilization Europe has ever known. One senses that the Englishman bears a burden of tasks and responsibilities which accompany the pleasure of certain privileges, of which the most precious is that of knowing oneself to be English. My goodness! *Il faut que je fasse attention, je crois que je deviens anglophile.*

It's fascinating to see myself transformed in this Gallic mirror. I've become a kind of Phileas Fogg, a cool nineteenth-century *anglais* with the burden of Empire and the arrogance of Waterloo written all over me. I think feel flattered.

I have an email from Amanda, whom I've told about my dream and the Babalawo's interpretation. Amanda writes, "I hope Ochún isn't going to take you away from me." I do my best to reassure her that no jealous goddess is going to come between us.

While I'm logged on, I decide to check on salsa venues in case I'm missing anything good. My search for "Puerto Rico + salsa" turns up some discos that look interesting, but also – bizarrely – a site from the Expansionist Party of the USA. "Has there ever been so ungrateful a bunch as the people of Puerto Rico?" it asks. Its chief gripe seems to be Puerto Rico's refusal to let the US Navy drop bombs on one of its offshore islands after someone there was killed in a military manoeuvre:

> If Puerto Rico, not the US, is your "country" [it rants], and you refuse to live up to any responsibility of US citizenship whatsoever – refuse to take statehood and thus your place in the House and Senate to fight, with votes, for the good and necessary things in society; refuse to pay taxes to the national treasury; refuse to speak English … then it's time for *us* to refuse to permit you to take from our treasury any longer… And the next time a hurricane hits, pay for the damage yourselves.

The tirade ends with some thoughtful comments on salsa:

> Most non-Latins regard it as loud, cacophonous, and tedious. Blaring trumpets, pounding drums, wood blocks, and a driving rhythm may appeal to some, but most non-Latins find it unpleasant save in very small doses.

I click the site off. "Blaring trumpets, pounding drums…" Yes, that's what I'm here for. I'm longing to hear some good live music.

My reflections are interrupted by Emma, a Bulgarian who's with the German group. We've talked a little before, and she's come now to tell me that the German group are going out this evening to the Placita de Santurce. Would I like to come? It sounds inviting, but I don't know what's at the Placita. "Oh, bars," Emma tells me, "clubs, music, maybe places where we can dance."

"I'm not very confident about dancing 'on two'," I tell her. "I've only just started, and I've never done it before. At home I always danced Cuban-style."

Emma's eyes light up. "Me too," she confides. "I find this dancing 'on two' incredibly difficult." She giggles conspiratorially. "Maybe we can dance Cuban together?"

That sounds tempting, though I wonder if I should let myself, since it'll probably set back my learning the new style. But Emma, who has short blonde hair, high cheekbones and loads of enthusiasm, is charming. I can see myself dancing with her. She says the group plans to be back at the Nuyorican Café in time to hear Juanra's band play, so the excursion looks like a bonus.

That evening I find the group of Germans clustering on the corner of Calle San Francisco, and ask the guide, Uli, if it will be all right for me to come along as Emma has suggested. Alas, Uli radiates disapproval. His German organizational sense is evidently put out by the arrival of another body. It affronts his sense of tidiness and he proceeds to give me a dressing-down. Of course, he tells me, I am perfectly welcome to come. But it would be better if people notified him in advance of exactly who was, and who was not, going to be present. He has ordered a minibus. It's possible that there might not be a seat for me!

Fine, I say, if there's no room I'll get a taxi of my own. No, no, says Uli, that's not the point. I realize that the point is that I can certainly come if there's room, but Uli feels that he must give me my reprimand first. So I stand there meekly and let him tell me off. Then I offer a ceremonious apology and promise never to do such a thing again. Uli is now perfectly happy and we settle down to await the transport.

When the minibus arrives, Uli asks if there's a seat for me and the driver says there is, at the back. When I climb in, however, there doesn't seem to be one. The driver gestures to the luggage space behind the rear seat. I struggle into it and find a frail, battered, tubular metal folding chair. I'd guess it's what the driver stands on when he washes the roof of the vehicle (a bucket of rags and sponges beside it confirms my intuition). I unfold this thing and bash the seat into position, then sit down. The chair feels ready to fold under me at any second. As the minibus moves off, it lurches around and I find that the only way to remain stable is to turn sideways, cling to the back of the seat beside me, and brace my feet against the wall of the bus. Even so, every time we turn left the acceleration makes the front legs of the chair float up from the floor and threaten to tip me over backwards. I imagine it's like being inside a space capsule. Fortunately Uli can't see me, or he'd stop the bus at once on health and safety grounds. As for me, I'm now so used to Latin American transport that it wouldn't have surprised me if I'd been asked to ride on the roof-rack.

We drive at breakneck speed down a long avenue – I see only odd glimpses because my head is jammed in a corner between the roof and the rear door – and turn into a labyrinth of smaller streets, coming to rest at a street corner between some low concrete buildings and an area of waste ground.

As soon as we pile out, we can hear music. The night sky is full of stars but the light down here is the pallid glare of strip lighting. We're in a side-street full of bars and cafeterias with neon signs advertising cheap beer. There are makeshift stalls selling roast chicken and fajitas. Crowds of people stand around drinking beer out of plastic cups. The area is much grittier than anything in Old San Juan. Salsa music pounds from speakers outside the bars. The noise is deafening, and to talk we have to yell at one another.

Our group gradually splits up. Emma and I buy a couple of cans of Medalla, the local beer, and walk up towards the Plaza del Mercado – the so-called Placita – in the centre of which is the *mercado* itself, a huge nineteenth-century market hall. We spot a pavement bar with a little band: just an electronic keyboard, a percussionist with congas, and a man playing a Spanish guitar. All of them sing as they play. Shamelessly commercial, they play well. We hesitate, watching them – and of course are instantly beckoned inside by a waiter. I raise my can to show I already have a drink but the waiter waves his arms, beaming. It doesn't matter! Come and listen anyway! So we sit under an awning in the warm night air and listen to the trio playing "Montón de Estrellas" and other salsa standards. The place is almost deserted. Two waiters lean beside the door under a neon Medalla sign. One or two people drift past, and a few stop. A heavily-built man in a blue uniform – is he a policeman? – starts to dance gently and lumberingly on the pavement with his plump, laughing wife or girlfriend. They're not doing salsa, just making simple to-and-fro movements with their feet. I watch the nimble rhythm of the man's huge boots with fascination.

We've heard so much music that it seems only fair to order a drink. Emma wants a *mojito*; I have another Medalla. Some of the Germans appear and join us. They're young and very blond. Two of them stand up to dance salsa and put on a flawless performance, New York-style, "on two". The waiters and some nearby locals watch, impressed. The pair are so tall that I'm worried the girl's head will hit the café awning as she spins, but they avoid disaster – just – and when the song finishes the spectators applaud enthusiastically. I'm longing to dance, so when the band begins again I ask Emma if she'd like to dance Cuban. She agrees at once and we join the first couple on the concrete under the awning. We can't compete with them in elegant insouciance but we enjoy ourselves, and by the time we've finished more people have gathered to dance beyond the tables, on the pavement. We shake hands with the musicians and walk back down to the Placita.

The crowds in the street below the market are now denser than ever, and the music from the bars is supplemented by the roar of engines. A police car with flashing blue lights circles the block every two minutes, as if on permanent patrol. There's a growing, low-pitched roar like distant thunder, building until a cavalcade of motorcycles appears round the corner. A procession of huge, shiny bikes, decked with fur, mirrors, elaborate lights and vast chopper handlebars comes and keeps coming. Are these Puerto Rican Hell's Angels? Or just people having a Friday night out? We watch, entranced, as the mirror-polished monsters glide past, throttled and growling, with their helmeted, leather-jacketed and miniskirted riders. The most spectacular bike, near the end of the line, has coloured lights mounted inside the engine so the fins and tubes glow an unearthly blue. The convoy is followed by yet another police car.

It's now nine o'clock and our group is reconvening around the minibus. Uli shepherds us in, I resume my humble seat on the gimcrack tin chair in the luggage compartment, and we're off.

Back at the hotel I take a leisurely shower and lie down until about eleven, when I stroll downstairs to see what's happening. The steep cobbled alley outside the hotel is full of people drinking, smoking and talking. A van at the top of the street is being unloaded. Men are heaving guitars, congas and speakers around. I wander into the darkness of the café. It's filling up: most of the tables are taken and people are drifting in from the street. The audience is completely mixed: there are old guys in their sixties, some with their wives; there are groups of teenagers perching on bar stools clicking their mobile phones. There are a few obvious tourists, including some Germans, and with them Emma, who joins me at my table. There's the usual mysterious work going on on stage, people wandering about with lengths of cable or turning the screws on drumheads. A broad figure I recognize as Juanra Fernandez is hunched over a microphone, tapping it and enunciating, "*A-si, a-si.*" The musicians assemble, puffing briefly on brass instruments, trilling out rolls on the bongo, putting out PA calls for band members who are off somewhere dragging on a last cigarette or closing a deal with someone in the street.

At last, when the place is packed and vibrant with suppressed expectation, the stage lights come up and Juanra settles himself behind the congas, leans into the mike and welcomes us. He counts the band in, the keyboards begin the *montuno* and the band launches into "A las Seis". It's quite a big band – a nine-piecer – with keyboards, stand-up double-bass, trombone, trumpet, two vocalists and three percussionists. The sound is chunky, rich, sonorous, with the percussionists putting a strong intricate network of sound on top.

After a few minutes Emma leans up close to my ear and says, "I am leaving, it is too loud for me." I raise my eyebrows in surprise. Is she sure she wants to go? But she is, and she does. How she's survived this long in the salsa world if she doesn't like loud music I can't imagine.

Soon people are clapping and moving their feet along with the big, solid sound. Despite the lack of space a few people get up to dance, which isn't surprising because the steady, relentless rhythms are highly infectious. They get right into your body, and most of the band members are dancing as they play.

Apart from the music, Comborican is a visual spectacle. The band members might have been chosen to exemplify physical and ethnic diversity. The guy on *timbales* has dreadlocks, a white T-shirt as big as a tent and an orange baseball cap worn sideways. The trumpeter is a small man sporting a 1970s-style Afro (I spotted him frizzing it out with a comb at a mirror behind the bar a few minutes ago), while the trombonist, another black guy, is tall, with a bald, domed head and glasses. The bongo player is a slight, pale-skinned, scholarly-looking Afro-Caribbean with a little beard. The slim, shy-looking Latino on bass looks suspiciously like the one who "mixed" my dancing shoes in the trash yesterday. Then there's Juanra on congas, with his huge build and blond, fair North American looks. The lead vocalist, Wilfredo Otero, is the quintessential Latino New Yorker with his skinny, wiry build, slicked-back hair, short-sleeved shirt and winkle-pickers. Beside him is a pretty, sharp-featured, red-headed female singer in a dress whose plunging neckline displays a truly spectacular cleavage. And behind them, playing keyboards, is a beautiful, fair-complexioned woman with long wavy hair who looks remarkably English. They're all so different: it's like watching a subtler, Puerto Rican version of the Village People.

They're also a bit like a family. They have a definite collective consciousness: I can see the musicians intuitively communicating, glancing at each other for a moment to co-ordinate a change in the music, someone counting a solo in or out with raised fingers. The music stays solid, a spontaneously organized pushing and pulsing river of sound.

After a couple of numbers Juanra introduces Herman Oliveras, the veteran Puerto Rican salsa singer, who steps up in white suit and white hat (somewhere between a pork-pie and a trilby, but it's not a Panama either), tall and elegant, with a certain resemblance to Buena Vista's Compay Segundo.

The band launches into another number. They play Fania standards like "Quitate Tu" and "Boogaloo", and soon Wilfredo and Herman are trading verses, improvising lines about members of the band, the audience, Old San Juan and salsa itself. Plenty of people are dancing now and the energy of the music is going through me like a current of electricity. But caught between the Cuban style I'm used to and the "on two" style I've just begun, I feel inhibited about asking anyone to dance so I just lean against a pillar near the stage, or practise a few steps, counting the beats, moving with the music. It's long after midnight but the dynamism of the band and the flow of the music seem inexhaustible. I feel it could all go on for ever.

At some point (my sense of time has gone completely) other musicians step in to give the Comborican members a break. During the first number I spot the beautiful pianist, released from her keyboard, making her way through the crowd. She approaches a grey-haired man at one of the tables, evidently inviting him to dance. I feel a momentary stab of envy – but the man shakes his head. She needs a partner, and I know I just *have* to dance with her. I hurl caution to the winds, go straight up to her and ask her. Smiling graciously, she accepts.

I dismiss any ideas of dancing "on two" and opt for a gentle version of Cuban. She seems fine with it. We sway and circle, and every so often I try a figure and it works well. I feel awed at the idea of holding those hands that have been pounding and coaxing the keyboard relentlessly for the past hour (or is it several hours?) and I'm terribly careful how I handle them: I don't grasp her right hand but simply press mine against it, palm flat. I try to express through my body how happy I am to be dancing with her. The music is far too loud for us to talk, but she smiles a lot and so do I. The band is playing a long number with lots of solos and improvisation, but we sustain it well and I have enough moves to keep it interesting without making things showy or complicated. When the song ends I thank her and kiss her on the cheek. I tell her her piano-playing is wonderful. I stroll back to my pillar walking, precisely as the cliché says, on air. There's now an elderly Puerto Rican leaning against the same pillar. He looks up at me, raises his eyebrows judiciously, and says, "Good dancing."

I've never been happier.

I wake at around eleven. Luckily my lesson with Norma isn't until one, because I didn't get to bed until three last night. I roll cautiously out of bed, have a shower (a wondrous cure for morning inertia) and walk slowly down to the cafeteria across the street, where the charming bilingual proprietor (who tells me he once spent a year working in Norwich) brings orange juice and coffee and cooks me scrambled eggs (*huevos revueltos*) with bacon. I take a taxi to Norma's place, a well-equipped dance studio out in a concrete wasteland between a Taco Bell outlet and a vast freeway intersection, and spend a couple of hours practising *sombreros* and right- and left-hand turns "on two". There are also exercises: moving my head, neck, shoulders and torso, "isolating" muscles so as to move one body-part while keeping the others motionless. Pushing my ribcage sideways without moving my hips is always difficult! By the time we finish, I'm aching all over. Am I storing up arthritis for my later years, I wonder, or protecting myself against it?

I go for a late lunch to a small café in the street next to my hotel. Juanra is drinking coffee by the window. He asks me what I thought of the gig last night, and I tell him it was some of the best live salsa I've heard. And the pianist was particularly good.

"Wonderful," he says. "Gwen is joining me here in a few minutes, so you'll meet her. Well, we play for dancers. Without a live audience it's just not the same. Old San Juan has this Bohemian community. These people live here, our audiences and our musicians. Our singer Wilfredo works at the hotel reception sometimes. The other people, they work around here one way or another. Several of them have their own projects too, their own bands. The guy you saw playing *timbales* – he's a record producer, he's just produced a reggaeton album. Everyone works with other bands as well as with the Comborican project. You want another drink?"

I say I'll have an orange juice and Juanra calls to the waiter for a "*china*".

"'*China*'?" I query.

"Yeah, Puerto Rico's the only place in the world where an orange is called a *china*. It's because the oranges used to arrive in crates stamped 'Made in China'. Hey, here's Gwen."

I look round and see the beautiful pianist approaching. "This is my partner, Gwen," says Juanra. (Partner? No chance of inviting *her* out for dinner, then.)

"Hi," says Gwen. "I've just taken the kids home from their karate class. They're five and seven," she tells me, "so I spend half my time driving them around – dance, music, martial arts, whatever."

I tell Gwen how much I enjoyed her playing the previous night. "You treat the piano like a percussion instrument," I say. "I'm sure that's how it should be played for salsa."

Juanra agrees. "She never ever uses the sustain pedal," he says proudly. "She keeps the *montuno* going all through the song, which a lot of keyboard players don't bother to do."

It turns out Gwen is American. She met Juanra at Michigan University; he was studying chemistry, and she was training as a physiotherapist. I look again at those hands I was so in awe of last night when we danced. They're powerful, with short stubby nails and broad fingertips – a sculptor's or potter's hands. "First I was a physical therapist, then I played percussion," she tells me. No wonder her approach to the keyboard is so punchy and tactile.

I ask how the band started. "I used to work on Wall Street," says Juanra, who evidently does most of the talking. "We got interested in drumming and started to try playing ourselves. On Sunday afternoons these fantastic drummers always met in Central Park to play *rumba*. We used to turn up early and there'd always be one good player there, so we'd accompany him and it made us sound good too." Then, it seems, Gwen got into piano. She found herself a teacher in New York. And when they got tired of New York they decided to move to Juanra's home, Puerto Rico. "We just used to play in our house. Friends who were musicians came around and we'd all play together. Then other people started coming, older musicians. We began playing in a bar called La Pregunta. It was like a workshop: old salsa artists would come along and jam with us. People like Juancito Torres. We learned so much from them. And younger people came too. It just took off from there. We used to play with people twice our age, and now we're playing with people half our age. We're handing on a tradition, the real tradition of salsa, the way the Fania people used to play it in the '70s, with real *rabia* – not the kind of *salsa romántica*, the pop salsa that's taken over in the last few years."

I can see Juanra is evangelical about this. "*Salsa romántica* has done so much damage. It's turned salsa into Hallmark sentiment, cheesy love-and-heartbreak stuff. We want to reclaim an urban relevance for salsa, to make it meaningful. We're taking the project into our own hands. We record ourselves and we sell ourselves. Johnny Pacheco sold seventy thousand records out of the trunk of his car! Why shouldn't we do the same?"

If salsa's to be political, I ask, what about Puerto Rico's relationship with the USA? Is that a problem?

Juanra shakes his head in despair. "It's a *huge* problem. We can't vote, we don't have our sovereignty, but that's linked to something people are prepared to die for, namely an American passport. It's very unfortunate that these two things are tied together. Because it prevents us from having a national project, it prevents us making something for ourselves."

"Project", like *rabia*, is an important word for Juanra. He uses it all the time: about his band, about Puerto Rico, about salsa. "My solution is, they should give us right of residence for a hundred years, which we have anyway; and they should give us independence. That way we have an interest in building a nation, but people can also say 'Well, if they fuck it up I can go to the States.' That way, people here would have an incentive *and* a safeguard."

Then he's back to salsa again. "I think what we're doing is the future of salsa, and San Juan is the ideal place to do it. People come here from the mountains, where they grow up learning guitar, *décimas*, country songs. And they meet people from the coast who learn percussion. They get together and spark one another up. Wilfredo, he's from the country, he's only just started singing salsa, and he's going to be a big star. We want to nurture people like that. He was invited to New York last year and the promoter wouldn't even pay his plane fare – so we found it for him, because we didn't want him to lose the opportunity to sing in front of all those people. And he wowed them; they thought he was fantastic. So many Puerto Ricans have missed out because they missed opportunities. You can't do that – you have to be there, and you have to give of your best. Once you start deciding how long you're going to sing that night according to how much they're paying you – or worse, if you start thinking how *well* you're going to sing – you're finished."

And how, I ask, does he come to be running a hotel as well as a band? "Well, we used to play at La Pregunta. They closed that, so we found the Nuyorican Café. Then some developer announced he was going to buy the entire block, including the café. That would have left us with nowhere regular to play. So I hustled around and found someone to lend the money and I said, 'I'll buy the block. We'll make it a hotel and gallery, and we can keep the café going.' Okay, so I'm running a hotel. But now the person who lent the money, he's setting up two more hotels and he wants me to run those too." He screws up his face and moans in comic despair: "*And all I wanna do is play my fuckin' drums!*"

I wonder if it's quite such an accident. Juanra has taken himself out of Wall Street, but maybe there's still a bit of Wall Street in Juanra? His belief that Comborican have the future of salsa in their hands raises another question. Some people say salsa *hasn't* a future; that the way forward now is with reggaeton. I challenge him on this.

"A lot of reggaeton artists actually want to play salsa now," says Juanra. "You know the reggaeton label White Lion? They've just called to ask if I'll be a consultant for them. They want to release a salsa CD!" He pauses to finish his coffee. "Look," he says. "This music has a three-hundred-year history. It's not going anywhere."

People say the live bands this afternoon will be on the Paseo Princesa near the harbour, so I take the coastal walkway under the sea wall, where I soon catch up with an elderly American couple I've met at the hotel, a courtly gentleman and his wife. They're in their eighties, and the other evening the lady told me she'd recently had two hip-joint replacements, but they're strolling steadily along the path and tell me they too are going to the Paseo to hear the bands. "And the girl in the hotel told us we absolutely *had* to dance!"

Five minutes later, we're turning a corner and strolling inland on a broad avenue between palm trees. There are people everywhere, walking, chatting, eating and drinking. Children yell and dash about. There are stalls selling toys and sweets and fast food. There's a whole series of bands playing salsa, spaced at intervals of a few hundred yards. We stop and listen to each in turn. "I can walk any distance," the lady tells me, "but I get tired standing about." The best band – a small group with percussion, keyboards, flute and vocalist – plays on a platform behind an open-air café. There's a fence covered with flowering vines, and inside it a space with some tables and room for dancers. Half a dozen couples are dancing: black people, Latinos, nobody doing anything showy, no one dancing "on two", just couples going to and fro or side to side, circling gently – the gentleman sometimes turning the lady or turning around once himself, the lady's arm floating around his waist. It's a very laid-back version of Cuban style.

"So are you going to dance?" I ask my companions.

"Not me," says the gentleman decisively.

"How about you?" I ask his wife.

"I'd love to," she says, "but I don't know how."

I feel inspired. "Come on," I say. "We can do this. I'll show you how, and I'll lead you." I take her hand and we go through the little gate. Still holding her hands, I ask her to look at my feet. I say, "All you have to do is this. Go back, forward with this foot; then forward, back with *that* foot. And keep doing it. If you get lost, just look down at my feet and follow them. Listen to the music: *one-two-three, five-six-seven.*"

And after a couple of false starts, it works. I take her gently into partner-hold, and we're dancing. All we have to do is move our feet forward or back on those four crucial beats. Forget all the clever stuff. I've discovered that salsa can be stripped down to just this. Once my partner's used to that simple step, we start gently turning around. Once she's used to that, I move back a little, lift her right hand in my left, and with the other hand gently push her round anticlockwise. I reckon it's taken me five minutes to get her started with salsa. I hold her very, very carefully. We dance on happily, with a few little turns, until the music stops. My partner is beaming with delight. Some people at the nearby tables applaud. Concentration and the afternoon heat have got to me so much that as we leave the café I see drops of my own sweat splashing on the concrete. But we've done it.

The lady rejoins her husband, delighted. I say goodbye, and as I leave I can hear her telling him, "Look, there's nothing to it. You just go like this…"

It strikes me that perhaps we've made salsa into something too complicated. If an eighty-year-old lady with two hip replacements can learn it in five minutes, anyone can – though since a lady can be led, it might take a little longer to get a man started. But maybe we *gringos*, with our competitiveness and obsession with technique, are in danger of forgetting the essence. It's actually so simple.

This suspicion is confirmed when I meet Emma later at the hotel. The Germans, she tells me, are discontented with Puerto Rico. They had imagined an island where everyone danced elaborate figures, perpetually spinning at high speed. Instead they've found the local people, in clubs and cafés and on the streets, dancing with elegant simplicity, expressing the music and their feelings for each other without a *setenta complicada* in sight. They've been reduced to dancing mostly with one another. They're looking forward to getting back to Frankfurt and Düsseldorf, where they can dance some *real* salsa again.

Juanra mentioned earlier that several bands, including Comborican, are playing tonight near the fortress, at something called the Totem Pole, so Emma and I decide to go. We've no idea where it is, but the fortress is at the top of the city so we make our way up the steep streets until we reach the humped, grassy mounds and white walls of the old Spanish fortifications. As we approach, the Totem Pole looms up. It's a towering, cylindrical sculpture, made of textured metal that, from a distance, looks exactly like tree bark. There are no faces carved on it. A flight of steps runs down to a plaza where a stage has been erected, with rows of plastic chairs for the audience. We find seats and listen to a group of African-style drummers playing *rumba*. A couple of women get up from the audience and dance in the middle of the plaza, in front of the musicians. A small girl – maybe three or four years old – comes out to join them, rotating her hips and shaking her shoulders to applause and indulgent laughter.

As the sun sets, it's Comborican's turn. Gwen spots me from behind her keyboard and gives me a wave. The band is well into a solid set when the electricity cuts out. Lights fail and the amplification dies. All we can hear is the percussion. Juanra looks around at the band, intensifies his conga-playing, and signals at the audience with one hand to get us all clapping. Soon the whole audience is one big percussion section, and everyone keeps going until the lights come on and the sound surges back. There's a wave of applause. The band goes on to finish the set, the final number levelling out into an obsessive chant, over and over again: "*¿Que pasa, Puerto Rico? ¡Levántate!*" – "What's the matter, Puerto Rico? Get up!" Juanra is putting out the message loud and clear.

Emma has already left (the music is too loud again). I stroll down to buy a Coke and a roast pork sandwich from a stall and return for the final act, a Puerto Rican band who currently have a big salsa hit. They're certainly very loud. The two singers dance energetically and shout a lot, but they lack the family ambience of Comborican. Each musician, intent on his score, seems to be playing to himself. A few people get up and begin frenzied dancing, but one by one they sit down again. Children look tired; the odd person yawns. After a couple of numbers people are checking their watches and drifting away. Rather cruelly, I stay on to see how many people will leave. When the seats are four-fifths empty I decide I've had enough. Tomorrow I'm going to the Dominican Republic and I need some sleep.

CHAPTER SEVEN
❊WORKING AT THE CAR WASH

To avoid yet another flight, I've decided to cross to the Dominican Republic by sea.

I've been warned that there will be political *manifestaciones* in the streets of San Juan this morning, so although the ferry doesn't leave until 8 p.m., and I needn't be on board until five, I've booked a taxi for mid-morning. The ferry sails from Mayagüez, in the far west of Puerto Rico, and the voyage will take several hours even if we escape from San Juan in good time.

In fact we see no sign of demonstrations as we move from the colonial picturesqueness of Old San Juan into the concrete sprawl of the newer city, then through suburbs between green hills and onto the *autopista*. We drive for hours along a plain dotted with drive-ins, factories and car showrooms, between tree-covered mountains, their lower slopes patterned with green stripes, which the driver tells me are coffee and banana plantations. Eventually we descend towards a margin of greyish sea. Reaching the nondescript outskirts of Mayagüez, we turn towards the harbour. As we pull into the car-park, the driver indicates a white ship looming over the single-storey concrete terminal. "There's your *Titanic*," he says. I hope it's not a bad omen.

I lug my rucksack into the terminal. A sign says that tickets must be booked twenty-four hours ahead. I booked mine weeks ago over the phone with a credit card, but I'm quite prepared for the smart girl in the blue uniform behind the counter to tell me they've never heard of me and there's no ticket. I'm not disappointed. There is indeed no ticket. After many comings and goings I'm told that they *have* heard of me, but my ticket wasn't booked because my credit card was rejected. I guess my English bank's computer didn't fancy risking money on a "customer not present" transaction in Puerto Rico. In the computer's place I'd probably have felt the same. But apparently my call satisfied the twenty-four-hour rule, and now I'm present the transaction goes through smoothly. The girl carefully levers the stapled green Visa Waiver form out of my passport – at severe risk to her spectacular, glitter-encrusted nails – and hands me my boarding pass.

Since the journey across Puerto Rico was much quicker than expected, I now have the whole afternoon to wait. I look around the hall with its rows of plastic seats. I'd counted on some sort of restaurant, but there's nothing, just a couple of vending machines, so I buy a can of Coke and a packet of Doritos and take my unappealing lunch to a bench outside.

Slowly people drift in. It starts to rain. By mid-afternoon the terminal's filling up. There are odd individuals with bundles, cases and bags; family groups with pushchairs, babies and bulging plastic sacks. By four o'clock the place is thronged, and at four-thirty, in response to some signal I failed to notice, there's general movement to form a queue. A door at the back of the terminal opens, and with agonizing slowness we filter through, then wait to be packed into buses which drive three hundred yards through the rain to the ship. The doors of the bus wheeze open and we plod up the gangplank, entering the ferry via the car deck, which is full of containers. An escalator takes us up to the passenger decks.

Many of the passengers have cabins booked. With my innate preference for doing things the unorthodox way, I haven't booked a cabin. I ask a sort of receptionist at a counter where I should go. The woman waves her arms vaguely. "Wherever you like." The whole ship, it seems, is my oyster. There are doors, carpeted corridors and companionways in all directions, with posters advertising the Casino, the Nightclub, the Bar, the Blue Ribbon Restaurant, the Cinema. Streams of people pour past. I feel disoriented already. Pulling myself together, I try to focus. I need to find some sort of saloon with seats where I can settle down. I try a corridor. It contains a featureless succession of identical numbered doors stretching into the far distance. It's like a shot out of *The Shining*, minus tricycle.

I go up one floor and try again. This time I find two doors labelled *Oslo* and *Stockholm*, which seems odd. Pushing one open, I enter a large, dim room full of high-backed chairs like airline seats. This is more like it. I find a seat over to one side, park my luggage and sit down to get my breath. I guess this is where I'm going to spend the night. Up near the door, families of travellers who evidently know exactly what they're doing are busy pitching camp, opening laundry bags, removing blankets, pillows, quilts and sleeping bags, laying claim to large areas of floor where they clearly intend to sleep, stretched out in comfort while I shall be writhing uneasily, scrunched up in my almost-upright airline seat. Never mind.

There's no secure place to leave luggage, so I extract my money and passport and leave the rest to take its chance on the seat. Then I set off to explore the ship. I find other saloons with names like *London*, *Berlin* and *Copenhagen*. All very un-Caribbean. Then I discover a door leading out onto the deck. Oddly, it's labelled "ISGLAT – EISGLATTE – ICE SLIPPERY". The penny finally drops when I go down one deck and am confronted by a bulkhead with a huge, pallid photograph of Tonbridge Castle, Kent, advertising some company that claims to be "giving colour to British Industry". Of course! The ship may be called *Caribbean Express* and registered in Panama, but it's actually a North Sea ferry. It must have been sold when it got too ancient, and wound up here. Even the piped music is dreary 1980s British pop. It probably came with the ship. Out on deck there's a locker full of life-jackets. The instructions are in English, Dutch and German – not a word in Spanish. I just hope they're never needed.

It has stopped raining. Leaning idly over the rail, I notice a group of people on the quayside pointing excitedly and gazing down into the water. It grows turbulent every so often and something – I can't quite see what – makes a curved slash along the surface, creating a flurry of ripples. I look enquiringly at a plump lady staring over the rail beside me. "*Tiburones*," she says. Sharks. "But only small ones," she adds reassuringly. A man on the quay tosses a piece of his burger in. The slashes grow frenetic, then subside.

I watch sunset from the upper deck. The stars come out. Soon after 8 p.m. the ship starts to vibrate, water churns furiously at our bows and the ropes are cast off. We move sidelong away from the quay. People stand on deck, mobile phones glued to their ears. The ship rolls soothingly. Puerto Rico very slowly fades to a faint galactic smear of light on the horizon. I go inside. In the bars people are settling down around tables, unpacking sets of dominoes or feeding children from packets of banana chips. I go to reception and rent a blanket for the small hours: it's chilly inside because of the air-conditioning, though outside it's warm and steamy.

I eat at the one-price all-you-can-eat dinner buffet, then wander again. The casino is open but I give it a miss. In the nightclub a man in a big Mexican hat sings comic songs. I buy a beer and sit on deck watching sea and sky until I'm too tired to do anything except try to sleep. Then I pick my way over the inert forms sprawled about the dark saloon floor and find my chair.

It's an uncomfortable night. The seat is too short, so my head lolls and my neck hurts. I sleep sporadically with scraps of weird, irritating dreams. In the pale dawn which comes far too soon I give up the idea of sleep and stroll stiffly about, stretching, rubbing my aching eyes. I brush my teeth in the washroom, stepping around shards of glass from a mirror that has fallen off the wall during the night. I go on deck into the warm, humid air under the overcast sky and look at a long thread of coastline tufted with tiny palm trees. That's the Dominican Republic. I've no appetite, but I go to the all-you-can-eat breakfast buffet and eat all I can – which isn't much.

When we moor at the quayside in Santo Domingo I can't see anything of our destination because by then, in obedience to instructions over the tannoy, I'm wedged in the midst of a gigantic queue which snakes to and fro up several decks of the ship. We shuffle slowly along and when at last I follow the long line of passengers off the boat, across the quay in the broiling morning sun and into the customs hall, I'm greeted by a sign in English: WELCOME TO INCOME TAX. But I find I've already paid my "in-coming tax" as an arrival in the Dominican Republic by buying a tourist card.

The customs hall is dark and stifling. Ancient fans twirl lazily, high up in the ceiling. There's another eternity of queuing. The customs staff, weary-looking women in jeans and blue tops, are opening every single box, bag and case, and scrabbling through the contents. The conveyor belts are all out of order, so exhausted people simply heave their luggage up onto them and drag it along to be opened. My turn comes.

"What's in your bag?" the lady asks.

"Clothes. And things for washing myself," I say.

The lady drags the zip open and roots about. "Also books!" she says accusingly.

What does she expect? I have a pen, shoes, and a compass too. Does she want me to catalogue those? Finally she slaps two blue stickers saying *VERIFICADO* on my bag and lets me go. I change some dollars into Dominican pesos at a grubby counter, stagger out into the blinding light and find a moderately decent-looking taxi.

We drive up a ramp where police are inspecting a battered van ("Smugglers", the wizened cabdriver tells me knowingly), and wait while a man opens gates in the sagging, rusted chain-link fence to let us onto the highway. We join the traffic. My driver is friendly, and proud of Santo Domingo. He points out the Spanish fortifications, the enormous bridge over the river (one of three, he says) and then, as we get into the old town, Colombus's house – a Venetian-looking building across a wide stone plaza. He jerks a thumb over his shoulder. "That street," he tells me, "was the first street built in the New World." If we're talking European building, he's right: the Dominican Republic is half of the island of Hispaniola, the first Caribbean island discovered by white men, and Santo Domingo was its first settlement. This is where the whole glittering, blood-soaked story began.

We bounce along the pot-holed street behind a rubber-tyred cart heaped high with green bananas and pulled by a skin-and-bone horse harnessed with knotted rope. Two men in shorts balance on the cart's edges, swinging their legs. When the street widens we overtake slowly. The horse wears blinkers, eight-inch squares of cardboard torn from a box. One has the word *Kellogg's* on it.

My guesthouse is in Isabel la Católica, a block away from the oldest street. We pull up in front of an iron grille – the characteristic *reja* of Spanish houses, covering the street door. My own name jumps out at me: there's a big card on the *reja* saying, in blue, "Grevel – Welcome, entrance in plaza", with an arrow underneath. I pay the driver, heave my pack out of the trunk and haul it round the corner of the building into a small shady square.

There's an open door on the right. I peer in, my eyes adjusting to the dim light. A woman's voice from somewhere in the depths calls, "Grevel! Welcome!" I step inside and find I'm in a treasure-house, a mass of colour and variety crowded with paintings, sculptures, furniture. In a carved chair opposite the door sits a lady with golden hair and huge glasses. She looks exactly like Angela Lansbury. She gets up, book in hand, and comes to greet me.

"Well how *are* you? And how was your trip?" She has a delightful Southern drawl. This is Bettye. She's hospitality personified, and I notice she's reading *David Copperfield*. "I just *love* Dickens," she tells me, waving it about. "I've read it before but I just had to read it again. And before that I was reading *Moll Flanders* by Daniel Defoe. Well, I come from Tennessee, and that's where she ended up. I could be a descendant. Sometimes I tell people I'm Moll Flanders's daughter – and you know? I think a few of them really believe me!"

I'm dazzled by Bettye, and by the abundance of our surroundings. The ancient, whitewashed room is crammed with brilliantly-coloured naïve paintings of landscapes, forests and flowers; there are icons, and sheet-metal sculptures delicate as paper-cuts; there are small tables covered with ornate little boxes, jewellery and carved animals. There are rugs and banners and textiles. There's furniture everywhere, and display cases between the furniture. We just about have room to stand amidst it all. Bettye, it seems, runs a gallery as well as a guesthouse. Most of the art, she says, comes from Haiti – the other half of the island. But there's a fair sprinkling of Dominican art and antiques too.

Bettye tells me I can choose between two rooms: one upstairs over the gallery, and one opening directly off the street. I take a look at both and opt for the one on the street. I'll be able to come and go as I like, and the furnishings are as rich and *outré* as the gallery's.

"I *knew* you'd choose this one," says Bettye with satisfaction. She shows me how to secure myself ("My dear, this place is *perfectly* safe as long as you are *sensible*"). Gong in or coming out, I must lock my door – a thick black oak slab – and close the *reja* over it. There are two bolts, one on the inside of the *reja* and one on the outside. I must make sure both are shut. If I'm going out, I must also padlock the outer bolt. We stand in the blinding light of the noontide street, going over the whole procedure, and I'm entrusted with a bunch of brass keys. Interested locals watch from a distance, leaning on walls or sitting on the pavement. Then Bettye goes back around the corner to mind her gallery. With much clattering of locks and slamming of bolts I shut myself into my cool, dark room, switch on the electric fan and fall thankfully onto the bed.

I'm tired, but I don't sleep. Instead I lie there, taking in the weird, battered opulence of my surroundings. The huge black door has small wooden shutters that can be opened to peer out onto the street. The room is full of *things*. There are two beds, and two ornate carved and gilded wooden chairs with worn, stained embroidered panels. There are four mirrors, two framed in old gilt and two with painted surrounds showing rainforest plants and birds. The mirrors are randomly placed around the walls, but each reflects at least one of the others, so the effect is disconcerting: wherever I look, further spaces seem to open at the edge of my vision. On one wall is a panel of sheet-iron fretwork, delicate as lace, depicting an enormous fish. Over the bed hangs an icon of the Virgin and Child in seventeenth-century dress: she wears a vast embroidered crinoline and lace cuffs. Opposite are two rainforest paintings and an icon showing a dandyish angel in long-skirted coat, lace collar, and plumed tricorn hat. Enormous feathered wings sprout from his shoulders and he holds a slender, elegant musket.

Looking upwards I gaze at a wooden ceiling supported on five immense, square-sectioned beams, black and lustrous as treacle toffee. A dusty chandelier hangs from a brass chain, its electric candles spreading a yellow light; next to it a brown electric fan rotates and wobbles.

A shower cubicle is squeezed into one corner of the room. In other corners are other bits and pieces – a small chest of drawers, a dusty coffee-maker, an ancient air-conditioning unit, a battered plastic water-cooler, a floor-standing fan, a lamp with a tarnished bronze pedestal moulded with cherubs. And right alongside the bed is the *pièce de résistance*: a wonderful screen of hinged sheet-iron panels, cut into intricate patterns. The first panel shows a little man, a strange quizzical look in his eye, marching through a forest. He wears a wide-brimmed hat, and carries a little hatchet over his shoulder. The next panel has a beautiful woman with long braids twirling around her head; she's surrounded by creatures: fish, a scorpion, and something like a chicken with a human head. The other panels show a lady who seems to be half peahen; and two figures – Adam and Eve? – under a tree, Eve kissing the serpent while Adam looks on, puzzled and anxious.

The effect of the room is overwhelming, even exhausting. In fact – I know I'm tired – it seems busy, positively *crowded*. It's as if the place is packed with people I can't quite see. I suspect Ernesto would say it was full of spirits. I lie on the bed and feel the place seething around me. After a while I decide to read. I open Borges's *Ficciones*…

I'm standing outside in the sunlit street, looking at the iron grille that leads to my room. Two women are bending down, heaping flowers on the doorstep. The flowers look like gladioli, but then I see they're red tropical blooms with long stems. They're piling the flowers outside the door because a powerful sorcerer, a *brujo*, once lived there. Someone is moving about upstairs. In the room over mine, two women are pulling the furniture back, making space for some kind of meeting or assembly that's to take place there.

I snap awake. I've lost the thread of the Borges. I get under the covers and try to sleep properly but I can't, so I take a shower and stroll round the corner to see Bettye again.

"Amazing room," I say. "So many wonderful things in it. Especially that metal screen. Fantastic."

"Isn't the screen wonderful?" says Bettye. "It's from Haiti. Those figures on it are Vodoun gods. Now, I don't know who they all are, but I *do* know that little man on the first panel, with the axe on his shoulder, is Legba, the god of the roads."

I should have guessed. It's my old friend Eleggua under his Haitian name. I thought I'd left him behind in Cuba, but here he is, right beside my bed. No wonder there's that cheeky look in his eye.

Realizing I'm hungry, I go out onto the blazing pavement. I evade the cluster of shoeshine boys in the plaza (I doubt they could do much good to my battered trainers) and pass a small bar with salsa music blaring from disproportionately large speakers. I turn the corner into the Conde, a wide space facing the Cathedral and filled with enormous, shady, deep-green trees, where I sit at a pavement café and watch the passers-by. The people here look more African, less Latin than in Puerto Rico. They carry things on their heads a lot. A small boy trots past topped with a sagging tower of bundled newspapers. Then it's a girl strolling along crowned with an enamel bowl full of waffles and bananas. When the waiter arrives I order a steak and the local beer, Presidente. Most of the other customers seem to be Spanish tourists; the man at the next table is absorbed in reading *The Power of Silence* by Carlos Castaneda, in Spanish. His copy is full of pencilled notes and blocks of text highlighted in yellow.

My guidebook recommends a club called Nowhere just a few streets away. Bettye confirms this: "I had two girls here last week from the Czech Republic. They went there *every* night and had a wonderful time. From what they told me, that place doesn't even *open* until sensible people like you and me are asleep in bed."

Determined not to be sensible, I sleep until around 11 p.m. and wake feeling as if I've got lead weights on my wrists and ankles. Getting up to go clubbing doesn't seem an appealing idea as I roll over in bed, groaning, to meet the cynical gleam in Eleggua's eye. But I pull myself together, take a shower, and go out to look for Nowhere.

It isn't hard to find – I can hear the bass thudding several blocks away. There are cars outside and a gaggle of people hanging about in the street. I go up the stone steps. Inside, a group of slightly intimidating men around a table tell me it'll be 100 pesos, so I pay, then go down some steps into a roofed brick courtyard. It's like being at the bottom of a shaft packed solid with people. It's barely possible to move. The crowd is mixed in age, race and style but the majority look like tourists in their twenties. The air shakes with deafening, percussive rap music. I fight my way to the bar and after an immensely long wait I secure a Presidente, hand over a 500-peso note and await my change. The change doesn't appear, and I soon realize that while half the people jammed around the bar are waiting for drinks, the other half are waiting for their change. Every time I catch the barman's eye he holds a hand up, fingers spread – "five minutes". A woman beside the till at the back is cashing up. We wait and wait, and the barman goes on serving, while she laboriously sorts notes into bundles, spikes receipts on a wire, consults a calculator. When the long-awaited distribution eventually begins, the barman has to ask me how many drinks I had and what I gave him.

"*¡Una!*" I yell. "*¡Quinientos!*" I get my money and turn my attention to the stage, where four or five black guys are rapping in Spanish to a backing track. The lead rapper is an enormous man in baggy red cut-off pants, a red-and-white windbreaker and puffy red-and-white trainers – the largest I've ever seen. They make my size 12s look like doll's shoes. He has a red baseball cap wedged on his head sideways. People jig about a bit and laugh, but no one is really dancing.

The sound comes and goes patchily, and after a couple of numbers the chief rapper says, in English, "We have some problems with the microphone so I want all the white people to come to the front." This puzzling *non sequitur* makes me a little uncomfortable. I stay where I am and so does everyone else. The rappers begin another number. After a while the chief rapper switches from Spanish to English and starts chanting, "I want a white woman up on stage. I want a white woman up on stage." Nobody volunteers.

Suddenly a white guy with long black hair and a vast, wavy, glossy black beard, who's standing near the front and who certainly has more guts than I have, grabs the microphone out of the rapper's hand. He shouts into it, "Look, man, we just want to fucking *dance!*"

The audience responds with a roar of support, and to my astonishment the rap artist simply caves in. He and his companions walk meekly offstage and the DJ puts on a reggae track. People sway about a bit – but still no one really dances. Next come some house and a bit of reggaeton but it's clear there won't be any salsa, and looking around I can see that this simply isn't a salsa audience. (Not that the crush would allow much salsa, even if the music did.) I finish my drink and go. Other people are streaming out too. Nowhere's evening doesn't seem to have been a success.

I drift up the steeply sloping cobbled street to XXO, another club warmly recommended by my guidebook. It's closed. So I stroll downhill again and out onto the vast plaza in front of Columbus's house. The wide expanse of moonlit flagstones is dotted with strange little mounds like molehills. Curious, I approach one. It's a small feral dog curled neatly into a furry circle, nose to tail, peacefully sleeping. The whole plaza is dotted with little curled-up dogs.

Beyond one corner and down a side-street I find Atarazana, which is supposed to be another good venue for live music. A dark, crowded, red-lit bar, it's almost as full as Nowhere, and the music is little different. Rap and reggaeton predominate. Most of the people look like locals, though there are some tourists too. Apart from a few Dominicans chatting up visiting girls, the two groups are pretty distinct; the tourists drink hard, while the Dominicans laugh a lot and push each other about. Occasionally a Dominican couple will dance to reggaeton for a minute or two. The dancing involves merely the man's standing behind the girl and synchronizing hip movements with her, so that they rotate pelvises together. The onlookers seem to regard this as a joke, laughing and clapping briefly before everyone loses interest. In truth, no one's making any real effort to dance here, either. I get a drink and go out to the courtyard at the back, where I can look up at the half-moon sailing – oddly on its back – in a clear sky. Then I watch the crowd again. Salsa here is unthinkable.

I finish my drink and drift out into the street. The other tourists are leaving too. A group of young women hurries past, heels clattering on the cobbles, one complaining bitterly in a strong Irish accent, "It's me last night on the island, and she goes and spoils it for me…"

I walk up to Isabel la Católica, ignoring voices from the taxi rank ("Nightclub, sir, very beautiful lady, check it out…") and passing a car-park guarded by a uniformed man holding a pump-action shotgun. Reaching my door, I'm about to start unbolting the iron *reja* when I hear a repeated glassy, clashing noise. Across the street a thin, bent woman is struggling to drag a supermarket trolley down the edge of the kerb. I go to help her. The trolley is completely full of empty bottles and cans. It weighs a ton. I haul it down the kerb, across the street and up the other side. She takes it from me, muttering weirdly, and goes on her way, dragging the rattling, clashing thing behind her. It's the recycling "system" I heard about in Panama. Bottles and cans are worth money, so vagrants trawl through the garbage at night and take them to sell. I hope she gets a good price. She's earned it.

✳

Over fried egg, toast, coffee and pineapple next morning, surrounded by carved tables and rainbow-coloured paintings, I ask Bettye how she comes to be living in Santo Domingo.

"I left a stressful job and a stressful marriage," she tells me. "I'd worked here for four years under the umbrella of the United Nations and liked it, so I came back. And now I've been here thirty years."

The phone rings from the other room and Bettye hurries to answer it. When she returns, an old man with a lined face, baggy trousers and a torn shirt is hanging about outside the door. After talking to him she comes back inside, sighing as she sits down.

"There are a lot of crazy people around here," she says, "but it's hard to tell how crazy they really are. There was this hard-rock alcoholic who used to come around; he used to do odd jobs and he was a nice man, only *ev-er-y* time he got money he'd spend it on drink. He'd drink himself insensible. I was certain he'd never stop. But then this crazy woman used to come around here too. She used to scream and shout – I had one visitor here and she terrified him, he said she pulled up her skirt to show him this scar on her stomach… Well, she used to sleep outside here sometimes and the police used to pick her up. And one night she just disappeared. She was never seen again. The gossip on the street was, the police had injected her. Given her a lethal injection, that's what people said. And this guy, this hard-rock alcoholic I told you about, he gave up drinking. Just like that! He said 'That could happen to me one night, they could find me lying in the bushes and inject me.' And he's never drunk since."

After breakfast I search Bettye's *Yellow Pages* for a dance teacher in Santo Domingo. Besides any local salsa style that may exist, it would be an opportunity for me to learn more about bachata and merengue, which are said to be popular. Santo Domingo has produced several leading salsa bands, so there must surely be salsa teachers. But I find nothing apart from a couple of ballet schools. An internet search is no more fruitful. I do, however, have an email from Mauricio in Bogotá:

Appreciated Grevel, I wish to know how is your marvellous and enigmatical life. I remember you now, reading your poems, and the magic of poetry summons mischievous little deities who cross the diaphanous air of the distance and reveal to me the meaning of the word FRIEND.

It sounds much better in Spanish, a language where poets actually write poetically. An English friend might just have written, "How's it going?" The thought that my life is marvellous and enigmatical consoles me for the frustration of not finding anyone to initiate me into local dance styles. I wish Mauricio were here now. I don't suppose he could find me a dance teacher, but it would be great to talk.

Since he isn't, I go for a walk along the Malecón. A narrow winding street takes me from the old town down to the sea wall and the highway alongside it. The Malecón here is smarter and duller than its namesake in Havana. The seafront is pleasantly lined with palms, and I can see the ocean rolling in, breaking on grey boulders just beyond the road. But the highway is a fuming, hooting inferno of nose-to-tail traffic, and the landward side of the road is lined with spotlessly clean, gargantuan, hideous hotels: ghastly fantasias of white concrete, gilded metal and black glass, with doormen in plum-coloured uniforms and peaked caps. Each hotel displays an enormous neon sign advertising its casino.

After walking past two miles of this ostentatious architectural rubbish I decide to return a different way, and go inland one block. Behind the hotels it's a familiar scene: little battered houses in stained pastel colours, only marginally less decrepit than those in Havana; pavements of fissured concrete; gutters broad as ditches, full of stagnant greenish water; makeshift stalls of bamboo and plastic sheet selling Coca-Cola or bananas. The buildings are festooned with electric cables so that everywhere I look the sky is criss-crossed with black lines.

By the time I've threaded my way back into the heart of the old town, I'm exhausted and soaked with sweat. I unlock my room and plunge into the comforting darkness, fumbling to slam the various locks and bolts into place behind me. I rest, take a shower, and go up to the Conde to eat a steak. (I seem to be living on steak these days.) Then I walk along to the Banco Santander to change some money. The bank is cool and palatial. I stand in a long queue beside a sign: *It is forbidden to enter with firearms, dark glasses, hats, caps, protective helmets etc.*

I take the money back to my room, sleep for a few hours and wonder what to do next. The clubs won't be open for a long time. Turning the pages of the newspaper an old man talked me into buying at the café, I see that today is a cockfighting day at the grandly-named Coliseo Gallístico Alberto Bonetti Burgos. Having heard that cockfighting is the national sport of the Dominican Republic, I'm curious about it – the more so because it was the main plebeian sport of England in Byron's day, the period I used to teach when I was a literature professor. I'm slightly nervous: I haven't watched blood sports before, and I have no idea what you do at a cockpit. But I go out and find a taxi driver who's willing to plough through the afternoon rush-hour to the Coliseo, on the far side of the city.

After an hour or so contending with the traffic, we pull into the car-park of a building that looks like a concrete flying saucer on stilts. The driver tells me he'll stay in the car-park; with this traffic it's simply not worth his leaving and coming back in two hours.

The entrance is like a cinema's. I join a small queue and ask the darkly beautiful girl behind the ticket window for one of the cheapest seats, which I reckon will give me a glimpse of what typical Dominicans might see and do. I can hear muffled sounds of crowing from somewhere in the background. I go up two short flights of concrete steps and find myself in a kind of circular miniature theatre. In the middle is an arena of bright green Astroturf about six yards across, with a white upholstered barrier around it, ringed by six steep tiers of red tip-up seats. A girl in a blue uniform directs me to my seat. Evidently the two front rows are the expensive ones. I'm not sorry to be a bit further away from the action. The place isn't full, but people are dotted around on all sides and it's filling up. There's a small bar opposite with a Budweiser sign, and girls are delivering beer to customers around the tiers of seats. The spectators seem to be of all types – mostly men alone or in groups, but others who are treating it as a family outing: there are several couples with small children, and two plump women on the tier behind me bounce a baby on their knees and share a milkshake in a plastic cup.

Odd pieces of apparatus hang over the cockpit. There's a clock, and a pair of perforated Perspex boxes on a sort of pulley. Two teenage boys are busy polishing the Perspex with rags. After half an hour or so, when the place is fairly full, we all stand up for the national anthem. An MC welcomes us with a series of elaborate rhetorical announcements, and then the proceedings begin. Two more Perspex boxes come gliding across the ceiling on wire, like miniature cable cars, each with a cockerel inside; one of them crows tentatively. The boxes are lowered into the arena, where the boys take the birds out and pop them into the first pair of boxes, which I now see are in fact a set of scales. Once weighed, the cocks are taken out by two men who proceed to show them to each other, each flourishing a rooster almost within striking distance of its opponent, whisking it around like an elaborately plumed fan. Each bird is then dropped onto the Astroturf and allowed to lunge at its rival – but pulled back at the last moment by a tail feather so it doesn't make contact.

The purpose of all this is evidently to work the birds up into a frenzy before they start fighting. It certainly has that effect on the audience. From the instant the birds are out of the weighing boxes, it's pandemonium: men all around the ring are shouting at their neighbours, jabbing fingers in the air, yelling or signalling to others across the ring. It's like the floor of the Stock Exchange. Everyone is placing bets. Someone taps me on the shoulder and I turn to find a man behind me waving a five-dollar bill in my face, wanting me to accept a bet. I wave him away (frankly, I haven't a clue what's going on) and he latches onto someone else. The clamour continues as the birds are released and fly at each other across the bright green Astroturf. They leap and tumble together a few times, then settle down to pecking each other's heads. The clamour from the spectators continues. After five minutes or so of head-pecking, one of the cocks is weakening, and it soon lies down. The other cock stands on it, still pecking. A buzzer sounds and two men carry the cocks off. They both still seem to be alive. The two boys run in, carrying buckets of white cleaning fluid and scrubbing brushes, and get to work briskly scrubbing the traces of blood off the Astroturf. There's a faint syrupy smell in the air, which takes me back to my grandfather's poultry shop in the old Liverpool market. It must be chicken blood.

By now another pair of birds is riding in overhead and being lowered into the arena. The whole procedure is repeated. By the time I've seen it half a dozen times I'm utterly bored with watching poultry pecking each other's heads. It's clear that the whole interest of the sport lies in the betting. Otherwise this has to be the most tedious sport ever devised. I've had enough. Surprisingly, not one of the losers I saw was dead when taken out. Are they killed and eaten? Do they live to fight again? As I leave, I notice a lad holding an injured bird in his hands, surrounded by a bunch of youths energetically debating. Perhaps they're arguing over whether it's worth saving.

On the way back, the driver asks me what I thought of the cockfight. "Interesting," I say. "No, actually – quite boring. Once is enough."

I'm wondering if I'll ever find any dancing in Santo Domingo. I've tried every club I can find; they're all full of house music, rap and tourists. But there's one other well-known club still on my agenda. I've been told it's worth going just for the venue, regardless of the music, so late in the evening I go to the usual taxi rank and ask for Guácara Taína.

We drive out to what looks like a suburban park: all I can see in the dark is a stretch of manicured grass by the roadside. I follow a path downhill to a small hut, where I buy a ticket and am directed down some concrete steps. Lit sporadically by electric bulbs, the steps go down alongside a rough, rocky cliff face, then turn and go steeply into the depths. Soon I am far underground, descending flight after flight of steps past walls of mottled, perforated, pinkish limestone. Then there's a sloping tunnel. Finally I come out into an enormous cavern with a vast, irregularly arched, rocky roof, from which hang clusters of stalactites like huge blobs of yellowish, melting wax. There are also lighting gantries up there, projecting disco lights downwards. The place is huge – and there are further depths ahead, beyond a floor covered with tables and chairs and a lower floor for dancing. The air is misty and cool, with a damp, slightly earthy smell. I remember someone saying this club was "in a bat cave". I didn't take much notice at the time, but now I understand what they meant, though I can't see any bats and the volume of the music must surely have jammed their radar by now.

There's a cluster of people on the dance floor so I go down (more steps) to take a look. They seem to be a group of friends, and although they're speaking Spanish I get the feeling they're tourists. The speakers are playing some very dull merengue and one or two couples are dancing, not well. I climb through the tiers of seats up to the bar, come back down with a Presidente and hang about on the edge of the floor until a salsa track comes on. Then I ask a young woman close by if she'd like to dance. She smiles and shakes her head, indicating a nearby man – her boyfriend, I suppose. Clearly I'm wasting my time here. The cavern has been worth seeing but there's no reason to stay. I finish my Presidente and climb the stairs. A couple of taxis are waiting by the grass verge and I take one into town. The taxi radio plays great salsa all the way back.

Walking the last block to my room I hear salsa music yet again. It's coming from the tiny bar across the street, with its long counter, stools, and bleak, bluish strip lighting. As I get my keys out, I see an elderly couple dancing on the pavement among the plastic chairs. He wears a blue mechanic's overall, she a red top and black skirt. They dance Cuban-style with a couple of nifty moves. When the music ends, the woman flings herself against the man; they kiss, and stay balanced in a long embrace.

The following morning, before it gets too hot, I stroll around the old town. Taking a turning I haven't noticed before, I find myself in a small garden behind railings between the end walls of two churches. At one side of the garden is a stone plinth with a green bronze bust, a tranquil-faced lady with her hair in a bun. I wander over. A young European is photographing the bust with a high-tech camera. When he pauses, I greet him: "*Buenos dias*." He replies in kind, and I ask if he knows who the lady is.

"No," he says. I ask if he speaks English; he does, and we chat a little. "I'm from Switzerland," he tells me, "but I spend a lot of time here."

An inspiration strikes me. "Do you know where the people around here go to dance?"

"What kind of dancing are you looking for?"

"Well, ideally salsa, but anything really. The discos all seem to be full of tourists, and nobody dances."

He ponders. "Mmm, salsa? You won't find much salsa. People listen to it a lot, but they don't know how to dance it, because when they were growing up it was all merengue and bachata. And you won't find much bachata because the middle classes disapprove of it; it's considered low and indecent. The discos in the city are all for tourists, really, and they're limited by the curfew these days. They have to close at midnight Sunday to Thursday, and 2 a.m. on Friday and Saturday. Anyway the discos are too expensive for most local people."

While we talk, a man in a smart cream suit and glasses – he looks like a businessman or a lawyer – strolls into the garden. He goes over to a corner and pees into the flowerbed; I can hear the splashing while we talk. Then he zips himself up and strolls away. I wonder if he's one of these middle-class people who disapprove of bachata.

The Swiss makes a wry face at the man's departing back. "No shame," he says. "But if you really want to dance," he continues, "what you need to do is go out to the suburbs and find a car wash. That's where people really dance."

I'm incredulous. "A *car wash*?"

"Yes. On Fridays and Saturdays the car washes turn into dance clubs. It's mostly merengue, but it's good merengue. It's a great evening out."

I thank him fervently, and a couple of minutes later we shake hands and go our separate ways. It looks as if my problem may just have been solved.

Back at Isabel la Católica I tell Bettye, "Okay. I need your help. I want to go dancing at the car wash tonight."

"The *car* wash?" Bettye has never heard of this either.

"Yes." I tell her what I've just heard.

"I'll try and find a driver who knows about this," she says doubtfully. "Amos is no good – he's not very bright and he's always reading his Bible. He might not know. Ramón is your man. He knows *all* about cockfighting so maybe he'll know about the car wash too. I'll give him a call."

Ten minutes later Bettye knocks on the door of my room. "Ramón knows all about it," she tells me in triumph. "He says he knows *exactly* where you need to go. He'll pick you up at ten tonight. Well … *I* never heard of this." She goes off, shaking her head.

At ten o'clock I go out into the street. It's Saturday, and everyone is doing something special, even if that means just relaxing in a plastic chair on the pavement with a cigarette and a beer. As usual, salsa is pounding from the bar across the street, but though they have plenty of customers, no one is dancing. I hear a car horn and a shout. A Mercedes taxi has pulled up opposite and the driver is waving at me. It's Ramón. I get into his large, comfortable car – he's evidently a very superior sort of taxi driver – and we set off, down to the river, over a vast suspension bridge and onto the Avenida San Vincente de Paul. As we power along through the night-time traffic my head is full of memories of the '70s disco movie *Car Wash* and its theme song…

How do you dance in a car wash, I wonder. Do people dance inside those things with the revolving brushes? I can't imagine it.

Ramón is a round and genial man. He enjoys telling me about the local customs. "Saturday night," he tells me, "people either go to the car wash, or dance at the cheap cafeterias." He indicates a grubby white single-storey concrete building, lit by the usual pallid neon tubes, in the strip-mall development by the roadside. It's swarming with people, inside and out. There are plastic tables and cars all over the pavement.

We cruise for another ten minutes, then pull in and park in a sort of lay-by. We walk a few yards up the road, alongside a high chain-link fence, to an entrance with a broad metal barrier. Overhead is a sign in big pink capitals: CANDY CAR WASH. We go into a concrete forecourt that's been transformed into an open-air café by being filled with plastic tables and chairs. Most of the tables – there must be getting on for a hundred – are already taken, but we find one and sit down. A waitress in bulging, skin-tight jeans wanders around taking orders. I order a couple of Presidentes.

Looking around, I can see that my fantasy of people dancing around the machinery of a drive-through car wash was completely wrong. It's a manual car wash, and what's being used is the space. The tables extend to the sides, even under striped canopies labelled "*Area de aspiradoras*" and "*Area de limpiando a presión*" – the places for vacuuming and pressure-hose cleaning. In front of us there's a bar on a tiled platform, under an awning edged with bright green palm fronds, and bunches of balloons in the trademark red and green of Presidente beer. At the sides of the platform are two large speakers, and instruments are propped up at the back.

Our beers arrive. A beer here costs half what I paid in the discos – and there's no cover charge. Ramón explains that in the Dominican Republic, every car wash has a bar, "so the driver can have a beer while his car's being cleaned".

"And then they drive?" I ask.

"Well, they have only one or two," says Ramón.

Come to think of it, he and I are having a beer right now and the night is young. Relaxing, I look around again. We are out in the open, under the moon and stars. The tables around us are full of people of all ages: groups, couples, a few children. Styles range from the elegant (long dresses, smart collared shirts) to the utterly casual (tight shorts, T-shirts and flip-flops); physiques from the tall, svelte and willowy to the bulging and frankly blobby.

A DJ behind the bar puts on a bachata track and a few couples go up onto the tiled platform to dance. I watch some very elegant bachata – in particular from a wonderfully slender black couple, the man dancing with stylish restraint, pointing his toes, making small, neat, accurate movements, and the woman tall and slim, her skin-tight white trousers stretched over a bottom that wiggles with incredible agility and rhythmic precision.

After a couple more tracks, which draw only a few dancers, the MC announces the band. The musicians step forward. The bandleader is a big man in a yellow shirt with a glitzy red button accordion strapped on his chest. There's a bass guitarist, a tenor saxophonist and three percussion players – one on congas, one on *guayo* (that thing that looks like a cylindrical cheese-grater, scraped with a stick), and the third taking his seat in the usual white plastic chair with a big, corded black-and-yellow drum across his knees. They launch into a merengue number, and instantly couples hurriedly thread their way between the tables and flood onto the platform. The music is loud, punchy and exciting. Merengue is a very limited form musically – just a fast, staccato, four-four rhythm, usually on three chords – but this saxophonist enlivens it with jazzy solos, and the accordionist sings with a rich, grainy voice and a good sense of timing.

I begin to feel like dancing. After a few more numbers and a couple of drinks I feel restless and confident enough, with a little encouragement from Ramón, to go over to a couple of women sitting together near the platform and ask one of them to dance. She agrees, and we go up onto the platform. Happily I had the foresight to take a lesson in merengue before leaving England, and since it's about the simplest dance ever invented, I can manage. To dance merengue, you simply hold your partner and walk briskly in time to the music: one-two-three-four, left-right-left-right… You can walk forwards or backwards or around in a circle, it doesn't matter. My plump lady partner, in a capacious skirt and brown blouse matching her friendly, round brown face, smiles away and seems perfectly happy to go backwards and forwards and round and round with me: left-right-left-right…

I've also been taught that you can do pretty well any salsa move in merengue; you just walk through it, taking as much time as you like. However, I soon find that I can't lead my partner into any of the fancy moves I learned at home. I can't even get her to do the famous "merengue arms", which people in England tell you is the typical merengue move. I can turn her clockwise, holding her right hand in my left, and that's all. Apart from that she's perfectly happy to go round and round, one-two-three-four, beaming at me and pressing her good-size bosom against my shirt, until the song ends. And I see hardly anyone else doing fancy moves either. A very few young and well-dressed people do some very fast salsa-type moves, but most people just do the occasional little turn, and you can see from their faces that they feel pretty cool when they do it. Simplicity rules.

And that suits me fine. Taking my partner back to her table, I ask her friend for the next dance but she says no. Undeterred, I invite a sizeable lady at the next table. She gets up readily, displaying a midriff that spills spectacularly from her bulging jeans, and away we go. The percussion gets really loud – and sets off the alarms in the cars parked outside, so the music is joined by a chorus of beeps, buzzes and wails. It's rather fun steering this bountiful body around, and though I can see people are amused by the two of us I don't care. From that point, in fact, I don't look back. Ramón is now dancing too, so together we find pairs of pretty girls and take one each up to dance. We look around for older ladies whose friends or husbands are up on stage dancing, and we take care of them. I notice that merengue, unlike salsa, can be danced perfectly well in flip-flops. The music never varies much, though at times the band gets into passages of extreme syncopation, so it requires some care to keep in time. It's all so simple and so much fun that I'm amazed when the band plays its final number and Ramón tells me it's two-thirty – time to go home. The car wash has been a great discovery.

Ramón's driving seems as steady as ever on the way back, and I've had such a good time that I take it pretty well when he announces the not inconsiderable amount I owe him for his evening's work. After all, fair's fair: I've kept him dancing and drinking for hours when he could have been earning. And his Mercedes *was* very comfortable. Damned if I'm adding a tip, though.

CHAPTER EIGHT
✳ROBOT BALLET

And so, finally, I'm on the plane to the USA. Again I affirm on the green form that I'm not a drug abuser or a Nazi war criminal, while over the PA the steward, relishing his role as airborne Master of Ceremonies, invites us to "Loosen your ties please, put your feet up on the furniture, and enjoy a beautiful flight to Miami, Florida."

I feel oddly apprehensive. After so long in Latin countries I don't really want to go back into Anglophone culture. I feel as if I'm about to lose some sort of security blanket. Maybe I've developed a different persona in Spanish and feel I'll be exposed once I'm speaking English again. But the flight is short and comfortable, the staff at Miami International Airport are friendly, and most of the people around me are speaking Spanish, so the transition isn't in any way harsh.

Outside the airport I get into a taxi and give the name of my hotel, which is on South River Drive. I've chosen a small hotel near South West Eighth Street, the road known in Spanish as Calle Ocho, because I want to be near the Cuban quarter, Little Havana. We leave the airport by a series of complicated intersections – freeways looping around like concrete ribbons – and head across the city. Miami is flat and surprisingly green, with a good deal of open space and palm trees everywhere.

The driver's cellphone rings; he picks it up and talks, driving with one hand. I can't tell what language he's speaking – I wonder if it's thickly accented Cuban Spanish.

"Where are you from?" I ask when he's finished.

"Haiti," he says. So the language was French patois. I tell him I've got a Haitian painting in my luggage – something I fell for in Bettye's gallery. We chat a bit, driving past mile after mile of small square single-storey houses. Then I notice we're heading towards another airport, a private one. That seems odd, and when we reach a sign saying *Airport Traffic Only* it strikes the driver as odd too: he stops, turns around, and heads back up the road.

"Do you know the way?" I ask him.

"South River Drive, isn't it?"

"That's right."

"Yeah, I think I started off the wrong way; we're going the right way now."

We head back into the city, come up with traffic, and crawl along a broad street lined with shops and office buildings. A sign says *NW Flagler St.* A river appears ahead of us, which gives me some hope. We drive alongside it for a while, stopping at a dusty dead end by a chain-link fence. The driver reverses and drives back the way we came, until we reach a T-junction. He stops, cranes his neck out of the window, and points delightedly at a sign. He reads aloud, "North River Drive."

"Yes," I say, "but we need *South* River Drive."

"Ah yeah, South River Drive." We start off again.

After another forty-five minutes in the traffic, we're back on North River Drive again. The driver points hopefully at the sign. "Yes," I say patiently, "this is North River Drive. But I want South River Drive. I think we should be on the other side of the river. Is there a bridge around here?"

The driver moves us off again slowly, muttering purposefully to himself like someone doing mental arithmetic. He gets on his phone again. While he cruises around I dig into my pack, which fortunately is on the seat behind me, and get out my map of Miami. I locate the river mouth, then North River Drive. Opposite, across the river, is South River Drive. Now I just need to find where we are. We pass a lot of numbered turnings but Miami is enormous, and the grid of many hundreds of streets on the map is giddying. It's like trying to read multicoloured graph paper. Eventually we spot a turning that leads onto a freeway crossing the river. Now I know where we are. I navigate, shouting "Turn left! Second right! Keep going!" until we reach a small, curving road alongside the river. South River Drive! And there's the hotel, a cluster of old green-and-cream clapboard houses shaded by trees. It's taken us more than two hours.

The driver looks sheepish. "How much do you want to pay me?" he asks humbly. I pay him probably too much.

I collect my key from the desk in one old house and lug my rucksack over to another. The buildings are carefully restored nineteenth-century cottages with chintzy fabrics, mahogany furniture and ceiling fans. My room seems positively decadent after the kind of places I've stayed in hitherto: it has a TV and an ensuite bathroom with a bath, not just a shower! The air-conditioning is cool – in fact rather too cold, but that can be adjusted in due course. I open one of the chintzy curtains and find, to my surprise, that there's a concrete expressway on stilts just yards from my window. It's weirdly like being back in Caracas. The difference is that here the double-glazing means I don't hear the traffic. I close the curtain again. I lie on the bed. I'm exhausted.

The air-conditioning comes on with a roaring sound every few minutes. It's freezing and I'm getting a headache. I hunt for the control. A remote? A wall switch? A knob somewhere? Nothing. It quietens down, then starts up again. I'll have to ask at reception. Meanwhile, I'll have the long-awaited luxury of a bath! I undress and go into the bathroom. I turn on a tap – and my head is immediately soaked. It's a mixer tap and it's set to supply the shower-head, not the bath. I pull up the little metal knob and start the taps again. But the minute I let go of the knob, the water goes back to the shower-head. After a few experiments I realize that the tap has been doctored to prevent it from supplying bathwater. The promised luxury of a bath was a mirage. Well, fair enough; I suppose water is a valuable commodity here. A pity their ecological awareness doesn't extend to the unstoppable air-conditioning. Accepting the inevitable, I take what feels like the millionth shower of my trip.

The hotel is close to Little Havana, the area populated by the thousands of Cuban exiles who have streamed over here, some legally and some illegally, some by air, some by ship and some – notoriously – braving the storms and sharks of the Miami straits on unseaworthy rafts and overloaded motorboats to escape the rigours of Castro's regime. It's too late to explore Little Havana today but I want to get at least a taste of it, so I leave the hotel to walk the four blocks to South West Eighth Street – Calle Ocho. It's still hot outside, the pale concrete pavements reflecting the blazing afternoon sunshine. I pass small concrete apartment blocks two storeys high, cross a street to a gas station and go inside to buy a paper. They have *El Nuevo Herald*, the Spanish-language local paper; I pick one up and join the queue.

The plump woman behind the counter is gossiping in Spanish with another customer.

A tall, stringy, dark young man queuing in front of me turns round. "Hey," he says in English, "You an inspector?"

"No," I say. I wonder what sort of inspector he has in mind. Tax? Gas-station safety? Illegal immigration? "I'm a visitor from England."

"Okay," he says as we reach the counter, "lemme show you something for Miami." He has a bottle of Budweiser in a small brown bag. "You get a bag like this" – he picks up another bag – "and you do this." He turns the second bag upside-down over the neck of the bottle, pushing until the neck tears through the paper. "Then you go out and you get drunk all day, because there's nothing else to do. No jobs in Miami. You got jobs in London?"

"Maybe a few," I say. "It's not so bad there right now."

Having paid, he turns back: "Okay, you have a nice day now."

I reach the till. "He paid for your paper," the lady tells me.

"Present from Miami," says the man as he goes out.

I take my paper and turn the corner into Calle Ocho, a wide street with a lot of traffic, lined with low concrete buildings. Havana it ain't. But it's interesting none the less. There are delicatessens, wine stores, copy shops, cigar shops, with all the signs in Spanish. It gives me a certain sense of security: it's a bit more like what I've become used to. I pass a shop with speakers out on the street playing salsa. Wondering if it's a café or a club, I peer inside. It's a hairdresser's. There's a woman in the chair and the hairdresser is dancing salsa around her. Whether he's doing her hair at the same time I can't tell.

I want to eat something, so I look for a restaurant – preferably one that isn't mainly a pâtisserie: I've already passed a lot of shops that specialize in sickly Cuban cakes, top-heavy with sweets and coloured icing. Eventually I find a Cuban diner advertising *pollo asado* and other good things, very cheap. I hoist myself onto a padded stool at the counter, getting curious looks from the ladies behind it – who look like mother and daughter – and the only other customers, an elderly man in overalls and a fat man in jeans eating beef stew. I guess *gringos* don't frequent these places. Anyway I soldier on, greeting the young lady in Spanish when she turns to me and ordering roast chicken with rice and beans, and a Corona.

Salsa music is playing in the background. When it stops I see that it's been coming from a juke-box on the wall. I haven't seen a functioning juke-box in years, so I decide to use it. It takes me a while to work out how, until I realize that it takes dollar bills, not coins. I feed one in and press the buttons to swing the old CD covers across in search of something good. There's a lot of unfamiliar stuff, but I find "El Cantante" by Hector Lavoe and "Monton de Estrellas" by Polo Montañez and select them. I go back to my stool and start in on my chicken again accompanied by the dramatic, haunting strings that open the Lavoe track.

The man next to me in the blue overalls, a brown, wrinkled veteran who I gather is a joiner, is telling the girl behind the counter about working on board a private boat at the marina. In the saloon, he says, they had a real Picasso, *so* big – he demonstrates something about a foot square. "*¡Vale millones! ¡Millones!*" He's wide-eyed, both awe and disapproval in his voice. "Worth millions!"

"Monton de Estrellas" comes on. The fat man beside me taps the *clave* on his beer-bottle with a spoon, then leaves when the song is over. His place is taken by a thin, younger man in jeans and a check shirt, who greets the women as friends. He nods to me, then we chat while he drinks his soup. He tells me he arrived here from Cuba just a few months ago; he's a musician but he can't get work. "The music's not so good here in Miami," he says. "Not like it is in Cuba." If I want salsa here, he says, the place to go is Café Mystique on 72nd Street.

I thank him; but already my attention is being drawn by the TV set up on the wall behind the counter. It's showing a place I recognize – in fact it's Caracas, and there are huge demonstrations. I can't follow the excited newscaster well enough to understand what's going on, but I hear the name Hugo Chávez. Maybe some of the discontent I noticed when I was there is starting to boil over.

Walking back to the hotel, I realize I'm here in Little Havana for the same reason as most of its long-term inhabitants: because I don't want to admit that I've left Latin America. At least here I'll have the luxury of watching TV in bed. Once I've made myself as comfortable as I can be with the howling air-conditioning, I switch on and start flipping through the channels. It's amazing how little there is to watch, actually. After checking out thirty-odd channels I've glimpsed a lot of people trying to sell things, a lot of sport and a lot of reruns of *Friends*. There are a few old movies. Finally I settle for a news channel. There's no mention of Caracas. Most of the news is about crime: crime as drama rather than reportage. Glamorous female presenters, wide-eyed and breathless with excitement, give minute-by-minute coverage of murders, bomb threats and hostage takings, with throbbing background music.

"More mind-boggling twists and turns in the Stacey Peterson case," exults a girl reporting on a murder case. "Religion and money – yes, money! – have now entered the story. Let's go *sterrraight* over to Keith Oppenheim, who's covering the case on the spot!" There's an interview with the poor man who found the suspect's second wife drowned in a bathtub. When he takes too long with his story, the interviewer cuts in briskly, "Get us to the body!"

In the morning I have breakfast under the trees beside the swimming pool and read the *Nuevo Herald*. There have been enormous demonstrations in Caracas. Led by the students, they're opposing changes Chávez wants to make to the constitution, changes that would let him remain President indefinitely. Photographs show the central avenues of Caracas filled to the horizon with hundreds of thousands of people. Music played its part too. At a recent summit meeting, King Juan Carlos of Spain challenged Chávez, "Why don't you shut up?" The students in Caracas played the King's words over loudspeakers, dubbed onto a reggaeton number. In Spanish, the question – *"¿Por qué no te callas?"* – fits the reggaeton rhythm perfectly. I wish I'd been there to hear it.

I decide to explore downtown Miami. The sun is scorching, but there's shade in the small park opposite the hotel, which has a view of the river where a little road bridge, surprisingly old-fashioned, lifts itself up with the melodious clanging of a bell every time a boat comes along. I walk towards downtown and find the Metromover, a light rail system that runs on elevated tracks around the centre of Miami. I hop onto a train; it runs without a driver like the DLR in London, and the views over the city are fabulous. I ride to Bayfront, then walk two blocks to the marina and waterfront shopping area. It's a good place to explore, even if you don't want to buy souvenir T-shirts or a dried baby alligator head. I climb to one of the upper decks and buy a beer, then sit in the sunshine looking at the amazing glitter of the turquoise water in the harbour, the multi-faceted, giant jewellery of innumerable glass-fronted skyscrapers catching the sunlight, and the state-of-the-art cruisers and private yachts moored at the quays with their streamlined prows, smoked glass and complicated satellite gear. Maybe it was on one of these that the Cuban joiner saw the Picasso.

Finishing my drink I stroll around the sunlit market. I find an information desk and ask the lady if there's somewhere I can use the internet. She gestures over my shoulder and says, "Pushcart." This seems odd, but I go in the direction indicated and find the pushcart: a kind of barrow with an awning and four computers, guarded by a young Latin-looking woman. I sit on a stool, check my email and write to Amanda – hurriedly, because at fifty cents a minute I don't feel inclined to worry about spelling. Then I head back to base.

The main thing on my mind has been the question of organizing some salsa lessons. Miami's famous dance school is Salsa Lovers and I'm looking forward to trying it. I imagine that, as in England and every other country I've visited, I can just turn up for a class and take it from there. But when I call the number, I find it doesn't work that way.

"Have you had lessons at Salsa Lovers before?"

"No. I'm visiting Miami and I'd like to take some lessons while I'm here."

"We have classes every evening, but before you can join a class we have to give you an assessment."

"Okay. Can I have an assessment this evening?"

"Uh… No, we don't have any places this evening."

"How about tomorrow?"

"No, we're fully booked tomorrow… In fact, we don't have any places for assessments until Monday."

"You don't have anything sooner? Maybe during the day?"

"No, we only do assessments in the evening. You could have an assessment at 5.30 on Monday and then go straight on to a class afterwards. The assessment only takes half an hour."

"All right, I'd better do that. Maybe you can book me in."

"The assessment costs eighteen dollars. What's your name, please?"

So I make the booking. I shan't be getting my lesson until shortly before I'm due to leave, but at least I'll have set foot inside Salsa Lovers. As I put the phone down the freezing air-conditioning comes on again.

I spend the late afternoon by the pool, reading and getting bitten by mosquitoes. The water is slightly greenish and despite the heat I'm not tempted to swim. Little brown birds, striped like tabby kittens, run about between my feet looking for crumbs. Towards sunset, when the insects get too bad, I go to reception and ask for the third time if they can turn down the air-conditioning in my room. Then I follow the paths between the trees over to my own building. Entering the strange little chintzy parlour, with its blinds, mahogany bookcases and pale green damask wallpaper, I'm struck that the place is oddly melancholy. There's something uneasy about the atmosphere, something restless and distracting. And although I'm the only person there, it doesn't actually seem empty. The odd thought strikes me that there are ghosts in the room. I wonder what's happened to me. I never used to have these thoughts, or these perceptions – if that's what they are. Is it the incessant travelling? Or is it possible that that initiation in Havana opened me to things I wouldn't previously have noticed? All I can do is shrug my shoulders and go upstairs. I turn on the TV and flip channels at random until something holds my interest. I'm startled by recognizing an aerial view of a city, and then a street leading to a waterfront jammed with glittering cruisers. Of course: I'm watching *CSI Miami*.

The tables out by the swimming pool are lively at breakfast the next morning. There's an art fair in Miami, and a team of art-movers – guys who've driven a van full of paintings all the way from New York

– are staying. They're young, lanky and long-haired and they wear interesting T-shirts with heavy-metal motifs on them. We introduce ourselves as we collect our orange juice, coffee and cinnamon cake from the unmanned self-service kitchen (the staff in this hotel are invisible: they do things when you're not looking and then leave). The art-movers, two of whom are called Dave, are really musicians, painters and writers; it's just that they have to move art to earn money. They know all about what's happening in Miami and they're excited about an event at the Wolfsonian Museum. It's a performance of *Ballet Mécanique*, a piece of Dadaist music composed in the 1920s by George Antheil for sixteen mechanical pianos, siren, electric bells, airplane propellers and various other bizarre "instruments". Naturally it isn't often performed. We agree that we really should go and hear this thing while it's on.

From Dada we get to talking about salsa. One of the Daves turns out, remarkably, to be a *tres* player as well as a guitarist. The *tres* is a Cuban instrument like a guitar but with its six strings grouped in three pairs tuned an octave apart – a bit like half of a twelve-string guitar. It has a wonderful silvery tone, and Cuban *tres* players improvise beautiful, intricate solos. "I just hope they never let all those musicians out of Cuba," says Dave wryly. "If they come to the States I'm gonna be out of a job. They play so much better than I do!"

Over coffee, as we fight off the mosquitoes, the other Dave asks me what I think of the hotel. "We were here last year," he adds, "and it doesn't look quite as well kept as it did, like maybe they've let it go downhill a bit."

"I don't know," I say. "There *is* something just a little… maybe depressing about it. In fact, last night when I came in I was thinking there's something *ghostly* about the place."

"Hey," says Dave, "I think you hit it. When we were here last year, we had this local taxi driver, you know? And he told us – we couldn't understand all of it because our Spanish isn't that great – but he told us, what the people around here say, this place is haunted. I guess you picked up on it too."

It's Friday night and I'm going to Hoy Como Ayer, a Cuban club on Calle Ocho. The club's name means "Today Like Yesterday", which surely says something about the Cuban exiles' feelings of nostalgia. I get the hotel reception to call me a cab. When it comes, the driver doesn't have good English so I try Spanish. He introduces himself as Juan Carlos and says he's from Venezuela. I ask what he thinks about Chávez and his referendum.

"Chávez is insane," says Juan Carlos. "My parents live in Caracas. Every day they go to the supermarket with money, and they come back with the same money. There's nothing to buy. No food, no milk." He reverts to English: "He's fucking the place up good."

He drops me outside Hoy Como Ayer and I join a small queue outside the door. When I get inside, a plump woman with long black hair, sitting behind a table, asks me, "Do you have a reservation?"

I'm thrown. You need a *reservation* to get in here?

"I'm sorry," says the woman, "we may not be able to fit you in. Let me go and check." She goes inside, returning to announce, "Yes! We can *just* squeeze you in by the bar!" I take a step forward. "The cover charge is forty-five dollars," she tells me, "*and* you have to buy at least two drinks."

Hey, we're definitely not in Latin America any more. That's nearly twenty-five pounds just to get inside. And a minimum number of drinks? Not that two drinks will be a problem. Well, I've come this far... I pay her and go in. The club is pretty dark inside. It's a single largish room, mostly full of tables. Down one side there's a long bar, where I perch on a stool and ask for a Corona. The tables are filling up rapidly, and the DJ is playing salsa. Everyone's speaking Spanish. A couple of the tables are taken by celebrating groups who sit around those cakes I've seen in the pastry shops, cakes the size of cartwheels piled with elaborate sculptures of coloured sugar icing.

Towards midnight a woman walks onto the small stage carrying an acoustic guitar. She settles herself on a stool, adjusts the microphone and sings a couple of songs. It's pleasant enough, nothing special, but the audience applauds wildly, as if they want to urge her on, or maybe convince themselves she's better than she is. While she's still acknowledging the applause, other musicians come on stage behind her and ready their instruments. She turns round, counts them in and they launch into a classic salsa number. They have a good, punchy style and the singer has a strong voice and plenty of energy. After playing some salsa they move on to other Latin styles. There's a lot of jazz and rock influence. The singer shouts, incites the players, gets the audience to clap with her.

It's a decent performance and I enjoy it. But it's a million miles away from real Cuban music. The percussion lacks that Afro-Caribbean, rhythmic dynamic that powers the best Cuban salsa. From the way audience members call out requests and what sound like jokes or personal messages, I guess this band is a regular fixture. However much energy the singer puts into it, there's a kind of mutual reassurance going on between artists and audience. No one's taking any risks. The feeling is confirmed towards the end, when everyone joins in to sing a couple of romantic-sounding ballads about Cuba. It's an exercise in nostalgia that doesn't connect with the Cuba that's there now.

After the band has played the two encores they were clearly expecting to play, the DJ puts some real Cuban tracks on; I recognize a favourite number by Adalberto Alvarez. That's interesting in itself: from what I've been told, a decade ago this club could have been fire-bombed for playing music by a band resident in Castro's Cuba. Things have changed a lot. I love Alvarez's music and I'm longing to dance, but there's no one to dance with. A few people are on their feet in close-knit groups, and two couples have managed to squeeze themselves alongside the tables with just enough room to dance, but there's no possibility of finding a partner. The music is so good I simply can't keep still, so I get up, walk about a little, and dance a few steps by myself. But the truth is that despite its reputation this isn't a dance club.

I leave at around 2.30 a.m. It's still hot. I decide to walk home along Calle Ocho and see what goes on around here at night. And I'm rewarded. A few blocks along, a bunch of black guys are playing drums on the pavement outside a café. People are dancing Cuban-style *rumba*, moving with the energy of the music, shaking their whole bodies, while a crowd watches and a police car, blue lights flashing, hovers in the background. After two minutes the drums stop and the police move everyone on, but it was worth seeing.

❋

The big news in the *Miami Herald* next morning is that Chávez has lost his referendum. He's lost it narrowly, but decisively enough to halt, for the moment, his plans to be President for life. I wonder which way my morose police officer voted.

The other lead story is that Mexican tomato-pickers have held a protest at the headquarters of Burger King. Burger King refuses to pay the pickers an extra cent for each pound of tomatoes they pick. The *Herald* reports that the workers get up at 4 a.m. and work ten hours a day. They pick two tons of tomatoes each, for which they get fifty-five dollars, a wage that hasn't changed since 1978. Taco Bell and Macdonald's have agreed to pay the extra cent but Burger King won't. The *Herald* mentions that the twelve top executives of the equity firm that owns Burger King shared $200 million in bonuses last year. I drove past Burger King's head office, a building bloated as a giant cheeseburger, yesterday. They look as if they could afford the extra cent.

I'm not feeling too good, though. The air-conditioning, or something, has given me a sore throat. I spend a lot of the day lying down.

By evening I feel better. I decide to follow the advice of that Cuban musician and go to Café Mystique. With the Hoy Como Ayer experience in mind, I call to see whether I need a reservation and how much it costs. This time, it seems, I can just walk in and the cover charge is minimal. I call a taxi.

The driver is Haitian and the drive is a long one (Café Mystique is miles away near the airport) so, between long phone discussions in patois, we have time to set the world to rights. The driver has heard about "Travis", as he calls him, losing his referendum. I say that when I was in Venezuela, a lot of people seemed not to like Chávez.

"Well, anyone wanna change things, they gonna be unpopular. Look at Kennedy, look at Martin Luther King now, look at Jesus. What happen to 'em all? They try to change things, people don't like it. See, same thing with Travis."

"I think Chávez wanted to change things so he could be President for ever."

"For ever? Listen, Papa! No one gonna be President for ever." He makes a sharp right and we hurtle up a ramp onto the Dolphin Expressway, cruising along with a magnificent view over the twilit city, glass towers and neon signs glittering under the stars in a deep turquoise sky. "You hearda President Duvalier in my country? He thought he gonna be President for ever too, and where's he now? You tell me, where's he now? Travis, he go the same way in the end, like we all do.

"And another thing, Papa, when you vote for someone to be President, you know what you voting for? You voting for one thing, for that man and his family to be rich. Only thing I know is, whoever gets to be President, I'm gonna be driving a cab. I drove a cab under Carter, I drove a cab under the other George Bush, I drove a cab under Clinton, I drove a cab under this George Bush, and whoever's next, I'll still be driving a cab." He points out into the city panorama unfolding beneath us, indicating an enormous concrete rampart. "See that?"

"Yeah, what is it?"

"That's the Orange Bowl, you hearda the Orange Bowl?"

"Yes, it's the big stadium. Football? Baseball?"

"That's right. Well you take a good look, Papa, 'cause in January they gonna throw him down. You tell everybody you seen him, 'cause they gonna throw him down. Thing is here, they don't got no landmark, see? In Europe, in the Caribbean, they got landmark! 1790! 1850! But here, they don't care, they got no landmark. And you know why?"

"You tell me why."

"It's because they don't *know* nothing, see. I'm not saying they dumb, 'cause they ain't. But they don't *know* nothing."

So I take a good look at the Orange Bowl. Seems a pity they're throwing him down. But then they did the same to Wembley Stadium, didn't they? It doesn't only happen in Florida.

We pull up in the Café Mystique car-park. The club is round the side of a drab-looking, concrete airport hotel. There's a group of stocky men in suits around the door, speaking Spanish. I feel a bit nervous, but they take my money without demur and direct me inside. The club is large, cool and softly lit, with a big circular bar, and tables at one side. There's a good-size dance floor. There are a few people at the bar and the tables but it's early, so I get a drink and wait. Gradually the place fills up. All age groups are represented, from teenagers up to couples who could be their grandparents, and everyone is speaking Spanish. Again I'm at a gathering-place of the *émigré* community.

The DJ has been playing salsa and merengue tracks from the time I came in, but now a few couples actually step onto the floor and dance. It still feels quite early so I don't try to find a partner, just make myself comfortable near the bar and watch. The couples mostly dance a fairly straightforward Cuban style without many fancy moves. They often seem to begin on the *five*, halfway through the *clave*. The music changes to reggaeton, and by midnight, when people really start flooding in, no more salsa is being played. At 12.30, musicians appear on the small stage behind the dance floor and begin tuning up. The DJ fades his music, an MC makes a long, intense announcement in Spanish, and the twelve-piece, Cuban-style band begins. There are three percussionists, and a proper brass section of two trumpets and a trombone, as well as a baritone sax (unusual), with keyboards, bass guitar, a vocalist and three backing singers. The playing is tight and professional, and they play from scores. Most of the music is familiar: they're playing standards – but they play them forcefully and well. Some people dance, though the floor is right in front of the stage where the sound is very intense; most just stand and listen, singing along at times.

The band finishes and the DJ resumes. I decide it's time to dance. Everyone seems to be in groups. Noticing a pair of friendly-looking middle-aged women at a nearby table, I go over and ask one of them if she'd like to dance. She smiles and shakes her head. No. Nor her companion? "*No, gracias.*" Oh, well. I wait a little, and when the next salsa number begins I go over to another pair. This time a blonde woman, probably in her forties, agrees to dance, with much smiling and laughing to her companions. We take to the floor and have a lively dance, though I soon find I have to keep things pretty simple: she's liable to go beyond my leads and set off all over the place if I try to move her too much. Still, it's pleasant and I'm finally getting some exercise.

I return her gratefully to her friends and go across to ask a young woman talking to her friends at the far side of the floor. She puts on a smile to say, "Thank you, no," and switches the smile off again like a light bulb before turning back to her conversation. No future there, clearly. I try another woman, older this time. The same thing happens.

So I wait a few minutes while the DJ plays a couple more tracks. Then I try again. But it's the same response every time. When I've asked six more women and had six more refusals, I decide it's time to accept defeat. I leave Café Mystique, go round to the hotel entrance and ask the desk clerk to call me a cab.

On the way back I ponder my experience. People here seem more closed-off than anywhere I've been so far. I had expected the Cubans in Miami to be more good-humoured and open-hearted than the surrounding society – in fact, more like *Cubans*. But my experience here is nothing like Cuba. What's happened to the relaxed cheerfulness, the constant partying, the sense of mischief, the instant friendliness, the inclusiveness? And what's happened to the *black* Cubans? Very few seem to be here in Miami. I can only guess that many Miami Cubans have come to see themselves as a separate, Hispanic enclave, and their strong group consciousness doesn't welcome an obvious outsider in their midst. They're not hostile, just vaguely puzzled by what I'm doing here; and they're not interested in finding out.

On Monday, after a day of sightseeing, shopping and eating, I get ready to visit Salsa Lovers. The taxi driver this time is Cuban, born in Havana, which he left as a child. He's excited to hear that I've visited Cuba, and everything I tell him astonishes him. He seems amazed that there are now many tourists there, and almost incredulous when I tell him the police no longer bother about people illicitly watching the TV from Miami. Are there many cars on the streets, he wants to know. Do they mend the roads? Do I think things are going to get freer, more open? I do. This plunges him into silent thought – something unusual in my experience of Miami taxi drivers.

After a while he emerges from his cogitations. "You find people here friendly?" he asks.

I hesitate. "To be absolutely honest, I have to say no, not very."

"Mm. Know what you mean. It's the stress. Everybody having to work too hard, push too hard, nobody can't trust nobody. This city, you don't work for two weeks, you can find yourself living on the street."

I'm still having trouble grasping just how enormous Miami is: more like some vast geological phenomenon than a man-made city. Salsa Lovers is a very long way indeed from downtown – a forty-five-dollar taxi ride, in fact. Its frontage is smaller than I'd expected, just a modest shop-front on a mall. I look at it dubiously but the driver assures me it's the right place. I go in and identify myself to the girl at the desk, who tells me I'll be assessed by Abel. I sit on a plastic chair to wait.

A few young people drift past, chatting in English and holding shoe bags. I pass the time by browsing the leaflets in a nearby stand. Salsa Lovers seems to have a highly organized system. It appears that they teach salsa by means of *rueda*, where couples dance in a circle, with the moves – including lots of partner-changing – co-ordinated by a caller. Salsa Lovers has no fewer than seventeen levels. You move up through these, learning a vast number of *rueda* moves on the way, and you can take two lessons to learn how to adapt these moves for couple dancing. It looks beautifully logical but also pretty inflexible. It's the exact opposite of the system in the UK, where you learn salsa as a couple dance, and at some later point get introduced to *rueda*.

After a few minutes Abel appears. He's a slight, wiry young man with dark shiny hair and a Spanish accent, wearing tracksuit bottoms and a red T-shirt. He takes me through into a studio at the side, a long room with a polished wood floor and mirrors along one side. At the far end a couple are dancing under the eye of an instructor.

Abel asks me what experience I have, and explains that new students have to be assessed because the *rueda* won't work unless everyone in the group has the same repertoire of moves. The assessment is to see how many of the prescribed moves I know, so I can be assigned to an appropriate level for my lesson. I'd expected that if the assessment involved dancing with a partner, a female would be produced, but no, I'm to dance with Abel. It feels odd to be dancing with a man, but I soon adjust. He's easy to lead and dances very well, and entirely without embarrassment, as a woman – or "follower", to use the neutral term. We do the *guapea*, then he tries me with *enchufla*, *enchufla doble*, *vacílala*, *sombrero* and other things, as well as checking that I understand what's meant by *da me* and *da me dos*. Unfortunately I go wrong with *exhíbela*. Amos shows it to me briefly, but I've placed myself and have to settle for being classified as 3A, which Abel tells me is the highest level of Beginners.

We return to the desk, and I'm told that my lesson will be starting soon. I pay the eighteen dollars for my assessment and the ten dollars for my lesson and am given a red plastic wristband, red being the colour code for my level, 3A. I go through into the main studio, a vast room with the usual shiny floor and mirrors together with a number of vending machines. People of all ages in all kinds of gear, from jeans and T-shirts to state-of-the-art purple and turquoise Lycra sportswear, are milling about in groups or sitting along the edges of the room changing their footwear. Salsa music is playing through large speakers.

After a while the teachers arrive: three or four men in tracksuits who walk to different parts of the room and then shout for their classes to assemble round them. Abel is there, but he's taking a more advanced class. The man shouting for 3A, my class, is a young, slender Hispanic guy with dark floppy hair. A few people go and stand around him. Rather too few, in fact: it's soon clear that we students are six men and only two women. The other dancers include a small, rotund, jolly, middle-aged Cuban woman, an angular bleach-blonde middle-aged Anglo woman, a grey-haired Hispanic guy about the same age as me, and a thin young Anglo guy with glasses. The teacher scans the horizon but no one else is coming to the rescue, so he calls a young girl from the office, who arrives wearing flip-flops. With the teacher turning himself into another follower, we'll have four "women". Two men will have to dance with imaginary followers, which isn't a great problem as *rueda* involves constant changes of partner, so a real follower will soon arrive.

We get started. The noise is colossal. Besides loud music from the speakers there are three *ruedas* circling in different parts of the hall, each with a teacher shouting instructions. What with the echo and the conflicting calls from different teachers it's almost impossible to make out what our own teacher is shouting. But fortunately *rueda* has a system of hand signals, and the teacher uses the full vocabulary. It doesn't take long for me to pick them up. A flick of the hand as if beckoning means *da me* (take the next lady – literally, "give me one"); tapping the head means *sombrero*; pointing to the eye indicates *vacilala* ("check her out" in Spanish).

After we've gone through a series of basic moves, we work on *adiós* (hand signal simply a wave in the air – "Bye-bye") which, as it happens, I already know but the rest of the group don't. We get this right and I'm able to polish mine up a bit – learning not to raise the lady's arm too early, nor hold on to it after I've passed underneath. We work our way round and round, learning to keep the circle the right size, not letting it collapse inwards or disintegrate outwards, occasionally getting things wrong and colliding with one another and laughing. And then the hour is over. I've had my lesson. I shake hands with the teacher. The girl at the desk calls a cab and suggests I watch another class while I wait. I go back to the first studio, where a large class is learning "shines" – the little solo dances people do when they separate from their partners for a minute or so in the middle of a dance and do some intricate steps and moves on their own.

I watch a tall, pretty girl in the front row, with a flat face and curly dark hair. She wears tight black trousers and wiggles her bottom wonderfully, a look of painful concentration on her face as she works at getting the steps exactly right. She chews gum strenuously while she dances, and in the pauses, standing still to listen to the instructor, she blows big, pink bubbles that burst with a resounding *smack* all over her lips. Then she sucks the gum back in and starts chewing again.

A yellow cab screeches up outside. As I open the car door and climb in, I glance back at the pink Salsa Lovers logo in the middle of the concrete mall façade and realize I'm saying goodbye to salsa in Miami.

"This is Alberto," the driver tells me, pointing to a young man beside him. "He's learning to be a cab driver. You don't mind him being here do you?"

"Certainly not," I say.

"I knew it but I had to ask you. Hey," he asks as we pull out into the traffic, "is that place famous?"

"Yes, I'm from England and I knew about it before I left."

"You see," says the driver to his companion, "it's like I told you. We had a Swiss guy in the cab, he'd heard about Salsa Lovers and he wanted to come here too. I guess that proves it's *world* famous."

I confirm this.

Talking into his mobile phone, the driver changes lanes and we power off down the expressway, accelerating so hard that I'm forced back into my seat. "You nervous?" he asks.

"No," I say.

"That's good. I'll bet I can get you where you're going faster *and* cheaper than the guy who brought you. You just sit tight." The car takes off again with acceleration that welds me to my seat. The driver alternates talking on the phone with giving his apprentice a running commentary: "I'm cutting down here, see, because that way we miss the traffic at 71st, then we take the next off-ramp, not the one that's signed Coral Gables..." He's so manic I wonder if he's on coke.

We hare down a glittering boulevard. I can see the pulsing blue lights of a stationary police car ahead. We change lanes smoothly without slowing. "Now when we pass a cop, we change lanes," he explains. "That shows respect, that's the right thing to do." We sail past the cop car. "The patrol cars, they know it's our living so they give us a break. The motorcycle cops though, that's another story, they got no mercy." He puts his foot down again and picks up his phone. In the midst of a long conversation in Spanish he makes a sweeping left with one hand and we storm onto South River Drive. Outside the hotel we brake so hard my ribs are forced against the seat belt. The driver gives me a high five over the seat-back. "Am I *good*?" he asks rhetorically. "Forty dollars," he adds. "I bet the guy who drove you out charged more."

Around ten next morning I ride yet another cab, along the MacArthur Causeway past the palm trees and the freight terminals and out across the dazzling blue waters of Biscayne Bay to the Art Deco hotels and clean white skyscrapers of Miami Beach. The cab drops me in cool air and fresh sunshine outside the Wolfsonian-FIU, Miami's museum of modern art and design. I wander into its vast marble halls, past a conceptual artist's work consisting of the words "Lo and behold" written on two facing walls ("his artworks embody the complexity of simplicity", says an accompanying plaque) and upstairs to the galleries of Art Deco mosaics, metalwork and stained glass. It's a strange, dreamlike panorama of African-, Egyptian- and Indonesianinfluenced glass, bronze and marble, and I gaze at it numbly like a goldfish watching the reflections on the inside of its bowl.

I make it to the top floor, where a few people are already assembled. At one end of the room is what looks like a musical junkyard: it's the orchestra that will play Antheil's *Ballet Mécanique* – a dozen or so mechanical pianos, two enormous metal fans in wire cages, several robotic xylophones, batteries of drums with automated sticks and beaters, a siren, and electric bells ranging in size from small buzzers to the ones they use for school fire alarms. There isn't a human performer in sight. In 1924 the Dadaist masterpiece (or outrage, depending on your viewpoint) needed musicians, except for the contingent of mechanical pianos, which worked off punched cardboard rolls. Now, with the benefit of computers, the entire orchestra is controlled from a laptop at the front.

As one o'clock approaches, a sizeable crowd gathers. People look at their watches. They stand poised, waiting for something to happen. Then there's an enormous pianistic crash and the whole spooky orchestra comes to life. The pianos trill and thump, the sticks dance over the xylophones, the percussion pounds. And over the top, every so often, the fans howl, sirens scream or an electric bell lets out a prolonged, piercing peal. The music is loud – deafening at moments. It's punchy and visceral. It's a bit like Stravinsky's *Rite of Spring*. It's also very funny. There are no ballerinas in the *Ballet Mécanique*, but the instruments themselves look as if they're dancing, piano keys busily pumping up and down, sticks dancing shakily over xylophone keys. Some people block their ears or reach for the free plastic earplugs thoughtfully offered by the museum. Others laugh. I just let it wash over me, or through me. The whole monstrous cacophony is wonderful, almost soothing. I don't have to dance, I don't have to talk, I don't have to do anything, I can just lose myself in this tidal wave of semi-musical noise. I wish it could go on for ever.

But it doesn't. I come out of my thoughts and find it's stopped. The gallery is emptying. The instruments are silent and the laptop sits there innocently as if it had never triggered that assault on our senses. I drift along a white wall and find the lift. It opens onto the cool marble lobby and I walk out into blinding, bleaching sunlight.

Where shall I go? At the corner of the block I look downhill and glimpse a slice of blue sea. It's the easiest thing to do, so I walk two blocks down the dusty pavement and onto the beach.

I trudge past a curved, modernistic, lime-green lifeguard post and sit down on the sand. I feel numb. Is it just the metallic battering my ears have had from Antheil? No. Watching those mechanical keyboards, I knew how they felt. I'm operating on autopilot. In fact, I think I've been on autopilot for some time. Two small memories swim up suddenly. There was a moment at Café Mystique, as I leant on a rail near the dance floor, when I came to with a little jolt and realized I'd fallen asleep standing up. Before that – was it yesterday, or the day before? – I recall being in some diner (Cuban, Mexican, I don't know) and, while I ate, watching a cockroach slowly circumnavigate the window frame beside me. I'm not squeamish, but normally the exploits of a cockroach next to me at lunch would have aroused *some* mental reaction. Not necessarily disgust, but maybe surprise? Amusement? *Something.* But I just watched it and thought nothing. It occurs to me that I'm utterly exhausted. I feel so tired I could almost die. Salsa? I can't even remember what it is. Music? I never want to hear it again. I sit on the beach watching families splashing in the shallow waves. Pink clouds float above the horizon. The toy-like Art Deco hotels turn apricot and then orange, glinting as the sun sinks. When the stars come out I force myself to stand up. I trudge up through the sand to the hotel strip. Then I stand and wait for a taxi.

❋Epilogue

And so I step off the plane, bleary-eyed, into Manchester's damp, late-autumn chill. I queue through immigration and customs, the latter deserted as always – do they observe us with one-way glass or hidden cameras? And on out into the concrete tunnel where the taxis are supposed to arrive. I haven't got a proper coat with me, so I shiver in the thin fleece that's the warmest thing I have. I wait for ages, but when a taxi finally arrives, at least I can be confident that the driver won't steal my luggage or kill me by overtaking on a blind corner, mobile phone in hand. Driving through the suburbs, everything looks so small and tidy, and in such good repair. It's around eleven in the morning but most of me is still somewhere in the middle of yesterday. I feel hollow and light-headed.

I also find I feel slightly scared. How much will things have changed while I've been away? How much have *I* changed? A return to Manchester means a return to work, and a return to relationships that last more than fifteen minutes. It means a return to *responsibility*, something I've been wonderfully exempt from for nearly two months. Underlying it all, I find that what I'm really scared about is how Amanda will see me. We've never been apart for so long before. It feels like much longer than six weeks. Emailing is all very well, but an awful lot has happened since I left. Will I have become a stranger? To put it bluntly, will she still love me? Will we, indeed, still love each other?

All this, in some nebulous form, swirls about inside my head as we pass the little green gardens and the little brick houses and the clean, carefully-driven cars. And then the taxi is rumbling to a halt outside my house (yes, it's still standing and looks pretty much the way I remember it) and I'm leafing through the residual bolívars and dollars and Colombian pesos I didn't have time to change, looking for some money that the driver might recognize. Then I heave my bag up the path and stand on the doorstep. I'm not going to ring the bell. I'll let myself in. So I do, and I dump my bag in the hall and go into the living room, and Amanda is sitting there pretending not to be waiting for me. She gives me a slow smile, and she's very beautiful, and she gets up and we hug each other: one of those tight, thorough, head-to-toe hugs where the two of you seem to blend into one for quite a long time.

When we've finished kissing, she says, "Did you have a good time?" Then she says, "It's going to take me a while to get used to you again."

It also takes *me* a while to re-engage with the details of normal life. For some time things have a slightly surreal quality. On my first afternoon at home, I fall asleep on the sofa. When I wake up, I stare blankly around me in a kind of panic. I have absolutely no idea where I am. It takes about ninety seconds for me to remember that I'm at home. Over the last few weeks I've been through seven countries and I always knew where I was when I woke up. Something in my mind must have relaxed at last, and now that I'm back I don't know where I am.

There are also, more obviously, signs of my neglected responsibilities. The dog is portly and urgently needs walks. The lawn has grown into a forest. The battery of my car has gone flat and I'll have to get someone out to see to it. Was it this kind of thing I wanted to get away from? I don't think so. In fact everything has a certain richness about it; it's fresh and interesting and rewarding. I'm enjoying being home – though I'm less enthusiastic about the two-foot-high pile of mail I have to go through, and about dealing with those two-hundred-odd emails I've been studiously ignoring.

I quite enjoy the unpacking. Apart from the souvenirs and presents, the T-shirts, the Haitian icon and the Panamanian needlework, there are the CDs I've collected, new and classic, bootleg and legitimate, some of them put together by people I've met and given to me as presents. It'll take weeks to explore them all properly. And somewhere at the bottom, under the mosquito net I never used, slightly crushed and still in its cellophane, I find that packet of condoms. I'd forgotten all about it.

The jet-lag goes on for nearly a week. It surges up a couple of times a day: an overmastering desire to sleep, combined with a dull ache in the pit of the stomach. Conversely, I wake up in the small hours, fully alert and unable to sleep. Rather than disturb Amanda, I lie silent and motionless in the dark, thinking. I think a lot about the places I've been to and the people I've met. In fact when I close my eyes at any time, day or night, after a moment I feel as if I'm still somewhere in Latin America. The truth is that my mind hasn't yet fully disengaged itself. I also find myself wondering why I went. Was it just to improve my dancing? Well, my dancing has improved all right. But clearly that wasn't the entire motivation. A detached observer would no doubt murmur "Mid-life crisis", and I have to admit that the detached observer would be right. The same observer might also mutter the word "Women". Well, yes, I must admit to liking women, and I certainly met some very lovely ones. In fact, a *lot* of very lovely ones. It hasn't done me any harm at all, nor – judging by the few days since my return – has it done my marriage any harm either. Amanda and I have often agreed that dancing salsa is a bit like having sex with your clothes on. Which is great. Though being home, and having a lot of sex with our clothes *off*, has been even better. After all, we have some catching up to do.

But there's something else. It seems clear that my encounters with *santería* were no accident. I can see now that the gods of the West African heritage were coded into the music all along. The rhythms of salsa are in essence African rhythms, and they descend directly from religious ritual. They're still fed by ritual today because the same rhythms, often played by the same percussionists, are the foundation of the *rumba*s and Orisha dances people use to commune with the gods in Cuba and other countries around the Caribbean circle. The gods were talking to us in the music of salsa all along, if we'd known how to listen.

Which reminds me that I have a promise to keep. Remembering the Babalawo's advice, I go to the supermarket with a small but unusual shopping list. First I look for *ñames*. They don't have any yams that look like the shaggy black pear-shaped things I was shown in Panama, so I buy sweet potatoes instead. Their orange colour seems coppery enough to please Ochún. I also buy five eggs (organic, free range) and a bag of those little wax tea lights. At home I set up my picture of

Our Lady of Charity of Copper on a small table, put the eggs on a plate and five stumpy wax tea lights on another. I boil up my "yams" as instructed and make five balls of their mashed pulp. I put these on a third plate. Then I offer the whole lot to Ochún, with thanks for a safe journey. I let the lights burn right down until they go out.

The next day the room is pervaded by a smell of slightly putrified yam. Never mind. I pick up the sticky balls, as per instructions, and move them around over my upper body. Then I put them into a plastic bag. I take the dog for a walk in the woods. I make my way into the centre of the most impenetrable hawthorn thicket I can find. Restraining the dog, I tip the pulpy balls out and arrange the five eggs around them. Then I leave, my task fulfilled.

A few nights afterwards I dream of a beautiful mixed-race woman, with the complexion a Cuban would unhesitatingly call *mulata*. She wears a long dress of a dull orangey colour, caught in at the waist by a sash. Around her neck she has a remarkable necklace: it's made of Ogun's miniature tools – the little shiny metal saw, hoe, anvil and everything, all hanging from a narrow silver collar. She unties her orange sash and holds it out, beckoning me to come closer. Then she ties it around my waist. I wake up; but this time I don't need to be told who she is. The copper-coloured dress makes it clear enough.

I wonder whether I can write poems about some of my experiences, but I know it's too early. Things have to sink in deeper. And there are so many things that are impossible to express in words. In particular I find I'm remembering a moment one Sunday afternoon in the Parque del Este in Caracas, the most wonderful city park I've ever seen, a great sprawling sun-drenched labyrinth of flowering trees, green lawns, palms, ponds and fountains, its paths littered with fallen frangipani flowers like children's toy windmills, their petals shading from ivory through yellow into a blushing pink. I sat under a tree and looked around me. There were family parties picnicking on the grass, teenagers laughing and arguing, old people sitting on benches, talking, couples kissing, children running and shrieking. Perhaps because I was a stranger, I watched it all like a visitor from another planet. It was a panorama of the human condition and something about it became completely overwhelming. Every single person, I could see, was of truly astronomical complexity, a whole universe in themselves. And there were thousands of people around me at that moment. And this was in one corner of one city in one country of one continent of a single planet. The inconceivable intricacy and richness of all this was utterly overpowering. I gazed and gazed, unable to think, feeling tears pricking my eyelids. Maybe I was tired, maybe I was jet-lagged. I can't put into words what I saw, but I saw something.

And of course we dance. First of all we dance in the kitchen, the only room we have with a smooth floor. I'm able to show off a few moves, but more importantly the dancing flows better. My feet stay closer to the floor. Somehow my centre of gravity has shifted. At our usual classes there's some curiosity about where I've been and what I've learned. But the truth is I've danced so many different styles over the past few weeks that I'm still not an expert in any of them. I know I never will be. Technical expertise as such doesn't really interest me. If I've learnt anything, it's that salsa is about fun and feeling. Though a Peruvian girl at one class does pay me the ultimate compliment. "Hey," she says, "you no longer dance like an Englishman."

But my travels aren't over yet. Long ago – so long that I've forgotten all about it – we booked to go to the annual salsa congress at Blackpool. No sooner have I got over the jet-lag than we're packing to drive north and spend a weekend immersed in Cuban salsa by the windswept Lancashire seaside. One Friday afternoon we drive up and follow signs through the town to a road that runs parallel to the shore behind a line of dunes. The venue is a Holiday Park – what used to be called a holiday camp. When we pull into the car-park, it's evident that the keynote – out of doors, at any rate – is sand. It blows continually across the road from the dunes, building up into little furrows on the windscreen, and when we step out onto the tarmac the soles of our shoes shuffle pleasingly on the fine dusting that covers the ground and lies in drifts against the kerbs.

We check in and receive the key to our chalet and two red plastic bracelets. Then we wander between lines of chalets, little concrete buildings in pastel colours, surrounded by thin, sandy grass.

"They're like prefabs," says Amanda.

Every few minutes the bloated, fish-like, silver underbellies of jets from the nearby airport slide, thundering, overhead. We find our chalet, unlock the door, step over the sandy threshold and drop our luggage. I force the door shut against a gust of sand-bearing wind and sit down on the bed. The room's not bad: a pleasant square space with a TV and an ensuite bathroom at the back. There are yellow patterned curtains, yellow walls, yellow pillows and a yellow duvet cover. The bed feels comfortable.

I take a look at the schedule we've been given. "Ah," I say, "the red bracelets are to show we've paid. We have to wear them to get meals and use the dance floors in the evening."

Amanda is turning hers to and fro. "I can't work out how they're supposed to fasten," she says. "Oh, that's it. This stud clicks in here. Wait a minute. God, it won't come out again. I can't get it open to put it on."

Evidently the bracelets operate one way only. Once fastened, they come off only when you cut them. Amanda has clicked hers shut without putting it on first. I wrestle with it a bit, but no, nothing on earth is going to get it open now.

"Bracelets will be replaced only on payment of a seventy-five-pound charge," I read.

"They won't make us pay seventy-five pounds, will they?" Amanda is worried now.

I have a feeling they won't, and I bet *someone* clicks their bracelet prematurely every single time. After standing in the queue at reception for twenty minutes – people tugging wheeled suitcases now arriving from every direction – I swap the closed bracelet for a new, open one and rejoin Amanda.

From there on it's plain sailing. We have dinner in one of the large dining rooms – the food is much better than the school-dinner fare I'd been half-expecting – and then try to decide what we're going to do later, and tomorrow. There are several hundred salsa enthusiasts swirling around us, and dozens of workshops and classes to choose from all day long. For this evening, we simply dance in the two ballrooms, walking briskly across in the freezing wind from one to the other whenever we fancy a change. More and more people we know from the Manchester clubs arrive.

Next day the workshops begin. We "warm up" until we're dripping with sweat, under the direction of lithe Cubans in silky tracksuits. We work on reggaeton under the tuition of Leandro, an immensely tall Cuban in baggy white trousers and a scarlet top, who's an astonishing dancer. He moves like a puppet, tensing and sliding every part of his body separately, springing upside-down and balancing on one hand before pushing himself upright again. He doesn't expect us to do that, but he works us strenuously on "isolating" different parts of our bodies so we can move them independently. We work at it until our hips and shoulders are aching. We practise *rueda* in a circle of fifty or so couples in a studio the size of an aircraft hangar. I take a class in Cuban percussion, and we both go to sessions where we can learn the characteristic dances of particular Orishas, gods from the *santería* pantheon. Amanda chooses Yemaya, the sea-goddess, who dances shaking her skirts like the waves of the ocean; I learn the dance of Changó, the thunder god, wielding his sword and pulling lightning down from the heavens.

I watch a teacher called Orestes taking another class, and notice that the handhold he's teaching – and indeed his whole style – is exactly what Geldys tried to teach me all those weeks ago in Havana. Talking to him after the class I discover that he's a former soloist in the same dance company, the Conjunto Folklórico Nacional de Cuba, and he knows Geldys. He tells me he used to be an art historian before becoming a full-time dancer. "It's not about learning moves," he says in Spanish. He puts his hands on his chest. "When two people dance together, the dance is an expression of what is in the heart. *El corazón.*"

When the dancing becomes too much we take a break and wander around Blackpool, past the rows of prim little hotels with their awnings and names like Avonlea, Sunnyhurst, Ingledene and Monteray (*sic*). We brave the buffeting wind to walk along the promenade among the screaming gulls beside the churning grey sea, past the Smoking Gun Paintball Centre, the countless pubs ("Stags and Hens Welcome") and the little consulting rooms of the many fortune-tellers called Gypsy

Petulengro. Each one has a purple curtain, an array of photographs and an elaborately-lettered signboard:

Famous Celebrities Seek Her Advice.

As known for Centuries, only a true Romany Gypsy
can read your palm.

Your Palm is the Map of Your Life.

Tony Christie will make a Big come back Later in his career
As predicted by Gipsy Petulengro 34 Years Ago.

No one seems to know whether to spell "Gypsy" with an "i" or a "y". In the background looms Blackpool Tower, a knobbly web of chocolate-brown girders poised over a cluster of strangely-tiled Art Deco buildings. A kind of giant Victorian cake-stand, it's rather beautiful against the racing clouds.

We buy fudge, and talk about the future. We decide that next year we'll go to Cuba together. I'm starting to miss it already and I want to introduce Amanda to the addictive, multi-layered world of Havana. In wintry Blackpool the Cuban climate seems especially appealing.

On Sunday night, after the final workshops, we dance as usual, changing partners sometimes but mostly dancing together. The time comes for the competitions. The MC incites couples to come out onto the floor, and enumerates the prizes: free holidays for two, gift vouchers, DVDs and CDs. Reluctantly, bashfully, people start coming forward. Amanda and I look at each other.

"D'you want to give it a try?" I ask her.

"Not very much. Do you?"

I think about it. I've done a lot of dancing in a lot of different styles but I don't consider myself a champion in any. I know I'll never win any competitions. Moreover, I'm not a showy or spectacular dancer. And if I've learnt one thing, it's that authentic salsa isn't about showy moves or competing. It's about love and freedom, about the heart, *el corazón*, and about letting the heart float in that music, the music that has such a depth of history and colour and magic in it.

I shake my head. "Not interested," I say.

We go and get another drink, and then we sit down and watch as the couples in the competition are whittled down to the last few. We make our own judgements about who's the best, and sometimes we agree with the judges. And when it's all over, the prizes distributed, the floor opened again for dancing, the DJ puts on a hard, driving, melodic salsa track, the kind that grabs you around the hips and seduces you and makes you feel you can't sit down any longer. We look at each other and our eyes light up together, and we're both thinking, *Yes!*

So I take her hand and we head for the dance floor.